Philosophical Issues in Sport Science

Philosophical Issues in Sport Science

Special Issue Editor
Emily Ryall

MDPI • Basel • Beijing • Wuhan • Barcelona • Belgrade

Special Issue Editor
Emily Ryall
University of Gloucestershire
UK

Editorial Office
MDPI
St. Alban-Anlage 66
4052 Basel, Switzerland

This is a reprint of articles from the Special Issue published online in the open access journal *Philosophies* (ISSN 2409-9287) in 2019 (available at: https://www.mdpi.com/journal/philosophies/special_issues/Philosophical_Issues_Sport_Science).

For citation purposes, cite each article independently as indicated on the article page online and as indicated below:

LastName, A.A.; LastName, B.B.; LastName, C.C. Article Title. *Journal Name* **Year**, *Article Number*, Page Range.

ISBN 978-3-03921-888-2 (Pbk)
ISBN 978-3-03921-889-9 (PDF)

© 2020 by the authors. Articles in this book are Open Access and distributed under the Creative Commons Attribution (CC BY) license, which allows users to download, copy and build upon published articles, as long as the author and publisher are properly credited, which ensures maximum dissemination and a wider impact of our publications.
The book as a whole is distributed by MDPI under the terms and conditions of the Creative Commons license CC BY-NC-ND.

Contents

About the Special Issue Editor vii

Emily Ryall
Introduction to Philosophical Issues in Sport Science
Reprinted from: *Philosophies* **2019**, *4*, 57, doi:10.3390/philosophies4040057 1

Matthew Hickson
The Necessity of Philosophy in the Exercise Sciences
Reprinted from: *Philosophies* **2019**, *4*, 45, doi:10.3390/philosophies4030045 9

John Gray
The Hazards of a Biomedical Exercise Paradigm: Exploring the Praxis of Exercise Professionals
Reprinted from: *Philosophies* **2019**, *4*, 54, doi:10.3390/philosophies4030054 20

Evan Thomas Knott
What Might a Theory of Causation Do for Sport?
Reprinted from: *Philosophies* **2019**, *4*, 34, doi:10.3390/philosophies4020034 33

Saana Jukola
Casuistic Reasoning, Standards of Evidence, and Expertise on Elite Athletes' Nutrition
Reprinted from: *Philosophies* **2019**, *4*, 19, doi:10.3390/philosophies4020019 44

Francisco Javier Lopez Frias
Unnatural Technology in a "Natural" Practice? Human Nature and Performance-Enhancing Technology in Sport
Reprinted from: *Philosophies* **2019**, *4*, 35, doi:10.3390/philosophies4030035 55

Pam R. Sailors
Chips and Showmanship: Running and Technology
Reprinted from: *Philosophies* **2019**, *4*, 30, doi:10.3390/philosophies4020030 71

Harry Collins
Applying Philosophy to Refereeing and Umpiring Technology
Reprinted from: *Philosophies* **2019**, *4*, 21, doi:10.3390/philosophies4020021 77

S. Seth Bordner
Why You Don't Have to Choose between Accuracy and Human Officiating (But You Might Want to Anyway)
Reprinted from: *Philosophies* **2019**, *4*, 33, doi:10.3390/philosophies4020033 84

Andria Bianchi
Something's Got to Give: Reconsidering the Justification for a Gender Divide in Sport
Reprinted from: *Philosophies* **2019**, *4*, 23, doi:10.3390/philosophies4020023 93

Jonathan Cooper
Testosterone: 'the Best Discriminating Factor'
Reprinted from: *Philosophies* **2019**, *4*, 36, doi:10.3390/philosophies4030036 106

Rory Smead
Sports Tournaments and Social Choice Theory
Reprinted from: *Philosophies* **2019**, *4*, 28, doi:10.3390/philosophies4020028 121

About the Special Issue Editor

Emily Ryall is a Reader in Applied Philosophy at the University of Gloucestershire. She is the author of Philosophy of Sport: Key Questions, Critical Thinking for Sports Students and other publications on philosophical issues in sport, games and play. She is currently the associate editor for the Journal of the Philosophy of Sport and former Chair of the British Philosophy of Sport Association. She has contributed to media discussions on philosophical issues in sport on outlets such as the BBC, New York Times, The Guardian and the Australian Broadcasting Corporation.

Editorial

Introduction to Philosophical Issues in Sport Science

Emily Ryall

School of Sport and Exercise, Oxstalls Campus, University of Gloucestershire, Gloucester GL2 9HW, UK; eryall@glos.ac.uk

Received: 4 November 2019; Accepted: 4 November 2019; Published: 8 November 2019

Abstract: The role and value of science within sport increases with ever greater professionalization and commercialization. Scientific and technological innovations are devised to increase performance, ensure greater accuracy of measurement and officiating, reduce risks of harm, enhance spectatorship and raise revenues. However, such innovations inevitably come up against epistemological and metaphysical problems related to the nature of sport and physical competition. This special issue identifies and explores key and contemporary philosophical issues in relation to the science of sport and exercise. The opening four chapters, focus on the nature of scientific evidence, and causation in sport; the middle four chapters on the influence of science and technology and its relationship to sport officiating; whilst the final three chapters consider the way in which science affects the construction of sport. It brings together scholars working on philosophical problems in sport to examine issues related to the values and assumptions behind sport and exercise science, identify key problems that result, and provide recommendations for improving its practice.

Keywords: sport science; epistemology; ontology; causation; technology; evidence

1. Introduction

This special issue arose because although there are individuals writing philosophically about issues in the sport and exercise sciences, there has not been a collection of articles that focus on the sports sciences itself since McNamee's [1] edited collection *Philosophy and the Sciences of Exercise, Health and Sport* published in 2005. McNamee's collection of essays provides a useful starting point for sports scientists to think about their practice and some of the assumptions behind it, and this edited collection attempts to pick up the baton a decade and a half later. Clearly, during this period, although similar philosophical issues arise, the application and context has changed. The evolution of sport, and particularly the way in which technology affects it, will always raise significant philosophical and ethical questions about both the value and concept of sport and its relationship to the sciences. As our technological capacity and scientific knowledge develops, there remains a place for philosophical thinking about if and how it should be utilized as well as the recognizing often-unintended consequences that may follow. Similarly, the importance of sport and exercise science as a means to affect and influence this evolution appears to directly correspond with the professionalization and commercialization of sport and provokes questions about what we want sport to look like and what we expect it to do. As I am writing, questions have been raised over the legitimacy and value of Kipchoge's sub two-hour marathon, and Kosgei's women's world record a day later. Both of whom were wearing highly engineered running shoes designed to conserve the runner's energy and cushion the impact, thus making it 'easier' to run. Controversy surrounds this footware technology and whether the advantage it provides is akin to the subsequently banned 'sharkskin' swimming costumes that broke a multitude of world records within a single swimming event in 2009 [2]. Similarly, questions are asked about the way in which athletes are commodified and their bodies are dissected into ever more discrete physiological and biomechanical components in order to achieve 'marginal gains' in competition. There are also continued questions about the accuracy of officiating in sport, with ongoing implementation of ever more elaborate devices to ensure the 'correct decision is made'. However, as can be illustrated by the recent introduction of video assistant referee (VAR) in football, technology is not infallible and does not necessarily provide the means to answers questions about reality as to what 'really happened', hence why there seems to be an equal amount of controversy over officiating decisions following its implementation. All of this demonstrates that although scientific and technological innovations are intended to make sport better by increasing performance, ensuring greater accuracy of measurement and officiating, reducing risks of harm, enhancing spectatorship and creating wealth, they inevitably come up against epistemological, metaphysical, ontological and axiological problems that cannot easily be solved.

The focus of the papers within this special issue is broad and covers a range of topics, from the way in which philosophical thinking can provide sport and exercise sciences with an underpinning rationale about the value of sport and its priorities, to the more specific conceptual problems that arise from the use of technology in sport, to the way in which science is used to defend the way sport is structured, particularly around the issue of sex segregation. The first four chapters deal with scientific evidence and the issue of causation in sport, the next four chapters with technology and officiating, and the last three chapters with scientific influences on the construction of sport.

2. Chapter Overview

The first four chapters consider some of the broader epistemological and metaphysical questions in sport and exercise science, particularly focusing on how sport and exercise professionals should construct their practice and acknowledge the underpinning assumptions it rests upon.

It begins with Matthew Hickson considering the place of philosophy in the sport and exercise sciences. Hickson contends that the predominance of a materialistic and reductionist perspective in the exercise sciences is concerning because it leads to a disregard of ethical considerations, such as the rightness or wrongness of genetic engineering and its application in sport. Hickson argues that a reductionist approach that sees humans as merely a sum of a collection of parts depersonalizes what it is to be human, and consequently, what it is to be an athlete. This criticism levelled at the sport sciences is not new (e.g., [3–6]) and has traditionally centered on the instrumental attitude adopted in the sport and exercise sciences that aims to fix and control the human body in an ever-greater attempt at quantification of performance. Where Hickson develops these arguments is in his focus on the notion of causality. Sport and exercise scientists, he argues, implicitly accept a Newtonian account of causality, in that there is a predictable and mechanistic theory of cause and effect, that is founded on a belief that changes can occur—or problems fixed—if one just interferes with this linear causal process. Here, Hickson shares Gray's concern set-out in the subsequent chapter regarding the medicalization of the exercise sciences, particularly in the 'soft' science of psychology. Such a simplistic view of nature does not adequately reflect human behavior, which is far more complex than a linear causal relationship at a micro-cellular, neural or genetic level. This is a point I have made in a previous paper [5] that draws upon Peter Winch's [7] reflections; we do not ascribe causes for human behavior but rather reasons for it, and therefore it is incorrect to view human behavior in Newtonian terms. Viewing human action in terms of reasons rather than causes enables us to accept the notion of agency and free will and, importantly, moral culpability as Hickson rightly indicates. Instead of falling into the reductionist trap, Hickson advocates that the sport and exercise sciences need to adopt an Aristotelian, holistic approach to their method. This, he argues, can be done through ensuring that those working in the sport and exercise sciences recognize the limitations that such a reductionist approach entails.

John Gray continues this line of critique in the following chapter. In particular, he is critical of the medicalization of the sport and exercise sphere and the techno-rational approach that he argues has become the dominant paradigm. He describes the way in which the biomedical model—in which human problems are viewed through a biological lens that can be solved through an application of scientific knowledge and technology—has been layered over the sport and exercise professions, and evidences this through a thorough examination of literature in the exercise sciences. As Gray notes, the situation is complex as the educational expectations and professional requirements of exercise practitioners has increased alongside its growth. It is arguably right that the professionalization of the exercise sciences now seeks a far greater reliance upon scientific evidence to underpin practice. Yet, this is at the detriment of an ontological and axiological understanding of the limits of science and the evidence it accepts. Gray argues that as a result, exercise science is reduced to, "a routine of linear action to fulfil the expectations of medical data as opposed to an immersive humanistic experience" (p. 26). This parallels criticism levelled at the professionalization of nursing which, similarly, became fixated on medical solutions at the detriment of a caring and human ethos which is arguably at the heart of what it is to be a nurse. As an antidote against this techno-rationalism in the exercise sciences, Gray turns to the work of Johan Huizinga and his conception of Homo Ludens (playful man) in maintaining that this needs to be the underpinning principle that exercise professionals should work from.

We return to the issue of causation in sport in Evan Knott's chapter. Knott attempts to answer the question implied as a result of Hickson's earlier criticism: what theory of causation can best be applied to sport? In many respects, a mechanistic account of causation seems intrinsic to sport, i.e. the physical properties of, and relationship between, sporting objects such as a boot striking a ball, causing it to move in a particular direction. As Mumford [8] has previously identified, we congratulate goal-scorers on the basis that there was a causal relationship between their actions and the goal being scored. And yet the issue of causation has been little considered in the sport philosophy literature. Knott notes the limitations of several theories of causation, such as agency, mechanistic/deterministic and probabilistic theories, and instead, draws upon Lewis' counter-factual theory. Counter-factuals can indicate what we believe to be the causal relation between events in sport by their omission, e.g., 'the Red team would have won if A had occurred' on the basis that A is causally linked to winning. A counter-factual theory of causation holds that since A was absent, the Red team did not win. In this, Knott seems right to suggest that although a mechanistic or probabilistic causal relationship might be usefully applied to some aspects of sport, it fails in others; most particularly, in complex events which cannot fully be understood by reference to physical laws, and which also involve social rules and human action. Instead, a theory that focuses on absent causes, omissions or counter-factuals may bear fruition in a causal analysis of sporting events. Knott's recommendations has implications for sports scientists and performance analysts in particular. One of the main criticisms to be levelled at performance analysis in sport is that it quantifies particular actions in sport, such as number of tackles made, percentage of possession held, or meters run, as if such indicators are causally linked to a particular outcome, when the reality of the situation is far more complex than this. As Knott suggests, if sport scientists and coaches use thought experiments to consider counter-factuals in their understanding of causal relationships it will arguably lead to a much richer level of performance analysis in sport.

The fourth chapter focuses on the issue of evidence and appropriate methods in sport science. Saana Jukola highlights the inherent problem of providing good quality, evidence-based nutritional advice in sport. She argues whilst individual case or laboratory studies are often dismissed as lacking credibility when compared to the 'gold standard' of RCTs, they can play an important role in bridging a gap between hypothesis and application. This is particularly the case in reaching judgements about the efficacy of nutritional advice for elite athletes. As she rightly notes, elite athletes, by definition, are not representative of the 'normal' population and therefore the results of randomized controlled trials (RCT) (if they can be carried out at all) cannot be straightforwardly applied. Instead, nutritionists must rely upon unverified assumptions, or extrapolation from small group observations, case studies and laboratory tests. Jukola therefore suggests that sports nutrition should be casuistic, in that reasoned judgements should be made for individual cases based upon evidence from multiple sources. Whereas casuistic reasoning is often criticized for being unsound in the way conclusions are reached, she notes it does have a precedence in bioethics where general principles may not apply to all cases. In the case of bio and medical ethics, judgements need to be made based upon the needs of affected individuals as well as the wider community and other interested parties. Jukola concludes by arguing that sports nutritionists, and sport scientists more generally, need to understand the methods and assumptions that underpin scientific research and be able to defend particular approaches with a robust philosophical underpinning. Jukola's assessment has implications for the philosophical training that sport scientists should receive and provides a call for greater philosophical input into sport science educational programmes.

The next four chapters continue this investigation into the practice of sport and exercise but narrows the focus to specific technological issues. It opens with chapters framing the notion of the natural athlete and the way in which technology can limit the richness of the sporting experience, then considers the relationship between good sport officiating and notions of accuracy and justice.

Javi Lopez-Frias begins this section with a consideration of the concept of 'natural' and its relationship to anti-doping policy in sport. As he notes, the construction of the concept designates a range of ethical and cultural values about what is or is not acceptable. In this context, our concept of what is natural and how it relates to good sport, influences the decisions we make about technological and scientific innovations. Lopez-Frias argues that contemporary conceptions of the natural human influence the way in which we medicalize the body, in attempts to restore natural functions when the body breaks down, but also the way in which we design sport as a competitive environment within which we test the natural capacities of the human. He examines the way in which this concept has affected the development of anti-doping policy and suggests it is heavily influenced by the Protestant, puritan conception of human nature. This is reflected by comments from those defending anti-doping policy who insist that victory in sport should be a result of hard work and natural talents. Such an argument equates the development of natural talent through hard work and effort with moral excellence. Yet, as Lopez-Frias notes, there is little evidence to suggest that hard work and effort do attain the moral excellences that such advocates imagine. Arguably, the Protestant work ethic can result in an emphasis on the value of winning and profit-making above all else. Lopez-Frias maintains an alternative, postmodern conception of the natural human, that focuses upon the value of freedom, could result in a very different anti-doping policy to the one which is currently administered. Such a conception of human nature as one that is free to create itself, is one whereby doping could feasibly be tolerated and even cultivated. He advocates that anti-doping policy should recognize other conceptions of human nature rather than just a 'thin' one founded on Protestant puritanism, which has implications for the way in which sport science is developed and practiced.

The next paper continues this exploration between the human athlete, technology, and good sport. Pam Sailors begins by highlighting the unintended consequences of using electronic 'chips' to accurately record race times in marathons. The use of timing 'chips' in addition to starting and finishing gates can result in disputes as to who is the winner and how many races are really taking place. The issue set out by Sailors is the way in which a dependency on constant technological innovation can drive flawed conceptions of sport. To illustrate, Sailors recounts a multi-national corporation's failed attempt to draw upon all possible technological innovations break the two hour marathon (although as noted earlier, this has now been achieved) as if the record time is all that matters rather than how it is achieved or what it actually means for the notion of sporting competition itself. The problem, she argues, is that an over-arching emphasis on technology reduces sporting competitions to mere quantifiable outcomes but this bypasses much of what makes sport, sport. Sport is not just a matter of 'testing' but rather 'contesting'. The meaning and value of sport is so much richer than anemic attempts to depict a quantifiable and fixed reality that is represented by mathematical calculations and statistical analysis. In her examination of the issue, Sailors' utilizes the work of philosophers, such as Kretchmar, Reid, Loland, and Elcombe, to demonstrate how the vital ethical and axiological elements of sport are eradicated when sport is reduced to mere quantification of performance.

In the following paper, Harry Collins' picks up some of the arguments he has previously articulated on how technology is used to make officiating decisions in sport. He rightly notes that there is a pervading myth in sport that technology can produce perfection in decision making, i.e. that we can defer to technology to determine whether the ball was out (as in tennis), over the line (as in football), or whether the ball would have gone on to hit the stumps (as in cricket). In dispelling this myth,

Collins maintains that we should frame the argument on the use of officiating technology in sport as one of justice not accuracy. Criticism of match officials is often a result of technology undermining the authority of match officials in their role of upholders of justice and it is this that needs to be addressed, not the issue of accuracy. The solution Collins provides is to use video assistance when it is obvious that an officiating decision is at odds with other accounts (i.e., the replay). In changing the debate, he advocates a 'Right If Not WroNg' (RINOWN) principle. This avoids the problem of determining accuracy (in what 'really happened') and the subsequent paradox that a decision can be overturned through the use of technological aids even though officials and spectators alike 'saw' the same thing. Collins illustrates this paradox through the real-life example of a video-replay seeming to support the referee awarding a goal but it being over-ruled by other, more complex officiating technology that provides mathematical predictions about the ball's 'real' position in space and time. If the officials judge that a goal has been scored, and the video-replays appear to back this up, then there is no injustice in awarding it, even if there may be questions about its accuracy. Collins' paper has important epistemological and ontological implications for officiating in elite sport and enters the philosophical territory as to the notion of reality. Perpetuating the myth that technology is able to determine what 'really' happened suggests that when it comes to officiating sport, human judgement is flawed and that the correct view of reality can be obtained through technological means. As philosophers and scientists are well aware, the notion of 'reality' is far more complicated than this and Collins is right to refocus the debate in terms of justice and consistency since it both sidesteps this philosophical quagmire and returns to the essence of good sport.

Seth Bordner continues this analysis of accuracy in officiating sport in his chapter and argues that a fundamental question has been neglected in the literature: what does accuracy in officiating actually mean? As Bordner notes, accuracy is relative to the criteria that determines outcome. If we construct sport in such a way (through its rules) that humans are likely to make mistakes, then we should not be surprised if there is an increase in 'bad calls'. Humans are limited in what they are able to accurately judge and poorly constructed rules will hinder the notion of accuracy in human officiating. To illustrate, Bordner gives the example of the strike zone in baseball. There is no clearly defined boundary in the air as to what constitutes the strike zone, and the ball travels at a pace too fast for the human eye to fully track, therefore accuracy in decision making as to whether the ball was inside or outside the strike zone is going to be limited. Technology, such as Hawk-Eye, could be set up to map out a strike zone so that a ball passing through an area could be tracked and information to be provided to an official as to whether a ball passed through it—hence a more accurate decision—but the problem arises because of an unrealistic expectation as to what humans are able to do. This, Bordner argues, is a problem created by deficient sporting rules. Similarly, Border notes that human officials are not infallible when it comes to determining intention of action, in the case of fouls or unsporting conduct. Again, the criteria that defines how intention is judged will influence the decision of officials. Bordner argues that in wrestling with questions over officiating, sports governing bodies need to look at the rules and not merely to expect technology to solve the problems. Officials (generally) know the rules but they don't always know when to apply them: it can be difficult for a human to determine what the correct officiating call should be. As such, if we construct the rules in such a way that it is easier to know when they should be applied, the accuracy of officiating will be greater. As Bordner notes, "It is very easy for a human official to be mistaken by an inch or two . . . ; it is much harder to mistaken by three feet." (p. 90?) Bordner's conjecture here seems reasonable. To illustrate, he provides the following example: consider the difference between a rule in American Football that states, 'the ball must be placed where it was grounded', and a rule that states, 'the ball must be placed on the last yard line that the ball carrier made contact with in the direction of travel'. Both rules may appear similar, but the latter provides criteria whereby it is easier for a referee to provide accuracy in their decision. However, the criteria are also determined by the values we believe to be inherent in sport. On the basis that sport is rule based, one of the primary values will be justice, as noted in Collins' chapter, but it could also be entertainment, flow or some other aesthetic value. It is the additional values that may affect how accurate we wish officiating to be. As I have previously noted [9], one of the reasons FIFA (the International Federation of Association Football) were resistant in utilizing goal-line technology was its disruption to the flow of the game since a game's flow is an important value in the game of football. In Bordner's example, the current rules in American Football provide a farcical situation whereby the game is stopped and attempts are made, through the use of a low-tech chain marker, to accurately determine the spot where the ball should be placed. If the rule were to be changed to accord with human ability to determine its correct application then such situations would not arise. He concludes it is possible to both have accuracy of officiating and human officials but there may be a trade-off with the aesthetics (and other values) of sport which we would not wish to make.

The final three chapters of this book consider the way in which science influences the way in which sport is constructed. The first two chapters focus on the issue of sex segregation in sport and the scientific evidence that underpins it. The final chapter considers how sporting competitions could be fairly constructed so that the best team wins.

In their consecutive chapters, Bianchi and Cooper consider the high-profile controversy that arises from separating sport along binary sex categories and the notion of fair and unfair advantage in sport. Bianchi focuses on the apparent physiological advantages that transgender women hold over their cisgender competitors and what this means for the notion of fair sport. She draws upon the 'skill thesis' which is used to defend sex segregation in sport, in that that sports should be divided according to levels of skill in order to maintain fair competition. If there is clear evidence of a difference of skill (Bianchi provides a broad conception of this) between cismales and cisfemales, it is legitimate for sport to be separated on grounds of sex. Yet this binary solution creates a problem for athletes that do not fall into these two categories. The problem as both Bianchi and Cooper note, is the situation is further complicated because in sport, testosterone is utilized as a proxy for determining sex and therefore it is not just trans athletes that get caught in the debate, but intersex athletes too. Ultimately, it raises the sensitive question of what it is to be a woman. Bianchi sets out two approaches to resolving this: to either discard the skill thesis and allow transwomen to compete in the female sport category, or to maintain the skill thesis and mitigate unfair genetic advantages that some (trans and intersex) women have. She advocates the second approach and parallels it to providing a handicap in golf. Bianchi has previously suggested that this handicap should be applied according to testosterone levels (as a proxy for sex) but in this paper, she concedes that this may be unsatisfactory since it is unclear whether testosterone is the correct determinant for performance. She accepts that it also raises some practical issues regarding testing for its effectiveness. As a result, Bianchi follows a path previously advocated by Tännsjö [10] and concludes that sports should be categorized along other relevant factors that are sport dependent, such as height, or muscle-mass. This would retain the skill thesis in sport but enable it to be more inclusive and sensitive to recent political and cultural changes without the need for determining binary sex classifications.

Whilst Bianchi considers the issue of sex categorization in sport more broadly, Cooper looks at the way in which sporting authorities have attempted to defend their policies on eligibility. This argument holds that testosterone levels are a primary determinant of sporting performance and since there are clear differences between the testosterone levels of men and women, it is reasonable for it be used as a proxy for determining sex categories in sport. Yet Cooper claims that there is a clear conflict between the International Association of Athletics Federations' (IAAF) Testosterone Regulations and human rights. Most notably, if the sporting authorities define what it is to be a woman by virtue of testosterone levels, and subject those not deemed eligible to medical intervention, it raises important ethical and legal questions on human rights grounds. Cooper concludes that the fact that such intervention is based upon little to no scientific evidence on the performance effects of testosterone and a lack of transparency over the way in which decision on this have been made, raises further concerns.

The final chapter is an exploration of the structure of fair sporting competitions. Here, Rory Smead applies social choice theory to sporting tournaments in order to ensure that the best team wins. However, as Smead notes, the concept of 'best' can fall foul of Condorcet's paradox whereby there is no clear means for establishing which this might be; as in the case of a 'round-robin' league where each team beats another and everyone ends on equal points. Smead notes that the use of leagues as a means of determining sporting superiority generally assumes that relationships between teams are transitive; that A is better that B, B is better than C, and therefore A is better than C. However, this is not necessarily the case if we categorize teams or players according to individual strengths and weaknesses, as demonstrated by the game of 'rock-paper-scissors', and as such, teams' relationships to others can be intransitive. Smead claims that one way of overcoming this paradox is by applying Arrow's impossibility theorem to sports tournaments and by advocating championship pluralism. This approach accepts that there is no single way of measuring the best team and as such, a pluralism of organizational structures should be provided to capture all aspects of athletic excellence in order to structure sport competition as fairly as possible.

3. Conclusions

As set out at the beginning, what this collection of papers seeks to do is to demonstrate the important relationship between the sport and exercise sciences and the notion of good sport itself. Those working with sport and exercise—whether at the harder end of the sciences in physiology, biomechanics, medicine, engineering, performance analysis and nutrition, or the softer sciences related to psychology, coaching, governance or athlete support roles—need to consider their practices and what their role brings to the development and attainment of good sport. This collection starts to bring together some key discussions in this area whilst recognizing there is still more to be said in relation to the underpinning methods and assumptions within sport and exercise science, that philosophers of science, such as Karl Popper, Thomas Kuhn and Paul Feyerabend amongst others have previously commented upon. There is ongoing development in contemporary debates in the philosophy of science, around conceptions of causation, prediction, truth and knowledge that could be usefully applied to the sport and exercise context that have sadly not been able to be included in this collection. But what this collection does hopefully indicate, is that those working within sport need to be able to evaluate and understand the inherent philosophical questions on the nature of sport, what part it should play in our wider lives and how sport and exercise science can assist in these aims. As this collection shows, the relationship between science and sport is a significant one that deserves our attention.

Funding: This research received no external funding.

Acknowledgments: I wish to sincerely thank all the authors and reviewers who contributed to this collection and for their good will and timeliness in meeting deadlines.

Conflicts of Interest: The authors declare no conflict of interest.

References

1. McNamee, M. *Philosophy and the Sciences of Exercise, Health and Sport: Critical Perspectives on Research Methods*; Routledge: Abingdon, UK, 2005; ISBN 9780415353403.
2. Ryall, E. Banned on the Run. *Phil. Mag.* **2012**, *58*, 90–94. [CrossRef]
3. Culbertson, L. The Paradox of Bad Faith and Elite Competitive Sport. *J. Phil. Sport* **2005**, *32*, 65–86. [CrossRef]
4. Loland, S. The Logic of Progress and the Art of Moderation in Competitive Sports. In *Values in Sport*; Tännsjö, T., Tamburrini, C., Eds.; Routledge: Abingdon, UK, 2000; ISBN 9780419253709.
5. Ryall, E. The notion of a science of sport: some conceptual considerations. In *Exercise, Sports and Health*; Schulz, H., Wright, P.R., Hauser, T., Eds.; Chemnitz University of Technology: Chemnitz, Germany, 2011; ISBN 9783941003415.
6. Williams, S.; Manley, A. Elite coaching and the technocratic engineer: Thanking the boys at Microsoft! *Sport Educ. Soc.* **2016**, *21*, 828–850. [CrossRef]
7. Winch, P. *The Idea of a Social Science and Its Relation to Philosophy*, 3rd ed.; Routledge and Kegan Paul: London, UK, 2008; ISBN 9780415423588.
8. Mumford, S. Metaphysics and Sport. In *Routledge Handbook of Philosophy of Sport*; Routledge: New York, NY, USA, 2015; ISBN 9781138294967.

9. Ryall, E. Are there any Good Arguments Against Goal-Line Technology? *Sport Educ. Soc.* **2012**, *6*, 439–450. [CrossRef]
10. Tännsjö, T. Against sexual discrimination in sports. In *Values in Sport*; Tännsjö, T., Tamburrini, C., Eds.; Routledge: Abingdon, UK, 2000; ISBN 9780419253709.

© 2019 by the author. Licensee MDPI, Basel, Switzerland. This article is an open access article distributed under the terms and conditions of the Creative Commons Attribution (CC BY) license (http://creativecommons.org/licenses/by/4.0/).

Article
The Necessity of Philosophy in the Exercise Sciences

Matthew Hickson

Department of Kinesiology, Mississippi State University, Starkville, MS 39759, USA; matthickson91@yahoo.com

Received: 2 May 2019; Accepted: 29 July 2019; Published: 7 August 2019

Abstract: The pervasive and often uncritical acceptance of materialistic philosophical commitments within exercise science is deeply problematic. This commitment to materialism is wrong for several reasons. Among the most important are that it ushers in fallacious metaphysical assumptions regarding the nature of causation and the nature of human beings. These mistaken philosophical commitments are key because the belief that only matter is real severely impedes the exercise scientist's ability to accurately understand or deal with human beings, whether as subjects of study or as data points to be interpreted. One example of materialist metaphysics is the assertion that all causation is physical- one lever moving another lever, one atom striking another atom, one brain state leading to another (Kretchmer, 2005). In such a world, human life is reduced to action and reaction, stimulus and response and as a result, the human being disappears. As such, a deterministic philosophy is detrimental to kinesiologists' attempts to interpret and understand human behavior, for a materialistic philosophy, must ignore or explain away human motivation, human freedom and ultimately culture itself. In showing how mistaken these philosophic commitments are, I will focus on the sub-discipline of sport psychology for most examples, as that is the field of exercise science of which I am paradigmatically most familiar. It is also the field, when rightly understood that straddles the "two cultures" in kinesiology (i.e., the sciences and the humanities). In referencing the dangers of the materialistic conception of human beings for sport psychology, I will propose, that the materialist's account of the natural world, causation and human beings stems from the unjustified and unnecessary rejection by the founders of modern science of the Aristotelian picture of the world (Feser, 2012). One reason that this mechanistic point of view, concerning human reality has gained ground in kinesiology is as a result of a previous philosophic commitment to quantification. As philosopher Doug Anderson (2002) has pointed out, many kinesiologists believe that shifting the discipline in the direction of mathematics and science would result in enhanced academic credibility. Moreover, given the dominance of the scientific narrative in our culture it makes it very difficult for us not to conform to it. That is, as Twietmeyer (2015) argued, kinesiologists do not just reject non-materialistic philosophic conceptions of the field, we are oblivious to their possibility. Therefore, I will propose two things; first, Aristotelian philosophy is a viable alternative to materialistic accounts of nature and causation and second, that Aristotle's holistic anthropology is an important way to wake kinesiologists from their self-imposed philosophic slumber.

Keywords: exercise science; philosophy; sport psychology; materialism; Aristotle; causation and nature

1. Introduction

This paper will argue that philosophy is necessary in order to be a good exercise scientist. Although often unconscious and largely unacknowledged by exercise scientists, materialism is the prevailing philosophy in the field. I will claim, this philosophic commitment is problematic for three reasons. First, the materialist's anthropology is wrong in its assertion that the human being is reducible to mere matter. Second, materialisms endorsement of casual determinism ultimately denies the possibility of human freedom, values and consciousness. Third, in taking the view that nature is inert and external to particular beings it must follow that human life is devoid of any inherent purpose or goal-directedness. To the extent that the exercise scientists buys into materialist arguments such as these, it calls into question the ethical soundness of their practice and research, as well as its supposed truth in terms of application to the lived experience of human beings. I will propose Aristotelian philosophy as a viable alternative for exercise science and the perfect antidote to the problems posed by materialism. Most specifically I will draw upon Aristotle's argument for anthropological holism and his anti-mechanistic, materialistic accounts of nature and causation.

2. Refuting Materialistic Accounts of Nature

The picture of nature that predominates in the hard sciences and as a result, exercise science is staunchly materialistic. It is physiology, chemistry and physics that are the heart of kinesiology, because they measure the material world and the material world is all that exists. For example, in sport psychology the relationship between anxiety and performance is often viewed mechanistically (Wilson, 2008 [1]). Broader accounts which view anxiety as part of human beings' ontological condition have been largely overlooked (Ronkainen and Nesti, 2015 [2]). The ontological approach proposed by Ronkainen and Nesti, views anxiety as a concomitant of our freedom to make choices and sees it as a challenge that must be confronted by the athlete. In contrast, the mechanistic approach attempts to eliminate rather than understand the influence of anxiety. In doing so it places a heavy emphasis on techniques and limits the athlete's personal responsibility. What follows from this mechanistic point of view, is the assumption that the nature of anything is not intrinsic to it. Instead "nature" is seen as something external to the objects of our experience as it is to ourselves as human beings. As philosopher Joe Sachs (1995) explained, from a mechanistic point of view, "nature is merely a name for the collective sum of things" [3] (p. 19). This view replaced the Aristotelian account of active powers within things, with the idea that natural phenomena are essentially passive. That is, there is no intentional direction to a thing which is internal to its own being. An acorn for instance, is not directed by its own internal organization and nature towards becoming an oak, instead physical laws are imposed upon it from the outside (Feser, 2012 [4]). As such, materialistic philosophy leads many hard scientists to falsely predicate that all events in the natural world occur accidentally, by which they mean not chaotically, but without any meaning, order or purpose. As Sachs (1995) described:

> The picture of the world assumed by the materialist physicist is of atoms and void there can be no cosmos, but only infinite emptiness, no life but only the accidental rearrangement of matter. [3] (p. 17)

In contrast, Aristotle viewed nature in a non-derivative sense. He thought that things possess natures of their own. This is most obvious with living things which are organized, and goal oriented. Contrary to the materialist conception of nature, Aristotle saw it as something active and dynamic instead of merely inert.

Yet, if the Aristotelian position is correct then, the regularity that we find in the cosmos implies a necessary connection between cause and effect. Living things have real and inherent causative power. A things own nature, not merely the laws of nature, is the source of motion and rest within living organisms (Sachs, 2001 [5]). Of course, critics might insist that materialistic, hard scientists' attribution of inertia to all things within the natural world is not meant to be antagonistic but merely methodological. It is read into the scientific method to fulfil a specific purpose: to use the tools of the scientific method to pursue a better understanding of the natural world. Moreover, haven't the scientific discoveries of the last several centuries justified this position? Two responses to this can be offered. First, methodology should not be confused with ontology. To say that the scientific method requires scientists to "remain silent regarding what they cannot measure" and to say "what they cannot measure is unreal" are two very different things. Second, history shows that the materialistic motivation of hard scientists, has not always been merely methodological, nor has it always been benign.

That is, materialism also allows scientists to treat nature as a mere object that is to be controlled and dominated. This fiction is extremely useful, but the cost is likewise high. This view fails to recognize a fundamental difference between living things and inanimate objects. These differences- so quickly denied and ignored by materialists- are real and profound. For example, unlike living things, inanimate objects don't have the capacity to stop and start themselves. Philosopher of science Mary Midgley (1992) explained the concept of an inert natural world through a common view of the purpose of the scientific project, by referring to a quote from Francis Bacon:

> Men ought to make peace among themselves to turn with united forces against the nature of things, to storm and occupy her castles and strongholds. [6] (p. 77)

This mechanistic picture of nature proposed by Bacon, if endorsed, is detrimental for kinesiology. Here is but one key example, if we follow Bacon's commitments through to their conclusion, we would have no principled reason not to limit genetic engineering or even eugenics in the practice of kinesiology. If human beings are merely material there is nothing sacrosanct about them, they are simply one more castle to be "stormed and occupied". As Brown (2009) explained:

> Surely there are few of us who would not welcome enhanced memories and immune systems, a prolonged healthy life span, and greater cognitive powers to create and appreciate the lives we have. Their wide availability would go far in remedying the failures of nature (as we see them) and promoting a more just and prosperous society. [7] (p. 135)

Brown's account is overly optimistic in that it overlooks a crucial danger associated with bio-technology. That is, we would come to value athletes in terms of the physical attribute's hard scientists have designed and produced instead of viewing them in terms of their inherent value as human beings. Moreover, what materialist scientists such as Bacon either ignore or fail to realize is if we depersonalize human nature it presents us all, scientists and non-scientists alike with a grave epistemological problem. If there is nothing akin to our human faculties of reason, will, desire and curiosity within the nature of things, then nature becomes utterly incomprehensible. In reducing their subjects to mere insentient lumps of matter, the materialist scientists reduce themselves to mere insentient lumps of matter. It is for this reason that those thinkers who have emphasized the intrinsic, living and animate character possessed by nature have tended to propose that there is a kind of 'rational structure' to the material universe. As C.S Lewis (1967) put it:

> Unless all we take to be knowledge is an illusion, we must hold that in thinking we are not reading rationality into an irrational universe but responding to a rationality with which the universe has always been saturated. [8] (p. 89)

Aristotle is again useful for addressing this problem for he argued that human beings are rational animals by nature, which, if true, means that human beings should be able to recognize the correspondence between the rational nature of man and the rationality of nature as such. Moreover, other scholars have argued, scientific inquiry cannot proceed if this correspondence is explicitly denied. Cardinal Joseph Ratzinger (2006) put it this way:

> Modern scientific reason quite simply must accept the rational structure of matter and the correspondence between our (human) spirit and the prevailing rational structures of nature as a given, on which its methodology has to be based. [9] (p. 16)

Such claims are not merely another attack by "reactionary clerics" upon progressive scientists. Ratzinger's endorsement of a rational structure inherent to nature is in no way a departure from sound scientific practice. The issue raised is philosophical not theological. The issue raised is also inescapable. As Albert Einstein put it, "what is most incomprehensible about nature is the fact it is comprehensible" (Pieper, 1989 [10] p. 94). This view held by Einstein implies two things. First, that the primary aim of hard scientists ought to be understanding nature, rather than controlling it. Second, that there is a basic order to things, which can be understood. Scientific enquiry is dependent upon basic foundational commitments such as these. That is, for scientific research to get off the ground these assertions must be already accepted (at least tacitly) for any scientific research to commence. Philosophy whether materialistic or Aristotelian, whether true or false, is baked into the scientific enterprise. As the philosopher Thomas Nagel (2012) insists:

> Materialism is incomplete even as a theory of the physical world, since the physical world includes conscious organisms among its most striking occupants. [11] (p. 45)

As a result, insofar as many exercise scientists uncritically accept materialism and deny any coherent account of human consciousness, they are ill-equipped to accurately describe or understand the animate life and nature of human beings. If Aristotle is right about mans nature, then the contemporary scientific image of human behavior, of neurons firing, causing other neurons to fire ad infinitum (Cave, 2016 [12]) as a comprehensive explanation for human behaviors, thoughts and actions simply doesn't fit the bill. The materialist picture of nature is a convenient tool for initiating the endeavors of the scientific enterprise, but it should not be mistaken for more than it is. As Aristotle told us in his ethics, we should not expect more from a science than what it can give. Scientific research is valuable, but it is also limited. To say that natural science is good does not mean it gives us an all-encompassing view of reality. The scientific method should not be applied haphazardly to the world which we experience. As Sachs (2001) argues:

> As long as the sort of explanation is doing pure mathematics with an imaginary world, it is safe from objection, but as soon as it is applied to the experiential world, it becomes subject to perception. [5] (p. 13)

This purely mathematical account is an attempt to deny that anything in the world has specific qualities, rather than mere quantities. It is also an attempt to deny or ignore the reality of the natural scientists themselves, upon whose conscious perception all scientific measurements rely. As such, it makes the perceptual activities common to us all, a matter of skeptical doubt. Yet, our lived experience tells us that qualities like color do in fact exist. Wherever this falsification or simplification of reality is not recognized, the mathematical, mechanical conception of nature should be dismissed as an object of fiction.

Merely explaining away perception as that which takes place entirely through the mechanisms of our sense organs and the events of the nervous system is inadequate. If perception was nothing but a mechanical process in the body, then the things we take in through perception should also be merely material. However, an often-heard phrase in sport shows that this cannot be the case. That is, that the "extra one percent is the difference between success and failure". But in what way could this "extra" 1% make sense as a material reality. It is asserted that this wholly immaterial idea plays an essential role in motivating athletes because our common experience- despite sophisticated philosophical denials- shows that when we perceive the nature of a thing, we receive that nature in an extra material way. The nature of a thing comes to us as more than the mere sum of its material parts. The human person both in our awareness of ourselves and our awareness of others, is the most obvious example of this truth. As Sachs (2001) insists:

> Living comes about just where material bodies cease to explain anything, where they are organized into active wholes. It used to be said that the human body is mostly water whilst the rest of it is $1.98 worth of chemicals. Obviously, those materials, which could be collected in a bucket, are transformed when they are a human body, and only form can explain the difference. [5] (p. 18)

A further example of this, would be when we open the shutter on a camera, the mechanism does not enable the camera to see anything (Sachs, 2001 [5]), because sight is more than mechanism. In brief, anything that is merely material doesn't have even the simple sensory capabilities that are common to human beings because mechanism and sensation aren't the same thing. As such, perception cannot solely be the physiology of the sense organs (Sachs, 2001 [5]). Physiology is necessary but not sufficient.

Yet, the uncritical acceptance of materialism in exercise science demands that all things can be explained by underlying mechanisms. For instance, in sport psychology it is common to reduce the existence of the human mind and see it merely as the workings of the brain which is then further reduced to the functions of a computer (Peters, 2012 [13]). Reductionism rules the day. This is deeply misleading and deeply dangerous to kinesiology. As Kretchmar (2005) emphasized, reductionists believe that:

> Causal direction always lies in the direction of underlying mechanisms all the way down to the subatomic level. [14] (p. 14)

However, both human experience and clinical practice shows that reductionism has serious limitations for enhancing sport performance or improving health. One such example, is the tendency in western medical practice to view mental illness as a "brain disease" over which the patient has little choice or responsibility (Watters, 2010 [15]). Such fatalism can result in a loss of meaning of which is central to mental well-being.

Nevertheless, materialists continue to insist that empirical data, that which can be measured and quantified, is all that is really needed. This viewpoint is commonly promulgated in the physical sciences and is based upon the authoritative power of mathematics to reveal objective knowledge. As such, many exercise scientists have adopted this approach whereby there has been an over-emphasis on the methods of natural science (Anderson, 2002 [16]). Yet, ironically this is due to exercise scientists' commitments to philosophical materialism. Kinesiologist are often oblivious to non-materialistic conceptions of the field (Twietmeyer, 2015 [17]). The belief of the materialist in mathematics proves the exact opposite of what many materialists think. In fact, mathematics shows that materialism is a self-refuting philosophy. In materialism's rejection of intangibles lays the seeds of its own destruction. As Twietmeyer and Johnson (2018) put it:

> Mathematics upon which science relies is an abstract reality which cannot be reduced to matter. Numbers cannot have weight or any other physical property. They are wholly immaterial, yet their reality is necessary to the materialists' project of measuring and counting physical reality. [18] (p. 7)

This philosophic insight shows how deeply problematic materialism is for exercise scientists, despite their commitment to materialism, they routinely rely on the intangibles of mathematics to get their research off the ground.

3. Examining Accounts of Causation

The mechanistic picture of nature first put forth by the natural scientists of the seventeenth century which promoted a deterministic view of causality, eventually prompted the counter-assertion that all causes are loose and separate. Thus, it led to the classic problem about causation and induction proposed by David Hume. The Humean perspective is that there is no causative reality in the world other than regularity or what he called "constant conjunction" (Mumford, 2015 [19]). For Hume the cause did not produce the effect. Instead, the effect merely happened to follow the cause. In short, the world was according to Hume, a patchwork of unconnected events (Lewis, 1973 [20]). As distasteful as many find Hume, it should be clear that this naturally follows as a consequence of viewing nature as somehow external to things-themselves. That is, a strictly empiricist metaphysics necessarily results in causal skepticism. This relates to what Aristotelian-Thomist philosopher Edward Feser (2012 [4]) would describe as a case of "as-if teleology". For example, "the chance arrangement of liana vines into a form looking vaguely like a cross, is a case of as-if teleology insofar as the vines were not really arranged for the purpose of representing a cross, but merely to appear as if they were" (p. 5). What Feser means by the notion of as-if teleology is that the movement towards a particular end is not intrinsic to the nature of the thing in question. As such, the fulfillment of a particular end, is a mere random occurrence or chance event. To return to the example, it is not of the nature of liana vines to move towards the fulfillment of the end of becoming a symbol like a cross. The view that causation happens accidentally is associated with what Feser describes as "teleological eliminitvism". For the eliminitivist, there is no genuine purposes at all in the natural world. This applies to both the Humean picture of the world and that proposed by the modern scientific mechanists. For the Humean, causation is merely arbitrary and for the scientific mechanist it is totally determinate. The crucial difference between the world pictures proposed by the Humean and the scientific mechanist and the Aristotelian picture of the natural world that I am endorsing is that for Aristotle a thing's nature was inherent to it and it derived its causal power from its own nature. Aristotle argued, this was true of all living things but especially of rational substances, most notably human beings. Rational substances possess the ends towards which they are naturally inclined within themselves in the most perfect possible way. As such, living things are not merely caused to act in a specific way by a set of routine laws imposed upon them from the outside, or by a set of random, external chance occurrences. Another way of viewing all of this centers around the distinction between, on the one hand, those objects that have substantial forms and those having only accidental forms. In rejecting the Aristotelian metaphysical claim that things have natures, modern, natural science rejected the Aristotelian notion of substantial forms in favor of accidental forms. For Aristotle the object's form was what caused it to be in a specific way. For example, the cause of an object's beauty, was the result of its form, with form being the organizational integrity it exhibits to remain the thing it is. This is known in Aristotelian philosophy as formal causality. Modern, natural science, in contrast, took on the view of causality presupposed by Newtonian mechanics; that is the accidental arrangement and rearrangement of matter in space according to nothing other than physical laws. It could be argued this was a result of the natural scientists' unwillingness to deal with the puzzles presented by Hume. Newton argued confidently that causes are deterministically connected to their effects. Yet, due to the widespread indifference towards philosophy within exercise science, issues of causality, including conflict between the Newtonian and Humean accounts has largely been ignored. The prevailing Newtonian stance on causation has encouraged exercise scientists to assume that causality moves in a straight line or linear direction. As sport philosopher Scott Kretchmar (2005) explained:

> Linearity suggests that doubling a cause (say the length of a lever between the fulcrum and point of force) results in a predictable increase in the effect (the ability to move objects). [14] (p. 15)

Yet, experience shows the limitations of applying such a model to human behavior. Sometimes large causes can lead to small effects. On the other hand, sometimes large effects can proceed from small causes. For example, a small degree of imagination can lead to immense creativity. Or, a large amount of time spent practicing penalty kicks in soccer can have a diminishing return in a shootout due to over-emphasis leading to paralysis of performance, and practice conditions not entirely replicating a match situation, etc.

There is a second common assumption associated with a hard deterministic conception of causality in the sciences, which can also be easily unmasked. That is, that causation only moves in one-direction whereby tangibles effect intangibles, but not vice-versa. Kretchmar (2005) expressed the claim this way:

> If ideas are simply the result of a chain of electrical, chemical, physiological and cultural events, then ideas become merely the dependent offspring of the chain. [14] (p. 16)

As one of the leading evangelists of the evolutionary scientific movement Richard Dawkins (1989 [21]) would put it, intangibles like ethics are nothing more than the complex workings of our selfish genes. The irony of this view is that it can be refuted by both philosophy and science. For instance, psychologists at Stanford University, found that just by telling people they have a high or low genetic risk for certain physiological limitations can influence how the person functions when exercising or eating, regardless of what genetic properties or variants they actually have (Turnwald,

Goyer, Boles, Slider, Delp and Crum, 2018 [22]) As such, ideas have the capacity to change human perception and evaluation concerning the effects of our genetics on behavior. In this sense, ideas can help us overcome supposed physical limitations. Philosophy (ideas) is as important for kinesiology as physiology (genetics).

However, if we accept the predominant views of materialist scientists, we must deny the existence of any values whatsoever (Feser, 2012 [23]). One example of the absurdity of such a position is the reality love. Love is a fundamental reality of human existence, yet materialists explain it away as mere chemicals in the brain (Earp and Savulescu, 2014 [24]). The absurdity doesn't stop there. Respected neuroscientist, Professor Larry Young [25] claims, "it will soon be possible for scientists to develop aphrodisiacs-chemicals that would make people fall in love with the first person they see" (p. 148). Not only is this a denial of all value, it is also a denial of free-will, which is fundamental to the reality of love. The nature of love is as such, that it requires a freely chosen act of self-giving, of one person to another. That is, it can in no way be forced or coerced by outside stimulus and remain what it is. What should be clear from my argument is that the idea of causal determinism is not an adequate explanation of human behavior, and that all philosophic commitments materialistic or otherwise, have significant implications for sub-disciplines in kinesiology such as sport psychology. To reiterate, the findings of natural science are not the only legitimate sources of knowledge. What Young is prophesizing is merely another article of crude 'scientism'. In reducing love to chemicals in the brain neuroscientists are attempting to make love an empirically verifiable concept. That is because for reductionists like Young there is no reality beyond that which can be weighed, counted and measured. However, that the human intellect is capable of grasping immaterial concepts such as love should be accepted as the common sense reality that it is. Just because the definition of love possessed by the man on the street is lacking scientific support does not mean there is any reason to doubt its existence. Neither psychological research nor the human beings who participate in it can be coherently reduced to purely material causes. Nonetheless one popular mode of predicting human behavior in the psychological sciences shares the view of deterministic causation held by the materialist scientists. This school of thought is known as behaviorism. Software engineer William. A Wilson (2017) expertly summarized the tenets of behavioral psychology as follows:

> Behaviorists believe all human and animal behaviors are merely reactions to external stimuli and previous conditioning. Moreover, they posit the internal states of individuals have no causal effects on their actions, regardless of what those individuals may claim. [26] (pp. 5–6)

In more recent times in sport psychology a cognitive element has been added to the original approach adopted by the behaviorist. Whilst this has provided a belated acknowledgment on behalf of the psychologists of the existence of the human mind, cognitions are still by and large viewed in a deterministic fashion. I would argue, the positions taken by the behaviorists and more recently the cognitive behaviorists are detrimental for professional practice in the field of sport psychology and stresses the need to reconsider the appropriate sites of intervention when working with clients. To be sensitive towards such concerns whether (sympathetic or antagonistic) requires respect for philosophy. A pragmatist would likely suggest, for example, that where it works the behaviorists model is fine to use. Nevertheless, I would argue, behaviorism's mistaken views surrounding causality lead behaviorists to incorrectly understand the nature of the human person. As a consequence, behaviorists are likely to encourage among other things, unethical practice. For example, it may lead a practitioner to deny the free-will of their client through the belief that change occurs solely through altering outside conditions. This is unethical because the faculty of the will is fundamental to our existence as rational animals. Therefore, to prevent the lawful free choice of another human being is to act towards them in a way that is contrary to their rational nature (Feser, 2018 [27]). In addition, numerous studies in sport psychology have demonstrated that the use of prayer by athletes is a common and valuable practice for enhancing performance and overall well-being through supporting the alleviation of stress and anxiety in uncertain situations (Watson and Czech, 2004 [28]; Czech, Wrisberg, Fisher, Thompson and Hayes 2004 [29]; Vernacchia, McGuire, Reardon and Templin, 2000 [30]). All this implies reasons to doubt behaviorism. After all, is the well-established effect of prayer on the well-being and the performance of athletes plausibly explained away as self-delusion? Does the fact prayer is both a free endeavor and an immaterial concept provide grounds for dismissing its efficacy? Despite the objections of both materialists and behaviorists, experienced sport psychologists have stated the importance of investigating the possibility of reconciling the use of religious prayer with conventional mental skills training (Watson and Nesti, 2005 [31]). However, prayer is not just one mere technique amongst all the others. The materialist sport psychologist is ill-equipped to incorporate the use of prayer into their work with clients potentially limiting their overall effectiveness as a consultant. This is because the materialist would in most cases deny the existence of free-will and any form of immaterial reality. As such, they must conclude that the alleged benefits of religious prayer are nothing more than pure fantasy or at the very best mere 'wishful thinking'.

4. Holism and Waking Exercise Scientists from Their "Philosophic Slumber"

The value of philosophical holism in kinesiology, and the related non-scientific sub-disciplines of kinesiology should not be undervalued. That is, because holistic practitioners both look globally for partial causes of a problem and are willing to intervene in multiple locations, they do a better job of relating to human beings (Kretchmer, 2005 [14]). Holists realize that the human person is more than the sum of its material parts. Materialists will no doubt disagree. However, such discussion cannot even get off the ground, if exercise scientists fail to recognize the importance of philosophy to the discipline. This is but one example of how philosophy necessarily impinges on the sciences. In contrast to the linear model of causation endorsed by many modern natural scientists, Aristotle viewed causality primarily as hierarchical. As discussed, all of Aristotle's causes stem from beings, and they are found not by simply looking backward in time, but also upward in the chain of responsibility (Sachs, 1995 [3]). An example of a hierarchical causal chain was provided by Feser (2017):

> The coldness of the coffee was caused by the coolness in the surrounding air, which was caused by the air conditioner, which was caused to switch on when you pressed the button and so forth. [32] (p. 20)

What this demonstrates is that each of the lower members in a causal chain derive their causal power from a hierarchically higher member. In short, all contingent change requires a changer. What Aristotle went on to conclude was that all such causes derive their causal power from a prime cause. This unmoved mover, as he called it, was identified by Aristotle as God. For present purposes the larger theological implications can be set aside. The only thing that needs to be emphasized now is that Aristotle argued for an ordered rather than chaotic universe. The things in the cosmos, which had natures unto themselves, were part of a larger whole. Human beings, Aristotle posited, are naturally curious and as a result stretch themselves out toward knowing (Sachs, 1999 [33]). Human beings are not machines, but rather "rational animals" (Aristotle, 2002 [34]). Again, this implies the importance of philosophy as we try to understand, debate and discuss the nature and meaning of this alleged order.

The metaphysical realist position taken by Aristotle in relation to causation is fundamental to the reality and nature of sport and a coherent (and holistic) account of human beings. As philosopher Stephen Mumford (2015 [19]) points out, if there were no causation anything could follow anything else. This has both crude and profound implications. Crudely speaking, this would mean that the football player who scores a touchdown would not be worthy of any credit, as he did not cause the touchdown. More profoundly, if we don't possess something like in-built causal powers, we can claim no responsibility for our actions. As a result, not only would we never be worthy of any praise, neither would we be worthy of any blame. Human responsibility would disappear. Yet, the assumption of human responsibility undergirds all human activity. As sociologists Clifford Staples (2016) put it:

> To live in this distinctly human world means holding and being held accountable for what we do, or do not do, against a standard of right and wrong that we alone do not establish and are not free to ignore without consequences. [35] (p. 2)

As such, to abolish responsibility is to make the world inhuman. It is clear that this has substantial implications in terms of professional ethics for all disciplines within kinesiology. Yet again the importance of philosophy is demonstrated. For if free-will is to be jettisoned, the commitment should be made deliberately rather than as a cavalier result of previous unacknowledged philosophic commitments.

It also follows from the model of causation proposed by materialistic science that all sporting outcomes are necessitated. This would make sport dull to watch and pointless to play (Mumford, 2015 [19]). We would lose the mystery, serendipity and human drama of sport which is a primary reason so many of us are attracted to it. As Mumford (2015) argues, the reality of sporting contests proposes the existence of a causal efficacy that lies somewhere in between arbitrary and deterministic causality.

> It is arguable that sport is premised on there being a modal strength that is less than necessity but more than mere possibility; an intermediate dispositional modality in which sporting abilities tend towards outcomes without guaranteeing them. [19] (p. 282)

What Mumford means is that the best team or individual wins most of the time, but not all the time. Though chance and fortune should both play a part, skill should by and large be the determinative factor. What is clear from these examples, is that one's philosophic commitments matter at both the theoretical and practical levels. Ignoring the philosophical conclusions of materialism do not make them go away.

Aristotelian philosophy offers a viable alternative in kinesiology to the accounts of causation provided by modern, natural science. If we recover his notion of "nature" or final causality, we will be able to view the discipline primarily in light of the end's values associated with it. That is, as Kretchmar (2005 [14]) insisted, we will be able to consider kinesiology as a jewel rather than as merely a tool. Too often the discipline is focused on selling itself on the basis of its usefulness. In short, we limit our contribution to human health. Yet, as Twietmeyer and Johnson (2018 [18]) put it, "nobody lives for health. Rather they live from health toward the world of love, play, family, career, and so forth" (p. 8). In this sense, we are selling ourselves short. Exercise science is a powerful and indispensable resource for understanding the biological and physiological nature of human movement, but it is still just a tool, which must be put in service of some further good or end. To adjudicate these ends, to debate what we ought to do, to see and understand the good requires philosophy, not further measurement.

In denying the proper relation of means to ends we have followed the lead of modern, natural science which reduced Aristotle's final cause to a mere series of efficient causes. From Aristotle's point of view, this is incoherent. To reject the idea that things are directed to certain ends or goals by virtue of their nature, is to render efficient causality as unintelligible (Feser, 2010 [36]). For example, human beings have feet in order to walk, without this function, having feet as part of the human anatomy would make very little sense. Therefore, despite many natural scientist's rejection of final causality, they attempt to smuggle it in through the backdoor via the affirmation of efficient causes. Moreover, our over-emphasis on health encourages kinesiologists to take the view that matter is all that really exists. In other words, we have taken human embodiment too seriously. For many kinesiologists "we are just bodies".

This view of human embodiment in the exercise sciences which is so common, aligns with the currently dominant cultural paradigm. Materialism rules the day. As physical educator Brian Pronger (1995 [37]) explained, "the body is a malleable, useful object in modern culture" (p. 428). Kinesiologists must reject thinking such as this. Just as embodiment is part of the larger human whole, kinesiologists must discover a larger sense of the whole in the discipline of which each sub-discipline is merely a part. Exercise science and sport philosophy need each other. This acknowledgment is vital, both for the sake of attaining a true conception of kinesiology and for a true conception of our clients, students, athletes and research subjects. Human beings are not mere atoms in motion, nor are they incorporeal minds for whom embodiment and chemistry and genetics and physiology do not matter. This insight relies not on measurement but rather reflection. To do scientific research in kinesiology well requires philosophy because those of whom we serve, as well as all kinesiologists themselves are more than mere bodies.

Funding: This research received no external funding.

Acknowledgments: The author would like to acknowledge both reviewers for their helpful and insightful comments.

Conflicts of Interest: The author declares no conflict of interest.

References

1. Wilson, M. From processing efficency to attentional control: A mechanistic account of the anxiety-performance relationship. *Int. Rev. Sport Exerc. Psychol.* **2008**, *1*, 184–201. [CrossRef]
2. Ronkainen, N.; Nesti, M. An existential approach to sport psychology: Theory and applied practice. *Int. J. Sport Exerc. Psychol.* **2015**, *15*, 12–24. [CrossRef]
3. Sachs, J. Introduction. In *Aristotle, Aristotles Physics*; Rugters University Press: London, UK, 1995.
4. Feser, E. Atheistic Teleology? Available online: http://edwardfeser.blogspot.com/2012/07/atheistic-teleology.html (accessed on 5 July 2012).
5. Sachs, J. On the soul: An introduction. In *Aristotle, On the Soul, Memory and Recollection*; Green Lion Press: Santa Fe, NM, USA, 2001.
6. Midgley, M. *Science as Salvation: A Modern Myth and its Meaning*; Routledge: New York, NY, USA, 1992.
7. Brown, M. The case for perfection. *J. Philos. Sport* **2009**, *36*, 127–139. [CrossRef]
8. Lewis, C.S. *Christian Reflections*; Eerdmans: Grand Rapids, MI, USA, 1967.
9. Ratzinger, J. Apostolic Journey of his holiness Benedict XVI to Munchen, Altoting and Regensburg. Available online: http://w2.vatican.va/content/benedict-xvi/en/speeches/2006/september/documents/hf_ben-xvi_spe_20060912_universityregensburg.html (accessed on 9 September 2006).
10. Pieper, J. *An. Anthology*; Ignatius Press: San Francisco, CA, USA, 1989.
11. Nagel, T. *Mind and Cosmos: Why the Materialist Neo-Darwinan Conception of Nature is Almost Certainly False*; Oxford University Press: Oxford, UK, 2012.
12. Cave, S. There's No Such Thing as Free-Will. Available online: https://www.theatlantic.com/magazine/archive/2016/06/theres-no-such-thing-as-free-will/480750/ (accessed on 2 June 2016).
13. Peters, S. *The Chimp Paradox: The Aclaimed Mind Management Programme to Help You Achieve Success, Confidence and Happiness*; Tarcher Penguin: New York, NY, USA, 2012.
14. Kretchmar, R.S. *Practical Philosophy of Sport and Physical Activity*; Human Kinetics: Champaign, IL, USA, 2005.
15. Watters, E. The Americanization of Mental Illness. Available online: https://www.nytimes.com/2010/01/10/magazine/10psyche-t.html (accessed on 10 January 2010).
16. Anderson, D. The humanity of movement or"its not just a gym class". *Quest* **2002**, *54*, 87–96. [CrossRef]
17. Twietmeyer, G. God, sport, philosophy, kinesiology: A MacIntyrean investigation. *Quest* **2015**, *67*, 203–226. [CrossRef]
18. Twietmeyer, G.; Johnson, T. A kinesiology conundrum: Physical activity requirments in kinesiology degree programs. *Quest* **2018**, *71*, 90–111. [CrossRef]
19. Mumford, S. Metaphysics and Sport. In *Morgan and McNamee, The Routledge Hanbook of the Philosophy of Sport*; Routledge: Abingdon, UK, 2015.
20. Lewis, D. *Counterfactuals*; Blackwell Publishing: Oxford, UK, 1973.
21. Dawkins, R. *The Selfish Gene*; Oxford University Press: Oxford, UK, 1989.
22. Turnwald, B.; Goyer, P.; Boles, D.; Slider, A.; Delp, S.; Crum, A. Learning one's genetic risk changes physiology independent of actual genetic risk. *Nat. Hum. Behav.* **2018**, *3*, 48–56. [CrossRef] [PubMed]
23. Feser, E. Aristotle, Call Your Office. Available online: https://www.firstthings.com/web-exclusives/2012/10/aristotle-call-your-office (accessed on 18 October 2012).
24. Earp, B.; Savulescu, J. *Love drugs: Why Scientists Study the Effects of Pharmaceuticals on Human Romantic Relationships*; Cambridge University Press: Cambridge, UK, 2014.
25. Young, L. Being human: Love: Neuroscience reveals all. *Nat. Int. J. Sci.* **2009**, *457*, 148.
26. Wilson, A.W. The Myth of Scientific Objectivity. Available online: https://www.firstthings.com/article/2017/11/the-myth-of-scientific-objectivity (accessed on 12 November 2017).

27. Feser, E. Violence in Word and Action. Available online: http://edwardfeser.blogspot.com/2018/10/violence-in-word-and-action.html (accessed on 27 October 2018).
28. Watson, N.; Czech, D. The use of prayer in sport: Implications for sport psychology consulting. *Athl. Insight* **2005**, *7*, 26–35.
29. Czech, D.; Wrisberg, C.; Fisher, L.; Thompson, C.; Hayes, G. The experience of Christian prayer in sport: An existential phenomenological investigation. *J. Psychol. Christ.* **2004**, *23*, 3–11.
30. Vernacchia, R.; McGuire, R.; Reardon, J.; Templin, D. Psychosocial characteristics of olympic track and field athletes. *Int. J. Sport Psychol.* **2000**, *31*, 5–23.
31. Watson, N.; Nesti, M. The role of spirituality in sport psychology consulting: An analysis and integrative review of literature. *J. Appl. Sport Psychol.* **2005**, *17*, 228–239. [CrossRef]
32. Feser, E. *Five Proofs of the Existence of God*; Ignatius Press: San Francisco, CA, USA, 2017.
33. Sachs, J. *Introduction in Aristotle, Aristotle's Metaphysics*; Green Lion Press: Santa Fe, NM, USA, 1999.
34. Aristotle. *Nicomachean Ethics*; Focus Philosophical Library: Newbury, MA, USA, 2002.
35. Staples, C. Abolishing the Moral Order. Available online: https://www.crisismagazine.com/2016/abolishing-moral-order (accessed on 15 December 2016).
36. Feser, E. Teleology a shoppers guide. *Philos. Christi* **2010**, *12*, 142–159. [CrossRef]
37. Pronger, B. *Body Facism: Salvation in the Technology of Physical Fitness*; University of Toronto Press: Toronto, CN, Canada, 2002.

© 2019 by the author. Licensee MDPI, Basel, Switzerland. This article is an open access article distributed under the terms and conditions of the Creative Commons Attribution (CC BY) license (http://creativecommons.org/licenses/by/4.0/).

Article

The Hazards of a Biomedical Exercise Paradigm: Exploring the Praxis of Exercise Professionals

John Gray

The Business School, Teesside University, Tees Valley, Middlesbrough TS1 3BX, UK; j.gray@tees.ac.uk; Tel.: +44-01642-738472

Received: 30 July 2019; Accepted: 4 September 2019; Published: 12 September 2019

Abstract: There is a belief that exercise has a major role to play in the current health and wellbeing agendas. Consequently, health interventions are implemented based upon the recommendations of the ACSM and similar exercise research organizations. However this development has been challenged through both social and political perspectives. Specifically accusations of medicalization have been raised against the increasing relationship between the exercise and medical domains. The purpose of this article is to present a similar critique of the growing emergence of a medical paradigm within the exercise domain. In this instance the focus will examine the relationship between exercise professional, exercise science and the proposed medical paradigm. Through the use of philosophical essay and systematic review of literature, it is argued that a continuing shift by exercise science to mirror the medical paradigm will cause a number of issues and potential hazards in the working practices of its professionals.

Keywords: exercise professional; professional knowledge; health; wellbeing; philosophy; medicalization; scientism; biomedicine

1. Introduction

In 2004 Fred Widland attended his first free personal training session at Manhattan's Crunch Fitness International gym, USA. As reported in the New York Post, Widland, the self-confessed couch potato and ex-smoker, undertook a supervised training session that left him with severe kidney damage through the toxic condition of exertional rhabdomyolysis [1]. More recently in 2013 Rebecca Johnson, from Brighton, UK, participated in a private personal training session. However, as reported in the Mail Online [2], after the session Johnson, an experienced exerciser, stated:

A few times I said to the personal trainer I was finding it tough and I didn't know if I could carry on. 'But he encouraged me to dig deep to do the best possible. As he was the professional I did as he asked. I thought no pain, no gain'.

As a result, Johnson's experiences ended with a similar outcome to Widland: after observing blood in her urine she was taken to hospital to avoid life-threatening complications and was left with debilitating ill-health for several months. A year later, in 2014, Daniel Popp undertook a supervised training session at SnapFitness in Queensland, Australia and suffered the same issues as both Widland and Johnson claiming: "my urine went as back as leather!" [3]. Again, the filed lawsuit stated that despite the exerciser claiming they were unable to undertake the given exercise regime, the trainer persisted to push the client to a point of physiological danger. Historically, there have been demands to recognize and deal with similar problems in exercise contexts (e.g., [4]) but evidence suggests these experiences are not an uncommon trend. For example between 2011 and 2014, the reported cases of exercise induced rhabdomyolysis admitted to a single University hospital increased four-fold [5]. Thus concern arises as to the increasing incidence of these and similar reports of other exercise-induced injuries and debilitation.

In attempting to locate 'blame' for the negative exercise experiences the primary focus has been on the exercise professional. As a result, the academic consideration is that "trainers need better education on using the guidelines to initiate and achieve health benefits and avoid problems." [6], (p. 698). Thus blame is considered to be found in the lack of professional education. Furthermore a philosophy for the 'individualism of blame' becomes evident with the recent growth in legal specialists. For example accidentclaims.co.uk now offer Gym Accident Compensation Claims Experts (100% no win no fee); whilst actionsinjurysolicitors.co.uk advertise they have successfully obtained £6000 for a gym client's finger injury[1]. Consequently the premise is made that the problem lies with the 'rogue' trainer due to their lack of consideration for, and/or knowledge of, ethical and contextual demands in delivering appropriate exercise experiences [7–9].

This essay is an attempt to present a critical and alternate argument to the current position of blame based on 'individual errors of judgement' and the conclusion that professionals fail to follow the educational guidelines. The thesis presented follows a parallel line to existing challenges of the implied assumption that exercise is a medicine in contemporary definitions, and specifically argues that a deference to the paradigm of medical science has initiated an increasing *scientism* within exercise science and, by association, the domain's professionals [9–11]. Stated explicitly, it is argued that an increasing belief in warranting scientific processes validation beyond their bounds is leading to an exercise nemesis with hazardous consequences for public health [12]. As a result, this paper argues an alternate proposition: the cause of the negative experiences may be due to a deference to the professional exercise guidelines themselves, as opposed to their avoidance in the choices of 'rogue' or, as assumed, insufficiently educated trainer.

In presenting this argument, firstly a very brief overview of the concept of scientism and the issues which have historically beset medical science is presented. There is insufficient space within this paper to comprehensively review the debates surrounding scientism within medical literature. Consequently, a summary is presented of the key issues which may emerge as exercise science aligns the practice of exercise professionals to this paradigm. Secondly, this paper will then explore the results of a systematic scoping review of the exercise professional's knowledge base and consider the implications of these findings.

2. Issues of Scientism in Medicine

Medicine has become regarded as a knowledge system which has shaken off the 'magical' and 'superstitious' past to stand alongside the natural sciences of physics, mathematics and chemistry [13]. Thus, once considered the domain of charlatans and quacks, medicine, through a scientific rhetoric, has emerged as a key factor in determining social policy, technological advancement and bureaucratic governance of 'day-to-day living' in the 21stC [13]. This success has been credited to the application of what is termed the biomedical model; a scientific paradigm which can be summarized through four fundamental assumptions [14]:

1. Disease is defined as a deviation from a statistical norm and measurable level of biological functioning.
2. Each defined disease is a specific and individual 'entity'; generic regardless of culture and context.
3. Medicine is a neutral, objective science without recourse to relational, metaphysical or existential considerations.
4. Medicine allows for an ontological foundation of mind-body dualism.

Furthermore the biomedical paradigm is a position in which the body is presented ontologically "as docile—something physicians could observe, manipulate, transform and improve." [15], (p. 221). Consequently, through a biological machine metaphor, medicine is able to rationalize the body as

---

[1] Websites accessed 15/07/19.

an object for discipline and control. As Nicholson states, it is this model which provides the most powerful theoretical tool of modern scientific medicine and biology [16].

Increasingly, society has embraced this biomedical and scientific mind-set. Health discourses have become almost singularly based upon a biological and mechanistic linearity, and taught through delineated categories of 'healthy versus unhealthy' [17]. As a result, a medical scientism has pervaded contemporary culture in search of therapeutic miracles and 'magic bullets' [18]. Defined as a position in which positivistic science is extolled as the only 'methodology' and 'real knowledge' needed to deal with the human condition, this scientism ultimately suggests that the science of the biomedical paradigm should be applied to the understanding all health and wellbeing discourses [19–21].

Ultimately, through a double hermeneutical process, biomedicine has re-created in secular terms a 21stC belief in Gnosticism [22,23]. That is a 'faith' in the power of science to eventually understand all of 'nature's secrets' leads to a medical science which will cure all the 'evils' of ill-health [24]. In line with Gnostic beliefs of a 'true' knowledge which will provide ultimate enlightenment, there is a faith in Western medical technologies to create a new evolution of society [23,25].

Yet despite this Gnostic scientism, it has been demonstrated that the underpinning biomedical paradigm is a key factor in a number of emergent medical issues. As highlighted 40 years ago in Illich's *Medical Nemesis*, whilst achievements over some major disease cannot be dismissed neither can the dangers of iatrogenesis which modern medicine creates [26]. That is, biomedicine is in a dangerous position through which it may become its own nemesis. As Illich argues: medicine generates as many problems as it solves. Hence, contemporary scientific medicine has brought with it issues of hazardous side-effects, the medicalization of normal functioning, declining wellbeing and the generation of a morbid society [17,20,26–30]. As a result, there are a number of concerns voiced as to the appropriateness of the biomedical paradigm to meet the demands of society's health needs e.g., [26,31].

Despite warnings of biomedicine's dangers inherent in its philosophical position, there is evidence of a growing demand to follow this paradigm in the exercise domain. This is exceptionally evident in the Exercise is Medicine™ (EIM) scheme, a joint project by the American College of Sports Medicine (ACSM) and the American Medical Association (AMA). Initiated in 2007, it is an attempt to align exercise practice with medical intervention [23,32,33]. The project's objective is the habitual implementation of exercise for the management, prevention and treatment of disease and to "ensure exercise is thought of as a medication to be prescribed to patients" [34], (p. 413). The EIM has now been adopted on a global scale by 43 countries and is considered a key component in the development of public health strategies [10]. Although, at present, there appears to be no formal UK affiliation with the EIM, the ACSM's philosophy is the dominant principle supported by the majority of UK researchers, practitioners, and related organizations such as the National Institute for Health Care and Excellence (NICE) exercise referral schemes [35].

The dominance of a scientific exercise paradigm is reflected in the mission statements of the major fitness professional organizations and leaders. For example:

The ACSM [American College of Sports Medicine] promotes and integrates scientific research, education and practical applications of sports medicine and exercise science to maintain and enhance physical performance, fitness, health and quality of life. [36], (p. 24)

Furthermore, the 'National Academy of Sports Medicine' (NASM) states explicitly its demand for the scientific process in its professional practices:

A new form of exercise may allegedly produce significant results, but if it is not supported by scientific research, it becomes a questionable trend. [37], (p. 8)

As a result, such organizations have created a form of scientism based on a de facto acceptance of a biomedical philosophy [34]. That is: exercise is not only the answer but a scientifically and medically justifiable solution. Yet, these organizations, which promote the advancement of a biomedical exercise science and increasingly call for a scientific evidence base, appear to ignore the considerable dissent to biomedicine's scientism [31]. Accusations of scientism have already been made in sports research [38], and the dangers challenging the 'loss of the person' in the pursuit of a scientific understanding of sport have been voiced [39–43]. But such critiques are limited in the exercise domain with the literature providing any critical analysis focused predominantly political or sociological perspectives as opposed to methodological e.g., [9–11].

The aforementioned lack of philosophical discussion through paradigmatic and methodological criticism may prove problematic. Specifically, it can be argued that through such perspectives evidence of the negative effects of a scientific approach may already be observable in exercise practice e.g., [1–3,7,8,10]. As a result, mirroring Illich's warnings of iatrogenesis, data would suggest that an increasingly 'biomedical' exercise science could lead further down a pathway already criticized as dangerous. Consequently, it is argued that a significant and deeper critical reflection should be undertaken concerning the appropriateness of the biomedical paradigm for exercise science. Crucially, this analysis should focus on the nature of knowledge presented to and utilized by professionals in developing exercise experiences [44,45]. Thus, the hazards of rhabdomyolysis and similar debilitations experienced by participants may be due to a 'nemesis of biomedical exercise' lying at the root of the exercise professional's praxis. As a result it is proposed that the foundational paradigm upon which exercise praxis is built should be the starting point of inquisition.

3. Evidence for a Biomedical Scientism in Exercise Praxis

3.1. Method

To explore the current understanding of exercise professional's praxis a systematic review was undertaken. Similar scoping exercises on the role's demands have been previously described by De Lyon, Neville and Armour [45]. However, rather than re-create De Lyon's et al.'s work, the intention here is to explore the possible formulation of the underpinning paradigm behind professional practice.

Literature searching was undertaken using multiple strategies due to the possible diversity and broad variety of work. The electronic databases—SCOPUS and SPORTSDiscus (EBSCO) were searched for the period 2009–2018. This time period was used based on the initiation of EIM project in 2009. Boolean operators were used and as a result the searches used the terms of "personal train*" OR "exercise profession*" OR "fitness instruct*". A total of nine hundred and thirty-two titles were found. Relevant papers, textbooks, websites and bibliographies were also manually searched for possible grey literature and omissions from the digital search strategy. This strategy yielded an additional seven papers for consideration.

On completion of the search strategy, the removal of duplicates, and the elimination of irrelevant studies, a total of five hundred and thirty seven references for consideration. The remaining references were then analysed via the inclusion criteria question "Does this research present information which allows for the working practices, knowledge base and methods of exercise professionals to become evident?" This criteria was applied via the reading of abstracts and led to the removal of four hundred and ninety six references. After the application of the systematic process forty one papers were available for a final read through. The final screening process utilized an exclusion criteria to remove those papers which did not provide a specific focus or representation of the education and knowledge base of exercise professionals. This final examination left a total of seventeen papers considered appropriate: twelve papers examined the content of the education and knowledge [46–57]; four papers examined the application of knowledge [58–61] and a single paper examined the nature of professional knowledge development [62]. A full schematic representation of the systematic process is provided in the following Figure 1.

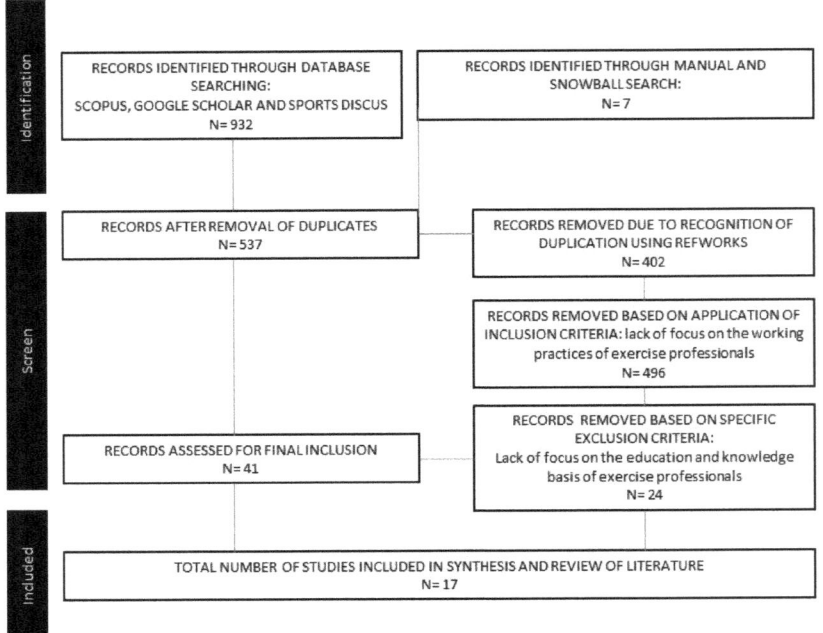

Figure 1. Schematic diagram of systematic process of literature review.

3.2. Analysis

Analysis was undertaken through a thematic categorization using a deductive framework of three themes: Epistemology, Ontology and Axiology. Papers emerging from the review were categorized into a single theme based upon the overarching research aims and objectives of the study in an attempt to begin to illustrate the scope of research being undertaken into the practices of exercise professionals. The theme of Epistemology was defined as research which explored possible interpretations of the knowledge base of exercise professionals. The theme of Ontology categorized research which examined the possible emerging 'models' of practice; whilst the theme of Axiology considered representations of the ethical and practical 'decision-making' factors considered by exercise professionals.

It is acknowledged that this philosophical and strict categorization is ultimately artificial. The limitations of such a thematic division of interpretation are recognized for their subjectivity and un-natural synthesis of experience in exploring the complexity of praxis. As a result the artificial division is undertaken with a sense of academic liberty. However, the process was undertaken from a perspective which considers that a professional first accumulates knowledge from which they develop a set of ontological propositions. It is these epistemologically derived propositions which guide practice. Thus professional praxis is understood to be the accumulation of professional knowledge for the analysis of a situation and the creation of action. It is conceded that an alternative view can be proposed. That is, the nature of the role, i.e., a professional ontology, is necessary before the recognition of the required knowledge for fulfilment of the role's demands. However, due to the nature of exercise professional development, students undertake academic study in vitro before experiencing the role in vivo. Therefore, it is argued here that students learn the 'true nature' of a role through a process of academic education. Thus professional epistemology precedes professional ontology. Consequently, the use of the particular boundaries in this work is recognized as an artifice of the underpinning assumptions and an accepted limitation.

3.2.1. Epistemology

In exploring the nature and expectations of knowledge presented to exercise professionals the scientific, propositional underpinnings can be readily observed. Importantly evidence of deference, and a belief in the superiority of a biomedical science is apparent.

Initial evidence of the dominance of science within trainer education is demonstrated in Gray, Smith and James's study of key textbooks from the major certificating organizations [51]. Their findings established that educational content was focused on the technical standardization inherent in biomedical science as opposed to instruction for developing personal exercise experiences. In 2015, Zenko and Ekkekakis surveyed exercise professionals concerning their knowledge of the ACSM guidelines for exercise prescription suggesting that the scientific knowledge was fundamental to practice [57]. This test included knowledge of such concepts as physiological ranges during exercise, metabolic functioning and understanding of similar biological markers. However, the grades suggested that the average score on the examination was less than 50%. As a result their conclusions argued trainers need greater knowledge of the scientific evidence which should underpin exercise practice. Similarly Bennie et al. surveyed fitness professionals concerning their level of education and sources of fitness knowledge [48]. Their exploration was based on the supposition that practice should "align with proven principles of exercise science and exercise prescription" [48], (p. 741). Yet their findings demonstrated that such academic content and sources of knowledge were accessed infrequently by exercise professionals. Consequently, Bennie et al. supports the work of Zenko and Ekkekakis, and Akerson in suggesting that exercise professionals should increase the use of scientific and academic evidence in their practice [48,57].

Accordingly, it can be demonstrated that the intention of the education of exercise professionals is an attempt to associate its content with a scientific propositional form of biomedical knowledge [51,63]. Thus it can be argued that the epistemological foundations of exercise praxis align with the key assumptions and determinants of the biomedical paradigm.

3.2.2. Ontology

A reading of the body of reviewed literature would suggest the epistemological foundations of exercise professional education present a biomedical ontology for practice. That is, the scientific epistemology generates a techno-rational ontology which defines exercisers through the quantification and measurement of physical capability. Therefore, following previous critiques from medical practitioners, it can be argued that any application of this ontological model by exercise practitioners would diminish the client to a biological paradigm. That is, the client is perceived through the lens of biomedical reductionism and statistical categorization [26–31]. This leads to a position of Gnostic scientism in which the client's needs, experiences and wellbeing, and the means for their fulfilment, are reduced to scientific processes. Thus any elements of existential wellbeing are removed and the training program becomes a mechanistic, techno-rational application of scientific data. Clients are considered in terms of their age, gender, weight, heart rate response and similar fitness parameters from which exercise programs are developed [51,57]. However as described in medical literature this ontology is problematic.

The perception of a differentiation between the educational content and the practical demands of the role is a consistent theme with research exploring professional knowledge [45]. Within exercise literature, De Lyon and Cushion examined the sources and acquisition of knowledge development in fitness trainers [62]. The findings of their work demonstrated a genuine discrepancy between theory and practice [62]. Specifically research has suggested the clients of exercise professionals seek a humanistic encounter based on personal interaction, alongside existential and social development [64,65]. However, these motivational factors appear at odds with the biomedical paradigm and the nature of method presented to the practitioner. Consequently, whilst the professional has been taught to approach the client's needs through quantification, the practical context, and language used within it, do not fully support this ontology. Ultimately, the ontology of exercise becomes one of a routine of linear action to fulfil the expectations of medical data as opposed to an immersive humanistic experience.

3.2.3. Axiology

It is acknowledged the term 'axiology' can be ambiguously defined or applied. Therefore, based upon the definition provided by Hart in which the word stems from the Greek *axios* or worth and *logos* or reason [66], the descriptor is utilized here to denote a consideration of the evaluative process through which exercise professionals undertake decision making. To be precise, this category represents the concept of praxis: the means by which, through reasoning, consideration of worth and thus value, professional knowledge is applied within the exercise context. Importantly, the position is taken that the ontology expressed through the educational epistemology creates an accepted set of values which define both the meaning of exercise and the rationale of decision making for the professional role. Therefore, due to the preceding discussion, it is argued here that the key issue facing current exercise professionals lies within the recognition of this philosophical relationship. That is, the problems manifesting within exercise experiences are ultimately a crisis of axiology generated by the biomedical contents of the professional epistemology and ontology.

There is little debate that exercise has a fundamental role to play in human health and wellbeing. An abundance of evidence that active exercise demonstrably reduces illness risk and increases experiences of health and wellness is readily obtainable and this message is presented throughout the exercise science literature [67]. Consequently data demonstrates the quantifiable and calculable impact of exercise on markers of cardiovascular, neuromuscular, endocrine and skeletal functioning. Thus, the value of exercise lies within the apparent irrefutable scientific evidence for accomplishing measurable health objectives. As a result, the axiological foundations would seem unquestionable and not worthy of consideration at this stage of exercise science's methodological development. However a counter-critique can be made as to the worth exercise has in the human health and wellbeing.

A counter axiological position of the value of exercise can be proposed based upon Huizinga's conception of *Homo Ludens* [68]. Explicitly, it can be argued that a quintessential element of human activity is the fundamental need for play:

> "... even in its simplest forms on the animal level, play is more than a mere physiological phenomenon or a psychological reflex. It goes beyond the confines of purely physical or purely biological activity. It is a significant function ... In play there is something 'at play' which transcends the immediate needs of life and imparts meaning to the action." [68], (p. 19)

Consequently within such philosophical considerations the value of exercise lies not just within definitions of health inherent in a biomedical paradigm but within a deeper existential purpose and humanistic conception of wellbeing [43,69]. Therefore the value is argued to emerge from transcendental qualities of experience beyond the mere expectation of a future utility or quantifiable outcome. [70].

However, the reading of the reviewed literature suggests that the major value of exercise appears to be derived not from a concept of *homo ludens* but from what may be coined *homo medicorum*. To be exact, exercise's value is judged on its ability to impact upon medically defined parameters. Thus, rather than transcendental and existential experiences, the worth is based upon the consideration of scientific, quantifiable, and definable objectives within a biomedical paradigm. As a result, this axiological position creates a linear, techno-rationale approach to decision making and a process of exercise prescription which mirrors the linearity of the medical encounter: test–diagnose–prescribe [71]. The exercise professional records medical data as a basis for diagnosis, and applies an 'algorithmic' approach to prescribe an intervention based on a scientifically derived formula. For example, considerations of a participant's limits within either strength, muscle growth or endurance, scientific resistance training requires a prescription based on intensities of '3–6', '8–12' or '15+' repetitions per exercise set respectively; within cardiovascular and aerobic considerations 220-age provides a formula for optimal zones of training intensity [36,37].

However it can be argued this axiological position of a medicalized value creates a situation in which the accusation of 'specialists without spirits' once levelled at nursing in the 1980's can be levelled at exercise professionals. Used to highlight the fact that nursing staff had lost their professional skills in 'bedside medicine', the 'specialists without spirit' was a label to demonstrate nurses had been reduced to the deliverers of precise, technical and linear instructions from a biomedical evidence base [72]. Thus, grounded in a model that claims deductive certainty through mathematics, it is argued biomedicine set the death knell for what has been termed professional 'Wisdom' [73] or the experiential art of bedside manner, prognosis, logic and observation [74]. As a result, the importance of existentialism, and the impact of phenomenological experiences of health, became lost [27,74–77].

Arguably with the rise in online personal training and exercise coaching, alongside the increase in fitness technology such as the Fitbit and similar apps for Smart phones, the work of the exercise professional may ultimately lead to similar consequences. The participant simply enters key medical data and quantified responses which trigger the 'correct' response from the trainer based upon reference to scientific propositions. Through a techno-rational application of prescribed anato-physiological interventions it is a believed a successful exercise experience can be achieved [71]. In such a role the professional is merely a specialist technician dispensing 'exercise medicines' without consideration for the spirit of either an existential client or of the value of play available in exercise experiences.

Furthermore this axiological position also brings an ethical dilemma: should the exercise professional stick to the 'book' or else apply knowledge not condoned within the current demand for a scientific basis of practice? [36,37]. The content of knowledge presented in professional education fails to appropriately reflect practical reality [62]. Although, research has suggested that trainers are aware of these tensions, the reported epistemology appears to provide limited understanding of a dynamic and humanistic process within the exercise experience [64,65,78]. As a result novice exercise professionals may be left without the understanding of the skills necessary within the role for health and wellbeing. Consequently, the evidence that trainers make the decision to step beyond the boundaries of their qualification, or else appear to fail to account for the individualism within a context, becomes comprehensible [47,60]. Yet, importantly, these tensions have been reported as leading to possibly dangerous and life-threatening occurrences through inappropriate decision making [79]. Therefore the end result of the trainer's actions may lead to the medical issues and debilitating experiences described in this paper's introduction. Thus the definition of the value of exercise based upon quantifiable biomedical objectives would seem axiologically inappropriate.

4. Discussion

An analysis of evidence leads to the argument that the praxis of exercise professionals is hindered by the philosophical foundations of knowledge upon which it is built. What becomes evident is that the biomedical paradigm underpinning exercise praxis does not appear to align to foundations of professional knowledge demonstrated as effective in related disciplines [80,81] Summarizing previous literature, Fox et al. identify that professional knowledge consists of four intersecting dimensions: propositional, process, personal and value-based [63]. As a result, successful professional knowledge is derived from an amalgam of theory, practice, experience and values. Therefore, the decision making process within a professional context is a judgement made based on a broad scopes of knowledge as opposed to the constraints of scientific propositions and mechanistic application [63,80,81]. Research suggests that in practice some trainers may draw upon all four elements described by Fox et al.'s summary [62]. Yet, despite this observation, sources of knowledge beyond propositional science do not appear to be presented as wholly appropriate within the educational process or academic literature. Thus it can be argued that other dimensions of professional knowledge are not considered with a similar level of authority as the biomedical proposition [48,51].

Importantly, it can be reasoned that the future advancement of educational processes will be primarily along increasingly scientific propositional lines and the implementation of the biomedical paradigm [51]. There is an increasing development of online and digital approaches to personal trainer education. For example, companies such as Origym and PTcareer now offer 4 and 5 week online courses[2]. Due to the nature of this delivery, the elements of professional knowledge beyond the scientific and propositional fact conceivably must be limited. Thus, arguably, the exposure to professional experiences and consideration of praxis which draws on, social and humanistic interactions beyond the linearity of data analysis and prescription, may not be limited [64,65]. Utilizing a pedagogical curricula based on linearity, uniformity, and digital efficiency in both teaching and assessment would seem a difficult means through which to express the dynamism inherent in the ludic exercise encounter. Therefore, it can be contended these emerging educational processes support the increasing medicalization of the exercise professional role and the promotion of a biomedical scientism in the supporting exercise science.

The current epistemological foundations demonstrate an emphasis on biomedical science, this in turn creates an ontology of a scientific process. From this position the exercise professional is challenged in the difficult axiological position of experiencing a dynamic, chaotic and humanistic encounter through the lens of a techno-rational biomedical intervention. But, as previously discussed, the dangers of a limited epistemological position have been articulated effectively and discussed in fields such as nursing, medical practitioners and teaching cf. [82–84]. Therefore, there is a need for exercise praxis to move beyond dichotomous assumptions of either/or in professional knowledge [85]. Professional knowledge should be maintained as a development of wisdom through the artful application of science [73,76,77].

As discussed, the reductionism to the biomedical paradigm brings inherent disadvantages and a stance which would appear counter to the expectations of those involved with providing health and wellbeing agendas. Thus, whilst academics argue that problems could be avoided through greater education on the scientific and academic guidelines, the argument is that the guidelines should first be questioned through a philosophical perspective [6,48]. As McNamee suggests, the use of science in the development of health, fitness and exercise is beyond debate [86]. However there is a need for critical philosophical reflection on the basis of the science being presented as the panacea for the current societal health and wellbeing issues.

5. Conclusions

Based upon this discussion it is recommended that a critical review of exercise professional education is required if these roles are to provide a key function in future health and wellbeing agendas. There is a need for a greater body of critical literature exploring the nature and construction of both exercise science and its professional praxis. Fundamentally this research should involve not only philosophical analysis but also utilize longitudinal, phenomenological, and case study explorations of both professionals and their contexts. Fundamental to this research should be the questions as to the relationship between science and experience; education and practice. However using the preceding arguments to initiate further discussion, the following considerations are made:

1. Exercise professional education should be structured in a manner which highlights the need for praxis. Professionals should be made aware of both the strengths and limits of a techno-rational process and its scientific foundations.

---

[2] Google search "online pt courses uk" undertaken 23/07/19 https://www.google.co.uk/search?source=hp&ei=8sg2XcKhKK2GjLsPlpa_kAQ&q=online+pt+courses+UK&oq=online+pt+courses+UK&gs_l=psy-ab.3..0j0i22i30l5.958.5348..5572...0.0..0.182.1322.19j2......0....1..gws-wiz.....0..35i39j0i131.PtOJ_zpOPD8&ved=0ahUKEwjC4uKd08rjAhUtA2MBHRbLD0IQ4dUDCAo&uact=5.

2. Exercise professional education should consider a greater holistic definition of professional knowledge beyond biomedical propositional concepts and theory.
3. Exercise professionals should be exposed to axiological notions of exercise beyond the linearity of medical data. The values of existential wellbeing and notions of play should be explicitly introduced into the educational process.
4. Exercise professional education should place greater emphasis on pedagogies which explore the issues of ethical programming, individualized physical activity, and client relationships. Consequently research should be undertaken into the appropriateness of utilizing online, digital and blended learning technologies within future education.

Funding: This research received no external funding.

Acknowledgments: I want to thank Emily Ryall, Ian Lawrence and Jim McKenna for their support and comments with this work. I also want to thank Claire, Paul, Kev, Piers and Alex on the Professional Doctorate at the University of Gloucestershire for their questions and comments.

Conflicts of Interest: The author declares no conflict of interest.

References

1. Greene, L. 'Fit' to Be Tried—$1.1M Workout Lawsuit. *New York Post*. 23 March 2004. Available online: https://nypost.com/2004/03/23/fit-to-be-tried-1-1m-workout-lawsuit (accessed on 15 July 2019).
2. Smith-Squire, A. One Hour with a Personal Trainer Put This Woman in Hospital for Four Days: Rebecca Suffered Rare Muscle Condition Brought on by Exercising Too Hard. *Mail Online*. 9 December 2013. Available online: https://www.dailymail.co.uk/health/article-2521007/Rebecca-Johnson-suffered-rare-muscle-condition-brought-exercising-hard.html (accessed on 15 July 2019).
3. Branco, J. National Gym Chain, Personal Trainer Sued after Man Spends Week in Hospital. *Brisbane Times*. 10 July 2017. Available online: https://www.brisbanetimes.com.au/national/queensland/national-gym-chain-personal-trainer-sued-after-man-spends-week-in-hospital-20170709-gx7q1p.html (accessed on 15 July 2019).
4. Sinert, R.; Kohl, L.; Rainone, T.; Scalea, T. Exercise-induced rhabdomyolysis. *Ann. Emerg. Med.* **1994**, *23*, 1301–1306. [CrossRef]
5. Aalborg, C.; Rød-Larsen, C.; Leiro, I.; Aasebø, W. An increase in the number of admitted patients with exercise-induced rhabdomyolysis. *Tidsskr. Nor. Laegeforen. Tidsskr. Prakt. Med. Raekke.* **2016**, *136*, 1532–1536. [CrossRef] [PubMed]
6. Khalil, M.A.; Saab, B.R. Resistance exercise-induced rhabdomyolysis: Need for immediate intervention and proper counselling. *Aust. Fam. Physician.* **2016**, *45*, 898–901. [PubMed]
7. Eickhoff-Shemek, J.M. An analysis of 8 negligence lawsuits against personal fitness trainers: 3 major liability exposures revealed. *ACSM's Health Fit. J.* **2010**, *14*, 34–37. [CrossRef]
8. Ciccolella, M.E.; Moore, B.; VanNess, J.M.; Wyant, J. Exertional Rhabdomyolysis and the Law: A Brief Review. *J. Exerc. Physiol. Online* **2014**, *17*, 19–27.
9. Pullen, E.; Malcolm, D. Assessing the effects of the exercise pill. *Qual. Res. Sport Exerc. Health.* **2018**, *10*, 493–504. [CrossRef]
10. Cairney, J.; McGannon, K.R.; Atkinson, M. Exercise is medicine: Critical considerations in the qualitative research landscape. *Qual. Res. Sport Exerc. Health.* **2018**, *10*, 391–399. [CrossRef]
11. Williams, T.L.; Hunt, E.R.; Papathomas, A.; Smith, B. Exercise is medicine? Most of the time for most; but not always for all. *Qual. Res. Sport Exerc. Health.* **2018**, *10*, 441–456. [CrossRef]
12. Lessl, T.M. Naturalizing science: Two episodes in the evolution of a rhetoric of scientism. *West. J. Commun.* **1996**, *60*, 379–396. [CrossRef]
13. Porter, R. *The Cambridge History of Medicine*; Cambridge University Press: Cambridge, UK, 2006.
14. Williams, S.J. *Medicine and the Body*; Sage: London, UK, 2003.
15. Freund, P.E.; McGuire, M.B.; Podhurst, L.S. *Health, Illness, and the Social Body: A Critical Sociology*; Prentice Hall: Upper Saddle River, NJ, USA, 2003.
16. Nicholson, D.J. The machine conception of the organism in development and evolution: A critical analysis. *Stud. Hist. Philos. Sci. Part C Stud. Hist. Philos. Biol. Biomed. Sci.* **2014**, *48*, 162–174. [CrossRef]

17. Kontopodis, M. Biomedicine, psychology and the kindergarten: Children at risk and emerging knowledge practices. *Sport Educ. Soc.* **2013**, *18*, 475–493. [CrossRef]
18. Quirke, V.; Gaudillière, J.P. The era of biomedicine: Science, medicine, and public health in Britain and France after the Second World War. *Med Hist.* **2008**, *52*, 441–452. [CrossRef] [PubMed]
19. Haack, S. *Defending Science-Within Reason: Between Scientism and Cynicism*; Prometheus Books: London, UK, 2011.
20. Williams, R.N.; Robinson, D.N. *Scientism: The New Orthodoxy*; Bloomsbury Publishing: New York, NY, USA, 2014.
21. Busfield, J. The concept of medicalization reassessed. *Sociol. Health Illn.* **2017**, *39*, 759–774. [CrossRef] [PubMed]
22. Giddens, A. *The Constitution of Society: Outline of the Theory of Structuration*; University of California Press: Berkeley, CA, USA, 1984.
23. Gray, J. *The Soul of the Marionette: A Short Inquiry into Human Freedom*; Farrar, Straus and Giroux: New York, NY, USA, 2015.
24. Sorell, T. *Scientism: Philosophy and the Infatuation with Science*; Routledge: Abingdon, UK, 2013.
25. Voegelin, E. *Science, Politics and Gnosticism*; ISI Books: Wilmington, DE, USA, 1968.
26. Illich, I. *Medical Nemesis: The Expropriation of Health*; Pantheon Books: New York, NY, USA, 1974.
27. Baron, R.J. Why Aren't More Doctors Phenomenologists? In *The Body in Medical Thought and Practice*; Leder, D., Ed.; Springer: Dordrecht, The Netherlands, 1992.
28. Pelligrino, E.D.; Thomasma, D.C. *A Philosophical Basis of Medical Practice*; Oxford University Press: Oxford, UK, 1981.
29. Jewson, N.D. The disappearance of the sick-man from medical cosmology, 1770–1870. *Int. J. Epidemiol.* **2009**, *38*, 622–633. [CrossRef] [PubMed]
30. O'Mahony, S. Medical Nemesis 40 years on: The enduring legacy of Ivan Illich. *J. R. Coll. Physicians Edinb.* **2016**, *46*, 134–139. [CrossRef] [PubMed]
31. Miles, A. From evidence-based to evidence-informed, from patient-focussed to person-centered—The ongoing "energetics" of health and social care discourse as we approach the Third Era of Medicine. *J. Eval. Clin. Pract.* **2017**, *23*, 3–4. [CrossRef] [PubMed]
32. Sallis, R.E. Exercise is medicine and physicians need to prescribe it! *Br. J. Sports Med.* **2009**, *43*, 3–4. [CrossRef] [PubMed]
33. Sallis, R.; Franklin, B.; Joy, L.; Ross, R.; Sabgir, D.; Stone, J. Strategies for promoting physical activity in clinical practice. *Prog. Cardiovasc. Dis.* **2015**, *57*, 375–386. [CrossRef] [PubMed]
34. Williams, O.; Gibson, K. Exercise as a poisoned elixir: Inactivity, inequality and intervention. *Qual. Res. Sport Exerc. Health.* **2018**, *10*, 412–428. [CrossRef]
35. Neville, R.D. Exercise is medicine: Some cautionary remarks in principle as well as in practice. *Med. Health Care Philos.* **2013**, *16*, 615–622. [CrossRef]
36. Bushman, B.A.; Battista, R.; Swan, P.; Ransdell, L.; Thompson, W.R. *ACSM's Resources for the Personal Trainer*; Wolters Kluwer Health: New York, NY, USA, 2013.
37. McGill, E.A.; Montel, I. *NASM Essentials of Personal Fitness Training*; Jones & Bartlett Learning: Burlington, MA, USA, 2017.
38. McFee, G. *Ethics, Knowledge and Truth in Sports Research: An Epistemology of Sport*; Routledge: Abingdon, UK, 2010.
39. Griffin, J. *Client-Centered Exercise Prescription, 3E*; Human Kinetics: Champaign, IL, USA, 2015.
40. Nesti, M. *Existential Psychology and Sport: Implications for Research and Practice*; Routledge: London, UK, 2004.
41. Corlett, J. Sophistry, Socrates and Sport Psychology. *Sport Psychol.* **1996**, *10*, 84–94. [CrossRef]
42. Fahlberg, L.L.; Fahlberg, K.; Gates, W.K. Exercise and existence: Exercise behavior from an existential-phenomenological perspective. *Sport Psychol.* **1992**, *6*, 172–191. [CrossRef]
43. Smith, A. Exercise is recreation not medicine. *J. Sport Health Sci.* **2016**, *5*, 129–134. [CrossRef] [PubMed]
44. Rejeski, W.J. Dose-response issues from a psychosocial perspective. In *Physical Activity, Fitness and Health*; Bouchard, C., Shephard, R.J., Stephens, T., Eds.; Human Kinetics: Champaign, IL, USA, 1994.
45. De Lyon, A.T.; Neville, R.D.; Armour, K.M. The role of fitness professionals in public health: A review of the literature. *Quest* **2017**, *69*, 313–330. [CrossRef]

46. Akerson, M. Investigating Personal Fitness Trainers' Qualifications. Ph.D. Thesis, University of Central Florida, Orlando, FL, USA, 2014. Available online: https://stars.library.ucf.edu/cgi/viewcontent.cgi?referer=&httpsredir=1&article=4014&context=etd (accessed on 15 July 2019).
47. Barnes, K.; Desbrow, B.; Ball, L. Personal trainers are confident in their ability to provide nutrition care: A cross-sectional investigation. *Public Health* **2016**, *140*, 39–44. [CrossRef]
48. Bennie, J.A.; Wiesner, G.H.; van Uffelen, J.G.; Harvey, J.T.; Biddle, S.J. Sources of practice knowledge among Australian fitness trainers. *Transl. Behav. Med.* **2017**, *7*, 741–750. [CrossRef] [PubMed]
49. Bratland-Sanda, S.; Sundgot-Borgen, J. "I'm concerned—What Do I Do?" recognition and management of disordered eating in fitness center settings. *Int. J. Eat. Disord.* **2015**, *48*, 415–423. [CrossRef]
50. Dietrich, J.; Keyzer, P.; Jones, V.; Norton, K.; Sekendiz, B.; Gray, S.; Finch, C. Train the trainers: Maintaining standards to minimise injuries and avoiding legal liability in the fitness industry. *J. Sci. Med. Sport.* **2014**, *18*, e3. [CrossRef]
51. Gray, J.; Smith, A.; James, H. An Aristotelian investigation into personal training. *Health Fit. J. Can.* **2014**, *7*, 33–47.
52. Keyzer, P.; Coyle, I.; Dietrich, J.; Norton, K.; Sekendiz, B.; Jones, V.; Finch, C.F. Legal Risk Management and Injury in the Fitness Industry: The Outcomes of Focus Group Research and a National Survey of Fitness Professionals. Available online: https://www.latrobe.edu.au/__data/assets/pdf_file/0004/589153/JLM-June-2014_Keyzer-et-al-article.pdf (accessed on 15 July 2019).
53. McKean, M.R.; Slater, G.; Oprescu, F.; Burkett, B.J. Do the nutrition qualifications and professional practices of registered exercise professionals align? *Int. J. Sport Nutr. Exerc. Metab.* **2015**, *25*, 154–162. [CrossRef]
54. McKean, M.; Mitchell, L.; O'Connor, H.; Prvan, T.; Slater, G. Are exercise professionals fit to provide nutrition advice? An evaluation of general nutrition knowledge. *J. Sci. Med. Sport.* **2018**, *22*, 264–268. [CrossRef] [PubMed]
55. Waryasz, G.R.; Daniels, A.H.; Gil, J.A.; Suric, V.; Eberson, C.P. Personal trainer demographics, current practice trends and common trainee injuries. *Orthop. Rev.* **2016**, *8*, 6600. [CrossRef] [PubMed]
56. Wojtowicz, A.E.; Alberga, A.S.; Parsons, C.G.; von Ranson, K.M. Perspectives of Canadian fitness professionals on exercise and possible anorexia nervosa. *J. Eat. Disord.* **2015**, *3*, 40. [CrossRef] [PubMed]
57. Zenko, Z.; Ekkekakis, P. Knowledge of exercise prescription guidelines among certified exercise professionals. *J. Strength Cond. Res.* **2015**, *29*, 1422–1432. [CrossRef]
58. Anderson, G.; Elliott, B.; Woods, N. The Canadian personal training survey. *J. Exerc. Physiol. Online* **2010**, *13*, 19–28.
59. Andreasson, J.; Johansson, T. 'Doing for group exercise what McDonald's did for hamburgers': Les Mills, and the fitness professional as global traveller. *Sport Educ. Soc.* **2016**, *21*, 148–165. [CrossRef]
60. Barnes, K.; Ball, L.; Desbrow, B. Personal trainer perceptions of providing nutrition care to clients: A qualitative exploration. *Int. J. Sport Nutr. Exerc. Metab.* **2017**, *27*, 186–193. [CrossRef]
61. Dias, M.R.; Simão, R.F.; Saavedra, F.J.; Ratamess, N.A. Influence of a personal trainer on self-selected loading during resistance exercise. *J. Strength Cond. Res.* **2017**, *31*, 1925–1930. [CrossRef]
62. Lyon, A.T.; Cushion, C.J. The acquisition and development of fitness trainers' professional knowledge. *J. Strength Cond. Res.* **2013**, *27*, 1407–1422. [CrossRef]
63. Fox, M.; Green, G.; Martin, P. *Doing Practitioner Research*; Sage: London, UK, 2007.
64. Brown, T.C.; Fry, M.D. Motivational climate, staff and members' behaviors, and members' psychological well-being at a national fitness franchise. *Res. Q. Exerc. Sport.* **2014**, *85*, 208–217. [CrossRef]
65. Campos, F.; Martins, F.; Simões, V.; Franco, S. Fitness participants perceived quality by age and practiced activity. *J. Phys. Educ. Sport.* **2017**, *17*, 698–704.
66. Hart, S.L. Axiology—Theory of values. *Philos. Phenomenol. Res.* **1971**, *32*, 29–41. [CrossRef]
67. Fletcher, G.F.; Landolfo, C.; Niebauer, J.; Ozemek, C.; Arena, R.; Lavie, C.J. Promoting physical activity and exercise: JACC health promotion series. *J. Am. Coll. Cardiol.* **2018**, *72*, 1622–1639. [CrossRef] [PubMed]
68. Huizinga, J. *Homo Ludens: A Study of the Play Element in Culture*; Temple Smith: London, UK, 1970.
69. Nesti, M.S. Exercise for health: Serious fun for the whole person. *J. Sport Health Sci.* **2016**, *5*, 135–138. [CrossRef] [PubMed]
70. Rodriguez, H. The playful and the serious: An approximation to Huizinga's Homo Ludens. *Game Stud.* **2006**, *6*, 1604–7982.

71. Heyward, V.H.; Gibson, A. *Advanced Fitness Assessment and Exercise Prescription*, 7th ed.; Human Kinetics: Champagne, IL, USA, 2014.
72. Hewa, S.; Hetherington, R.W. Specialists without spirit: Limitations of the mechanistic biomedical model. *Theor. Med.* **1985**, *16*, 129–139. [CrossRef]
73. Rubenstein, R.E. *Aristotle's Children*; Harcourt Inc.: Oakland, CA, USA, 2003.
74. Bergdolt, K. *Wellbeing: A Cultural History of Healthy Living*; Polity: Cambridge, UK, 2008.
75. Robbins, B.D. The Medicalized Body and Anaesthetic Culture. In *The Medicalized Body and Anesthetic Culture*; Robbins, B.D., Ed.; Palgrave Macmillan: New York, NY, USA, 2018.
76. Louis-Courvoisier, M.; Mauron, A. He found me very well; for me, I was still feeling sick': The strange worlds of physicians and patients in the 18th and 21st centuries. *Med. Humanit.* **2002**, *28*, 9–13. [CrossRef]
77. Baron, R.J. An introduction to medical phenomenology: I can't hear you while I'm listening. *Ann. Intern. Med.* **1985**, *103*, 606–611. [CrossRef]
78. Markula, P.; Chikinda, J. Group fitness instructors as local level health promoters: A Foucauldian analysis of the politics of health/fitness dynamic. *Int. J. Sport Policy Politics* **2016**, *8*, 625–646. [CrossRef]
79. Rawson, E.S.; Clarkson, P.M.; Tarnopolsky, M.A. Perspectives on exertional rhabdomyolysis. *Sports Med.* **2017**, *47*, 33–49. [CrossRef]
80. Schön, D.A. *The Reflective Practitioner: How Professionals Think in Action*; Basic Book Inc.: New York, NY, USA, 1983.
81. Eraut, M. *Developing Professional Knowledge and Competence*; Routledge: London, UK, 2002.
82. Kavanagh, J.M.; Szweda, C. A crisis in competency: The strategic and ethical imperative to assessing new graduate nurses' clinical reasoning. *Nurs. Educ. Perspect.* **2017**, *38*, 57–62. [CrossRef] [PubMed]
83. Eastwood, J.L.; Koppelman-White, E.; Mi, M.; Wasserman, J.A.; Krug, E.F., III; Joyce, B. Epistemic cognition in medical education: A literature review. *Int. J. Med. Educ.* **2017**, *8*, 1–12. [CrossRef] [PubMed]
84. Schraw, G.; Brownlee, J.L.; Olafson, L.; Brye, M.V.V. *Teachers' Personal Epistemologies: Evolving Models for Informing Practice*; IAP: Charlotte, NC, USA, 2017.
85. Renedo, A.; Komporozos-Athanasiou, A.; Marston, C. Experience as evidence: The dialogic construction of health professional knowledge through patient involvement. *Sociology* **2018**, *52*, 778–795. [CrossRef]
86. McNamee, M. Positivism, Popper and Paradigms: An introductory essay in the philosophy of science. In *Philosophy and the Sciences of Exercise, Health and Sport: Critical Perspectives on Research Methods*; McNamee, M., Ed.; Routledge: London, UK, 2005.

© 2019 by the author. Licensee MDPI, Basel, Switzerland. This article is an open access article distributed under the terms and conditions of the Creative Commons Attribution (CC BY) license (http://creativecommons.org/licenses/by/4.0/).

Article

What Might a Theory of Causation Do for Sport?

Evan Thomas Knott

School of Humanities, The Department of Philosophy, The University of Glasgow, Glasgow G12 8LP, UK; e.knott.1@research.gla.ac.uk

Received: 30 April 2019; Accepted: 14 June 2019; Published: 18 June 2019

Abstract: The purpose of this research is to articulate how a theory of causation might be serviceable to a theory of sport. This article makes conceptual links between Bernard Suits' theory of game-playing, causation, and theories of causation. It justifies theories of causation while drawing on connections between sport and counterfactuals. It articulates the value of theories of causation while emphasizing possible limitations. A singularist theory of causation is found to be more broadly serviceable with particular regard to its analysis of sports.

Keywords: counterfactuals; absence causation; causal necessity; causal contingency; david kellogg lewis; prelusory goal; possible sport worlds; metaphysics of sport; causation in sport

1. Introduction

Stephen Mumford states, "Causation is what connects distinct phenomena. [David] Hume . . . called it the cement of the universe . . . . [and] in sport, it is the absolutely vital metaphysical notion for without causation there could be no sport." [1]. Mumford asks, "What then is this metaphysical glue, which seems to bind one kind of event reliably with another and thus provides us with a basis for action?" [1]. Theories of causation are attempts to account for the basis. Two related questions will be answered: (1) What kind of theory of causation might be unifying in sport? (2) How would a theory of causation help to provide a theory of sport? This article answers the latter questions using Bernard Suits' definition of game-playing [2] and David Lewis' theory of causation[1] [6]. This article concludes that Lewis' theory is more broadly serviceable in answering these questions and that it offers valuable metaphysical import more generally. Lewis' approach belongs to a cluster of related theories known as difference-making approaches to the conceptual analysis of causation.[2]

2. Prelusory Goal and Causation

Why is the notion of a prelusory goal associated with causation? There is a link between Suits' definition of games and causation in sport. I will offer a conceptual analysis of this connection.[3] The analysis will support taking into consideration several theories of causation.

Suits looked closely at the elements of sports, by attempting to define games in contrast to Wittgenstein who took such definition to be impossible. There are reasons to think Suits was correct. Papineau recently stated that Suits provided " . . . a wonderful account of games, and [I] shall raise no objection to it. Wittgenstein held that there is no set of necessary and sufficient conditions for being a game. I take Suits' account to refute him outright. It captures the essence of games perfectly." [8]. Yet,

---

[1] For a recent discussion on notable problems for Lewis' theory and possible solutions see Maar [3]. For a summary of common objections to Lewis' theory see Menzies [4]. For an argument on the general value of counterfactuals, including the association between counterfactuals and causation, and notable critiques of the latter connections see Nolan [5].
[2] For a technical critique of Lewis' difference-making approach see Menzies [7].
[3] I thank Reviewer 1 for their suggestions which helped focus the use of Suits' theory of game-playing.

there are any number of critiques of Suits' account, including Papineau's own response.[4] Moreover, on Suits' account of sports as games, "sport is the unnecessary attempt to overcome unnecessary obstacles" [8], or the voluntary attempt to overcome unnecessary obstacles to achieve some goal. Sport can be construed as a kind of goal-oriented activity. Suits first treats sports as simply that sub-class of games that involve physical skills and offers a definition of game-playing [8]. Suits later revised the view below, and yet sport remained a goal-oriented activity [15].

Theorem 1. *To play a game is to attempt to achieve a specific state of affairs [prelusory goal], using only means permitted by rules [lusory means], where the rules prohibit use of more efficient in favour of less efficient means [constitutive rules], and where the rules are accepted just because they make possible such activity [lusory attitude]* [8].

Upon further analysis, the participants of sports accept the rules, which function to permit or prohibit physical actions, which are oriented towards achieving the goal(s) of the sport. Yet, there are discussions in the literature about the possible need to break rules.[5] Furthermore, participants achieve the prelusory goal through physical means. Yet, exceptions apply where there is seemingly no prelusory goal.[6] That said, Suits' account is laden with causal concepts. Mumford notes, "The competitor in sport is aiming to cause some distinct outcome ... [and] aims to cause some event or state of affairs through their bodily movements ... " [1]. Furthermore, from a practical standpoint, rugby union uses the notion of materiality when analyzing, among other things, referee decision-making (e.g., Did Red 3's action(s) have a material effect on Blue 7?).[7] I take these latter points as good reasons for introducing several theories of causation for further consideration.[8]

Sports are goal-oriented. In addition, where events appear to repeat themselves, as they do in sports, there is an increased motivation to engage with imaginative exercises such as developing *alternative antecedent conditions* for the purpose of obtaining better future results [18]. Conceptually, thinking *counterfactually* can be associated with the prelusory goal. Moreover, the prelusory goal is an important notion in what follows, and I will use football as my primary illustration. The prelusory goal stated immediately below is not intended to be exhaustive, but it is sufficiently comprehensive enough for the purposes to follow. In football, the prelusory goal involves achieving a higher score than the opposing team. The prelusory goal is to direct the ball into the opponent's net while preventing the same on one's own net.

3. Theories of Causation

I have argued that Suits' account of sports as games employs causal concepts and that counterfactuals might interrelate. A theory of causation could then interrelate with Suits' account because causal concepts already do. A theory of causation that is apt at handling counterfactuals might add value by improving understanding of causal concepts employed in thinking about the prelusory goal. I will go on to argue that Lewis' theory has the potential to achieve the latter. Before doing so, I will note the causal theories on offer and the conceptual level of interest in what follows.

---

[4] For an analysis of Suits' prelusory goal and lusory means, see Schneider [9]. For a response to Kreider's objections to formalism and non-formalism see Royce [10]. To understand how Suits' later work on play undermines the earlier definitional project of games, see Morgan [11]. For objections to Suits' notion of utopia as the ideal existence of game playing, see Thomson [12], Kretchmar [13], and Holowchak [14].
[5] See Royce [16] for a recent argument in favour of this position.
[6] See Hurka [17] for a discussion on the exceptions and Suits' revised account of games.
[7] I thank Reviewer 2 for this insight.
[8] If there is any doubt about the value of causation, Mumford also states, "Suppose there were no causation. Then anything could follow anything else. And then [for instance] when one kicks a football, instead of it moving in a direction roughly 180 degrees to the kick, it could do something else completely, such as evaporate. Or it might do nothing at all. Action [in sport] would then have no point. Its outcomes would be entirely unpredictable: and sport could not then be." [1].

An account of, approach to, or theory of causation involves defining, logicizing, modeling, or offering an explanation or understanding of causation. I am assuming that the theories of causation under discussion below are metaphysical apparatuses, conceptually engineered for various purposes some of which I have mentioned immediately above. My target is the conceptual level of analysis and assessing the merits of each theory in that respect. I am developing upon the cognitive aspects of causation and how theories of causation interrelate in understanding causation in sport.

In sum, sports can be conceived of as, among other things, causal activities, and a good theory of sport would capture that assumption or otherwise remain consistent with it. The best way forward when explicating causation involves referring to the developed theories of causation and then seeking out the possible value for sport. Moreover, offering an argument in favour of an elected theory of causation entails advocating the import of other metaphysical concepts. The same was true of causal concepts, which were implied in Suits' definition. There are three concepts that are associated with the recent and historical development of theories of causation. The three concepts are *causal necessity*, *causal contingency*, and *absent causes* or *omissions*. I will offer examples of each. If it is conceptually useful, such notions may also be referred to as *causal necessity in sport*, *causal contingency in sport*, *absent causes in sport*, and so on.

In cricket, when the batsman is caught out, but also knocks the bail off as they strike, it makes sense to refer to this as *causal overdetermination*: the player being out is overdetermined by more than one sufficient cause. This would be a token case of causal necessity. Likewise, it is reasonable to state: *had* there been one less cause, the player would still have been out. Moreover, in football, it is reasonable to construe a scored goal as causally contingent on a deliberate and preceding action of some player. If the player actually heads the ball into the net unfettered, the effect of scoring a goal is contingent on the player as the cause. One can appropriately ask, what if the player did not direct the ball into the net? It follows, the team would not have been awarded that particular goal.

The causal concepts employed above are analysable using counterfactuals. The "had" or "what if" are the kinds of alternative antecedent conditions that signal the use of counterfactuals in this context. By *counterfactual* or counter-to-the-actual in the context of this article, I mean something that did not happen. The counterfactual is introduced as an alternative antecedent to the actual world of events. Furthermore, the third concept is absence causation, and I propose that it is presently best understood using counterfactuals.[9] For example, had a referee exhibited better judgment (an absent cause), a particular goal would not have been scored.

Counterfactuals are normative in sports analyses. They are implied in sports commentary (e.g., Blue Team would have won if Blue 7 was not injured by Red 3), coaching strategy (e.g., Blue 7 would have scored that point on Red Team), reflections by athletes post-competition, and so on. In football, the use of the term missed opportunities implies a *what if* or *had* or counterfactual. Generally, if one is justified in assuming that counterfactuals are commonplace in sport, then one could be motivated to discipline those imaginings with an additional but relevant metaphysics suitable for analyses of sports, especially when the counterfactuals are associated with or directly concern causal claims. This is one sense in which a theory of causation might be serviceable to sport.

To analyse what any of the various theories of causation might do for sport, but which among them might be unifying, one first needs to understand the variants on offer; and what they might tell us about causation if anything. The standard approaches to causation include *generalist theories of causation* (e.g., the Regularity Theory or the RT), *singularist theories of causation* (e.g., Lewis' counterfactual theory of causation), *probabilistic theories of causation* (hereafter, *probabilistic approaches*), *causal process theories* (or *causal process approaches*), and *agency interventionist theories* (hereafter, *agency approaches*).

---

[9] See Dowe [19] for an argument in favour of this position and see Mumford [20] for an opposing view.

4. Possible Limitations

I will begin by arguing that the agency, causal process, and probabilistic approaches are inadequate to the task of this article's aim. The purpose is to identify a possible unifying theory of causation for sport and one that best supports or connects with what was previously set out with Suits' definition. I will then explore how the RT and Lewis' account, which are often put in opposition to each other, might be useful. Moreover, there are two general problems raised for agency approaches, which are the anthropocentric problem and the issue of circularity. Before outlining why those are possible issues for applying agency approaches to sport, I will offer a definition of causation on this account:

Theorem 2. *If c causes e, then if c were to be manipulated in the right way, there would be an associated change in e* [21].

This approach addresses the associations between causes and effects through a mediating manipulation concept. In a more developed account, manipulation is characterized as an intervention. One concern is that this proposal excludes things that humans cannot manipulate. That general concern is not enough to rule the proposed definition out, because causation in sport involves human activities, and one can accept such anthropocentricism for intrinsically humanly defined activities. In addition, the more interesting causes in sport analyses will be of the manipulatable type.

The other concern is that an appeal to manipulation as a kind of causal concept to understand causation requires applying one kind of causal language to explicate another, i.e., there is epistemic circularity. A possible workaround might involve construing manipulation without causal concepts, and one such attempt involves introducing the further notion agency. In the revised view, an agent has implicit awareness of causes and their associated effects. If an athlete causes a goal, then if the athlete were to make such and such interventions on the ball, the ball would go in the net. However, further theoretical problems ensue. An athlete may be able to rely on their awareness of associations for localized interventions, but what about knock-on-effects or effects that are distant from their cause?

Suppose a basketball ball is thrown and bounces off the rim. How would agency play an explanatory role in subsequent bounces of the ball? One way of addressing these latter questions is to propose that an agent projects a similar agency to the basketball rim, which then supports the implicit awareness of causes and their associated effects [21]. Yet, is that proposal generally true of human nature or does it appear to project agency with an ad hoc basis? If the basketball ball happens to bounce predictably off the rim to the backboard, does a subsequent ball movement follow from a projected agency on to the backboard? This same question should be raised where the agent had made no intervention. Moreover, how could agency control for the confounding variables in the analysis of sports? For example, assuming that they are not the one doing the scoring, how does agency support knowing that Blue 7 causes Blue Team to score more often in light of the possible confounding variables?

One can raise concerns about how the agency approaches handle complicated cases of association between cause and effect. Does it then seem appropriate to rely on agency in causally complicated or even causally complex cases? The agency "approaches ... [which] stress the connection between manipulation and causation [,] have been [most] popular within experimentally oriented disciplines ... " [21]. Unlike the experimental context, sports cannot be re-run in a laboratory, to experimentally measure the possible causal relationships. Given that competitive sports lack the possibility of experimental objectivity, there is a prima facie reason that the agency approaches to causation are not going to be broadly serviceable to the goals of this essay. An agent will implicitly understand causation, but to what extent is that basis formally useful for the needs of sport analyses? I had proposed looking for a theory of causation that might be unifying and one that helps provide a theory of sport. In any case, an elected causal theory ought to accommodate or remain consistent with introducing alternative antecedent conditions in light of the analysis of Suits' account.

What might significantly matter in the quest for a potentially unifying theory of causation, is an account that supports counterfactuals, which takes one beyond the immediate actual world of events and causes. The latter implies the use of broader causal possibilities, which is supported by Lewis' approach. One of the virtues of Lewis' approach is that it could accommodate the exploration of possible worlds beyond the actual world of causes in sport—a kind of virtual understanding of causation. There is a motivation for this approach: Analyses will not be limited to accounting for the actual world of sport, but they will go beyond actual causation to absence causation. The latter associations are applicable to goal-oriented activities. Generally, it may be that the agency approaches are consistent with difference-making approaches to causation in sport, or that a particular agency approach and difference-making account can be combined in some hybrid model. I am not going to address the latter possibilities.

Before proceeding to probabilistic approaches, I will note that it is tenable that causal process approaches and some of the associated theories are reducible to one of the other theories of causation being discussed here. The general idea of a causal process approach is that any facts about causation as a relation between events obtain only on account of more basic facts about causal processes and interactions. Causal processes are the world-lines of objects, exhibiting some characteristic(s) essential for causation [22]. Therefore, causal processes and interactions are more fundamental than causal relations between events, and, " ... [if] causation can be understood in terms of [these more basic] causal processes and interactions ... [then] the 'appropriate relations' [which will be used to define them, will] tend to be counterfactual dependence, chance raising, or lawful sequence ... " [22]. In terms of what has been stated in this article thus far, counterfactual dependence is captured by Lewis' approach, and the notion of chance raising by some suitable probabilistic approach, and lawful sequence by the RT. Moreover, one of the important accounts associated with causal process approaches is Wesley Salmon's mechanistic approach [23], which takes "[a] causal processes [as having] the capacity to transmit marks, namely various sorts of signals or information." [22]. However, Salmon abandons all probability, and the account fails to accommodate absent causes [22], which are normative and explanatory, as previously shown above. How can there "be [actual] mechanisms linking non-existent [or non-actual] entities [?]" [22]. For example, the absence of a key player Blue 7 could be viewed as explanatorily useful for assessing a win or a loss for Red Team or Blue Team. Yet, in Salmon's account, there is no mechanism that links the non-existent causes to the actual events.

A probabilistic approach would be useful for informing analyses of some kinds of causes or perhaps even identifying or realizing specific causes. In addition, I am not proposing the desertion of mechanistic or probabilistic theories of causation, which, when successfully applied to sport, would obviously be serviceable to understanding aspects of causation in sport. Yet, probabilistic accounts suffer from an obvious shortcoming. A probabilistic account of causation can be stated as follows:

Theorem 3. *Probabilistic Dependencies—normally when c causes e the former raises or lowers the probability of the latter* [24].

In other words, causes raise or lower the probability of their effects. Yet, the general concern for invoking probabilities alone applies to sport. Let us assume the following: *Some C's raise the probability of E's*. For instance, some kinds of players would seemingly raise the probability of their team scoring points. There will be instances or counterexamples where the same kinds of players lower the probability of the same team scoring. Without the underlying and accompanying mechanism spelled out for possibilities, probability says nothing about what we take to be the actual cause of the points scored. If Blue 7 raises the probability of their team scoring, then *why*? There are cases where one wants more than probabilistic statements. Notably, "probabilistic theories [ultimately] flounder because they admit counterexamples and because they fail to accommodate the important connection between causality and physical mechanisms." [24]. In addition, it is safe to state that, "an account that seeks to characterize or analyse causality just in terms of probabilistic dependencies, or just in terms of physical mechanisms, will be inadequate." [24]. More is needed for each account or perhaps the theoretical approaches can be combined in some other way.

One solution to the theoretical conflicts that arise between competing accounts of causation might be to adopt some kind of pluralist view of causal theories or even to abandon all reference between theories of causation and the actual world itself [25]. The assumption that there is no actual correspondence, between any of the theories of causation and the world, may dissolve some conflicts about which theory best accounts for the causal nature of some target phenomena. Yet, any radical proposal could raise further philosophical grievances and concerns, likely exasperate theoretical issues, and/or may simply lead to a generally impoverished metaphysics about causes in sport.

5. The Value of Difference-Making Approaches to Causation in Sport

David Lewis provided a kind of singularist theory of causation broad enough that it could be applicable to sport. Articulating the use of Lewis' approach to the analysis of causes in sport entails advocating that adherents to that view become counterfactualists in a much stronger sense than that in which they might already be. By *counterfactualist*, I mean that one believes that knowledge can be derived from counterfactual thinking. In the sense being discussed here, that knowledge concerns causation in sport. Lewis initially defines causation with the associated counterfactual dependence as follows:

Theorem 4. *Where c and e are two distinct possible events, e causally depends on c if and only if, if c were to occur e would occur; and if c were not to occur e would not occur* [4].

On the assumption that counterfactual thinking is already employed in sport, I argue for the application of Lewis' approach, which entails structuring those assumed imaginings. I argue that Lewis' approach might be unifying for sport, in so far as counterfactuals, which interrelate with absent causes, can be broadly utilized in thought experiments for the analyses of sports.

Concerning the two remaining theories yet discussed, they are sometimes set up in contention. The Humean generalist theory of causation (the RT) can be taken to be at odds with the Lewisian singular theory of causation. I am not supposing that they are ultimately irreconcilable. Conceptually, it is practical to apply the notion of law-like regularities to sport, and specifically, to instances that could be spelled out in terms of physical laws. For instance, projectile motions in sport are captured or understood through physical laws. Yet, not everything causal in the analysis of sport will be captured by the generalist's account, which is a requirement of the RT.

The issue I will dwell on concerns the impracticality of the RT's broad application to sport. When attempting to vindicate the invariant use of a generalist theory of causation for sport, there will be difficulties fitting all cases of causation into the logic of the generalist framework, which states: *All A's are B's*.[10] It simply is not the case that all causation in sport can be put in this form. For the RT, all instances of causation in sport would need to be invariant in the sense that B-events necessarily, or always follow, or are constantly associated with, or conjoined with A-events as follows:

Theorem 5. *c causes e if and only if it is the case that c temporally precedes e, and all type-C events are always followed by Type-E events* [3].

Let us test the generalist's model with an example. Take, for instance, George Weah's 1996 goal against Verona. Under the RT, one would have to look at other instances of goals to know if George Weah caused the specific goal. There are instances of causation where generally similar events should be irrelevant. It would be useful to make this distinction broadly clear ontologically because what

---

[10] In this context, either A-events and C-events or B-events and E-events are equivalent notations.

value a generalist theory of causation does not offer in understanding causes in sport is important for identifying what a singularist theory of causation might be able to do for sport more generally.

One can think of the world of sports as a subset of the social world, all of which is a subset of the physical world. However, just because a generalist theory can be seen to, conceptually speaking, range over all of these sets (e.g., physical laws apply to all sets) it does not follow that a generalist theory can do all the conceptual work related to all instances of causation among the sets. This leaves open a conceptual space for Lewis' theory to be serviceable. This is another way to state that more causal theories are needed than the RT. Moreover, if the RT could account for all instances of causation, then counterfactuals could still be supported by such laws. A physical law can be used to predict or explain what-if such and such happened as much as it explains what actually happens. Conceptually, one can imagine building out possible worlds based on full knowledge of the physical laws as they pertain to sport and all relevant levels of analyses of the sets. Yet, one cannot presently achieve the latter, epistemically speaking, or for other reasons it might not be possible, which again creates a space for a singularist theory of causation to offer understanding and insight.

In the application of Lewis' account to follow, I would characterize the inquiry as targeting the individual and/or collective level of analysis of causation in sport. At that conceptual level, there are complex features, which are not, at this present state of knowledge, immediately amenable to the RT's interpretation of causation. We cannot apply physical laws to account for all or even most of these features of sport. In addition, one may try to utilize robust tendencies from psychology or sociology (e.g., social laws), but even the best examples of propensities do not fit the RT's *All A's are B's* formulation. A statistical law takes the form *Some portion of A's are B's*, which is not typically if ever understood as causation. Moreover, there would be in retrospect of many professional sporting events, an attempt to identify causes that have more weight or bearing on a specific win or loss. Yet, conceivably, such analyses would not be carried out using general causation. Understanding causation in this latter sense is more amenable to Lewis' theory, but in particular with respect to absence causation.

A straightforward way to introduce absent causes into causal analyses is either as *causation by prevention*, *causation by double-prevention*, or *causation by omission* [26].[11] I will focus exclusively on the latter. I will suppose the following case of omission: *c actually causes e; but, if a happens, then e does not*. What is implicit in this case of omission, and makes for an additional cause of *e* (conceptually) is the counterfactual: *had a happened, it would have or might have prevented e*. Under a deterministic framing, the reading would be: *had a happened, it would have necessarily prevented e*.

These formulations might be viewed as problematic for a natural ontology, which supposes some correspondence with the actual world's nature, but they are not problematic in that one sense, in so far as they are assumed in a thought experiment. A counterfactual thought experiment, about an alternative sport scenario or outcome, is not bound to actuality, but it can engage with a variety of causal possibilities, of which, absence causation is an example. The appropriateness of a supposed thought experiment is a notable concern, and specifically whether it is disciplined, reasonable, or otherwise satisfies as a good, rational, but not too speculative reconstruction of the sport, which is supported by the right facts in the right way. From the standpoint of a skilled analyser of sport, a thought experiment can yield better and more accurate conclusions about the reasonable possibilities one can appropriately conjecture using counterfactuals.

For instance, it is safe to say that good professional-level coaching will involve evaluating the wins and losses (especially the losses) by thinking about what might or what would have been the case if the relevant causes had been different. One way that these counterfactual analyses could proceed involves adding possible causes and then imagining the possible effects of achieving the prelusory goal. A similar strategy could be to subtract actual causes away and then likewise imagine the outcomes.

---

[11] Both *causation by prevention* and *causation by double-prevention* are kinds of *causation by omission* for Paul [26]. Paul also uses the notion of *causation by omission* to refer to a specific instance [26], which is how I am using the terms.

Yet, absent causes are not necessarily part of the actual world of events. However, they can be made relevant to analysis. If I am late for work, a normative explanation could be that my bus never arrived. The omitted cause is the bus. Likewise, if Blue Team lost the game, it could be explained by the absence of the key player Blue 7. An explanation is not necessarily limited to the actual gameplay.

For illustrative purposes in football, let us suppose the following case: the referee actually causes the loss of the game for Orange Team, because of a decision that benefits Green Team. Let us further suppose that the decision is a bad call and also leads to a successful penalty kick. If it is helpful, let us suppose that this is the World Cup, where penalty kicks more often end in success. This is a sample case where poor judgment explains the loss of the game for Orange Team. Let us assume it is reasonable to speculate that the following holds true at the end of the game: had a member of Orange Team not been called for a penalty, which caused a subsequent penalty kick, then consequently, the winning goal would not have been scored by a member of Green Team. The actual goal is not guaranteed before it happens, but if it does occur, the referee's poor judgment will be seen as the cause of the unwarranted opportunity.

Continuing this line of thought, the absent cause can be straightforwardly identified. The referee is normally expected to make reasonable and accurate judgments and not to inappropriately award advantages. The referee fails to do the latter, and another way of re-stating the latter is to express that good decision making by the referee can help a team win the game, and in its absence, bad judgment can cause, determine, or contribute notably to a loss. One could also state, in a stricter analysis that remains closest to the actual world of causes, that only a bad decision caused the match to be lost, full stop. However, the latter construal overlooks the associated analysis for obtaining the prelusory goal.

To achieve the prelusory goal in reflection, one needs to import the cause *good decision making* to form the relevant thought experiment, i.e., the relevant absent cause has explanatory significance in light of the prelusory goal. In this sense, the counterfactual is a kind of conceptual go-between, which allows assessment of the factors that determine whether one team achieves or fails to achieve certain ends when conceptualizing causes aimed at achieving the prelusory goal. The referee's decisions can be seen as the more weighty cause in the penalty kick scenario.

In the illustration above, the cause, which is the false perception of a foul is actually present with its effect which is the loss of the game. The relevant counterfactual, more simply stated, is as follows: Had good judgment been the case (*a*), the Green Team's winning that particular win would have been prevented (*e*)—*no bad call, no-win* (or not that specific win). This singular cause is taken to be more essential among the various causes one could elect to explore. One might object that bad calls are just part of the game. Assuming that this is so, let us explore another nearby world in light of that view.

Another way of construing things from above is to state that, what it takes to win a football match, is not to elicit false judgments by referees at a critical time. If so, the player's ability to not do something is also part of the actual causal landscape with respect to the prelusory goal. Again, the cause could be stated non-counterfactually: a member of Orange Team exhibited poor judgment, causing a false perception by the referee, thus causing the loss of the game for their team. Yet, in retrospect of the actual loss, one must subtract away the actual cause *bad judgment*, and make it absent, in order to reconstruct events more favourably. The richer explanation involves a counterfactual anyway. There are two plausible counterfactual readings for the absence of good decision making, in Lewis' account, where I take Proposition 1 to be the more appropriate construal based on Suits' lusory means:

Proposition 1. Where *the referee's bad decision (c)* and *the winning goal (e)* are two distinct possible events, e causally depends on c if and only if, if c were to occur e would occur; and if c were not to occur e would not occur.

Proposition 2. Where *the player's bad decision (c)* and *the winning goal (e)* are two distinct possible events, e causally depends on c if and only if, if c were to occur e would occur; and if c were not to occur e would not occur.

What is important to address at this juncture of the counterfactual analysis is further thought that Orange Team could have just lost the game anyway. However, in contrast to guaranteeing a win, a particular loss is connected with a particular referee's bad decision. In a different possible world where the referee makes a normatively good call, events can still unfold unfavourably for Orange Team. However, in the thought experiment above, I have assumed an illustrative case that constrains the possible variables. My point in doing so was to provide a clear example, and a contrastive view to the RT, rather than to oversimplify sports more generally. In short, where the referee makes the same bad call, and Green Team goes on to win anyway by some other means, a different *possible sport world* from the one I have stipulated above is being employed.

The RT, as is, would lead to an impoverished analysis. Lewis' singularist theory of causation is more amenable to the evaluation of causes in sports. Lewis' theory is apt at handling absent causes, which can be made important for understanding the events that precede the wins or losses of games. In most conceptually developed sports, such as football, which I assume here as a paradigm case, the analyser of events will also want to understand the larger terrain of causation, in light of the prelusory goal or just because sport is goal-oriented.

Generalizing, for a theory of causation to be serviceable to the conceptual analysis of sport, it should accommodate counterfactuals in the senses discussed above or remain consistent with that possible normative use. In contrast to the view being advocated, a dispositionalist's view maintains that "[the] regularity theory and the counterfactual theory are judged merely to describe phenomena that follow from real causal connections. They are attempts to avoid acknowledging the reality of causal necessity [20]." Importantly, there are no contenders that provide an alternative to Lewis' theory, although the *causal modelling approach* does seek to formalize it by " ... establish[ing] interconnections between causal relationships on the one hand, and regularities, counterfactuals, interventions, and probabilities on the other ... " [27]. This approach links theorems and may be applicable to sport. Moreover, Lewis' theory has the potential to be unifying in sport, not only because it can support absent causes, and how the latter can be shown to conceptually function in thought experiments with respect to the prelusory goal, but because Lewis' theory can support the analysis of singular causation more generally. Moreover, Lewis' metaphysics assumes law-like regularities or laws of nature as the basis of a possible world [6], and the revised theory is consistent with the use of probabilities [28]. Lewis' view can accommodate many types of causal claims that may be used in sport. Last, Lewis' more developed account bears some resemblance to Salmon's approach, where "Causation as a pattern of influence is similar to the idea that a causal process entails transmitting a mark." [3]. Lewis later defines the pattern of influence as follows:

Theorem 6. *Where* c *and* e *are distinct events,* c *influences* e *if and only if there is a substantial range of* c1, c2, ... *of different not-too-distant alterations of* c *(including the actual alteration of* c*) and there is a range of* e1, e2, ... *of alterations of* e*, at least some of which differ, such that if* c1 *had occurred,* e1 *would have occurred, and if* c2 *had occurred,* e2 *would have occurred, and so on* [4].

In the revised account, Lewis' establishes a "pattern of counterfactual dependence of whether, when, and how on whether, when, and how (. . .) C causes E ... [if and only if] there is a chain of stepwise influence from C to E." [3]. In addition, "under this amendment[,] we are in [a] good position to say that there are different degrees of causal influence ... " [3]. which is likewise serviceable to analysis in sport. Lewis claimed that the revised theory was better at handling specific cases of pre-emption [4]. For example, suppose that there is a well-placed corner kick and two teammates happen to both be in a scoring position such that if one misses the goal another would have scored. Lewis' original theory cannot explain the judgment that the first player was the actual cause of the goal. There is no dependence between the player and their goal since if they missed heading the ball in the net, the goal would have been scored anyway. In other words, there is no counterfactual dependence for defining the causal relationship between the player and the goal that they are causally responsible for. In the revised theory, if the first player's physical actions are slightly different (e.g., the ball is a little higher and their position is different) while holding fixed the second player's physical actions, we find that the goal is different too. However, if we make similar alternations to the second player's physical actions while holding the first player's fixed, we find the goal is the same. The dependence between the player and their goal is more well defined in Lewis' revised account.

6. Conclusions

Mumford states, "Sport typically involves notions of winning and losing, based on some comparative measure: [for instance,] who scored more goals ... [and it] ... makes sense to reward winners ... on the ground[s] that ... [they] are causally responsible for the outcomes that are produced. Hence, the goal scorer is congratulated only because they caused the goal ... " [1]. Causation is relevant to sport and several theories of causation are shown to be connected with the analyses of sports. However, the Regularity Theory requires a problematic construal of many instances of causation in sport. Yet, associating causation with counterfactuals and embedding that proposal in an appropriate singularist theory of causation is broadly serviceable to sport. One theoretical upshot of Lewis' counterfactual theory of causation is made clear. Lewis' theory is particularly apt at handling absence causation, which is shown to play a useful role in the analyses of sports. In such analyses, counterfactuals support a kind of virtual understanding of causation by allowing for engagement with a larger conceptual space of possible causes in sport. Engaging with a broader conceptual space has practical application in planning for as many events as possible including non-events, and for good practices regarding player development and team preparation.[12] In addition, as this article can improve understanding of causal responsibility it might support new insights into the debate about the role of chance in sport.[13] Some might think it is better to be prepared than lucky. In player evaluation, it is useful to know whether success is attributed more to chance or causal responsibility. In addition, causation in sport is interlinked with philosophical views on bodily movement in sports.[14] Hence, further insights might be supported in the latter area of sport philosophy. Last, concerns over risks, dangers, safety [32], and injuries in sport are all possible candidates for counterfactual analyses.

Funding: I would like to thank the Scottish Graduate School for Arts & Humanities and the Arts & Humanities Research Council for the Doctoral Training Partnership and the associated opportunities.

Acknowledgments: I would like to thank Stephan Leuenberger and Neil McDonnell at the University of Glasgow for helping me prepare to write this article. I would like to thank the two anonymous reviewers for helpful comments in revising this article. I would like to thank Emily Ryall at the University of Gloucestershire for the encouragement and opportunity to write this article.

Conflicts of Interest: The author declares no conflict of interest.

References

1. Mumford, S. Metaphysics and Sport. In *Routledge Handbook of Philosophy of Sport*; Routledge: New York, NY, USA, 2015.
2. Suits, B. *The Grasshopper: Games, Life, and Utopia*; University of Toronto Press: Toronto, ON, Canada, 1978; p. 41.
3. Maar, A.; Applying, D.K. Lewis's Counterfactual Theory of Causation to the Philosophy of Historiography. *J. Philos. Hist.* **2016**, *10*, 349–369. [CrossRef]
4. Counterfactual Theories of Causation. Stanford Encyclopedia of Philosophy [Online]. 2014. Available online: https://plato.stanford.edu/entries/causation-counterfactual/ (accessed on 15 April 2019).

---

[12] I thank Reviewer 2 for their insights as an active rugby union coach and former match official.
[13] See Breivik [29] and De Wachter [30] for opposing views on chance in sport.
[14] See Breivik [31] on the philosophy of bodily movement in sport.

5. Nolan, D. Why historians (and everyone else) should care about counterfactuals. *Philos. Stud. Int. J. Philos. Anal. Tradit.* **2013**, *163*, 317–335. [CrossRef]
6. David, L. Stanford Encyclopedia of Philosophy [Online]. 2014. Available online: https://plato.stanford.edu/entries/david-lewis/#5.1 (accessed on 25 April 2019).
7. Menzies, P. Difference-making in context. In *Causation and Counterfactuals*; The MIT Press: Cambridge, MA, USA, 2004.
8. Papineau, D. The Nature and Value of Sport. In *Games, Sports and Play: Philosophical Essays*; Oxford University Press: Oxford, UK, 2019; pp. 194–195.
9. Schneider, A.J.; Butcher, R.B. Pre-lusory Goals for Games: A Gambit Declined. *J. Philos. Sport* **1997**, *24*, 38–46. [CrossRef]
10. Royce, R. Game-players and game-playing: A response to Kreider. *J. Philos. Sport* **2012**, *40*, 225–239. [CrossRef]
11. Morgan, W.J. Some Further Words on Suits on Play. *J. Philos. Sport* **2008**, *35*, 120–141. [CrossRef]
12. Thomson, K. Sport and Utopia. *J. Philos. Sport* **2004**, *31*, 60–63. [CrossRef]
13. Kretchmar, S.R. The Intelligibility of Suits's Utopia: The View from Anthropological Philosophy. *J. Philos. Sport* **2006**, *33*, 67–77. [CrossRef]
14. Holowchak, A.M. Games as Pastimes in Suits's Utopia: Meaningful Living and the "Metaphysics of Leisure". *J. Philos. Sport* **2007**, *34*, 88–96. [CrossRef]
15. Suits, B. Tricky Triad: Games, Play and Sport. *J. Philos. Sport* **2012**, *15*, 1–9. [CrossRef]
16. Royce, R. Concerning a moral duty to cheat in games. *J. Philos. Sport* **2015**, *42*, 317–325. [CrossRef]
17. Hurka, T. On Judged Sports. *J. Sport Ethics Philos.* **2012**, *6*, 323–335. [CrossRef]
18. Markman, D.; Gavanksi, I.; Sherman, S.; McMullen, M. The Mental Simulation of Better and Worse Possible Worlds. *J. Experimen. Soc. Psychol.* **1993**, *29*, 87–109. [CrossRef]
19. Dowe, P. Absences, Possible Causation, and the Problem of Non-Locality. *Monist* **2009**, *92*, 23–40. [CrossRef]
20. Mumford, S. Causal Powers and Capacities. In *The Oxford Handbook of Causation*; Oxford University Press: Oxford, UK, 2009.
21. Woodward, J.F. Agency and Interventionist Theories. In *The Oxford Handbook of Causation*; Oxford University Press: Oxford, UK, 2009.
22. Dowe, P. Causal Process Theories. In *The Oxford Handbook of Causation*; Oxford University Press: Oxford, UK, 2009.
23. Wesley, S. Stanford Encyclopedia of Philosophy [Online]. 2018. Available online: https://plato.stanford.edu/entries/wesley-salmon/#CausProc (accessed on 25 April 2019).
24. Williamson, J. Probabilistic Theories. In *The Oxford Handbook of Causation*; Oxford University Press: Oxford, UK, 2009.
25. Beebee, H.; Hitchcock, C.; Menzies, P. *The Oxford Handbook of Causation*; Oxford University Press: Oxford, UK, 2009.
26. Paul, L.A.; Hall, N. *Causation: A User's Guide*; Oxford University Press: Oxford, UK, 2013; pp. 173–175.
27. Hitchcock, C. Causal Modelling. In *The Oxford Handbook of Causation*; Oxford University Press: Oxford, UK, 2009.
28. Interpretations of Probability. Stanford Encyclopedia of Philosophy [Online]. 2014. Available online: https://plato.stanford.edu/entries/probability-interpret/ (accessed on 25 April 2019).
29. Breivik, G. Against chance: A causal theory of winning in sport. In *Values in Sport: Elitism, Nationalism, Gender Equality and the Scientific Manufacturing of Winners*; Taylor & Francie: London, UK, 2009.
30. De Wachter, F. In Praise of Chance: A Philosophical Analysis of the Element of Chance in Sports. *J. Sport Ethics Philos.* **2012**, *12*, 52–61. [CrossRef]
31. Breivik, G. Bodily Movement—The fundamental dimensions. *J. Sport Ethics Philos.* **2008**, *2*, 337–352. [CrossRef]
32. Ryall, E. What is the value of dangerous sport? In *Philosophy of Sport Issues and Ideas*; Bloomsbury: London, UK, 2016.

© 2019 by the author. Licensee MDPI, Basel, Switzerland. This article is an open access article distributed under the terms and conditions of the Creative Commons Attribution (CC BY) license (http://creativecommons.org/licenses/by/4.0/).

Article

Casuistic Reasoning, Standards of Evidence, and Expertise on Elite Athletes' Nutrition

Saana Jukola

Department of Philosophy, Bielefeld University, 33501 Bielefeld, Germany; sjukola@uni-bielefeld.de; Tel.: +49-(0)521-106-4586

Received: 4 April 2019; Accepted: 23 April 2019; Published: 25 April 2019

Abstract: This paper assesses the epistemic challenges of giving nutrition advice to elite athletes in light of recent philosophical discussion concerning evidence-based practice. Our trust in experts largely depends on the assumption that their advice is based on reliable evidence. In many fields, the evaluation of the reliability of evidence is made on the basis of standards that originate from evidence-based medicine. I show that at the Olympic or professional level, implementing nutritional plans in real-world competitions requires contextualization of knowledge in a way that contravenes the tenets of evidence-based thinking. Nutrition experts need to be able to combine and apply evidence from multiple sources, including the previous successes and failures of particular athletes. I argue that in this sense, the practice of elite sport nutrition embodies casuistic reasoning.

Keywords: elite sports; sport nutrition; standards of evidence; evidence-based practices; randomized controlled trials; philosophy of medicine; casuistry

1. Introduction

The right kind of nutrition programs are essential for the success of elite athletes [1]. Athletes competing at the Olympic or professional level strive for optimal performance at physiological and biomechanical limits. Sustaining high speed or power while maintaining an adequate level of technique is possible only if fatigue does not occur. Thus, the correct intake of energy, nutrients, and fluid during the training period and competitions is crucial [2]. As a consequence, nutrition coaches have an important role in supporting athletes. However, the scientific justification of the advice from these experts is questionable when evaluated according to typical evidential standards: The practice of sport nutrition is seldom based on high-quality evidence according to often-used criteria. Instead of randomized controlled trials (RCTs), the use of small group observations, case studies, and laboratory studies is widespread [2,3].

This paper assesses the epistemic challenges of giving nutrition advice to elite athletes in light of recent philosophical discussion concerning evidence-based practice. Our trust in experts largely depends on the assumption that their advice is based on reliable evidence. In many fields, the evaluation of the reliability of evidence is made on the basis of standards that originate from evidence-based medicine (EBM). According to the EBM approach, guidance based on outcomes of meta-analyses or RCTs is taken to be more reliable than guidance drawn from observational or laboratory studies, previous experiences of the specialist in question or anecdotal testimonies. I show that at the Olympic or professional level, implementing nutritional plans in real-world competitions requires contextualization of knowledge in a way that contravenes the tenets of evidence-based thinking. In the context of elite sport, relevant evidence that would be ranked high according to the criteria of EBM is often not available or sometimes even impossible to acquire. Moreover, even if such evidence was available, it alone could not inform nutrition protocols of athletes. Instead, nutrition experts need to be able to combine and apply evidence from multiple sources, including the previous successes and failures of particular athletes. I therefore argue that in this sense, the practice of elite sport nutrition embodies casuistic reasoning, that is, reasoning on the basis of multiple sources of evidence including existing, solved cases. Casuistry[1] does not abandon universal theoretical rules or population-level regularities (such as, in the case of sport nutrition or clinical medicine, outcomes of RCTs) but emphasizes the details of individual cases and accepts that, depending on the circumstances, the same rules may not always apply.

It has to be emphasized that the focus of this paper is on the epistemic challenges that practicing elite sport nutrition coaches face, not on critically evaluating the methods of sport science or sport nutrition research. I do not deny that these fields could have methodological problems [3,4]. However, they are not the target of the analysis here. I want to argue that even if all published sport nutrition research was of impeccable quality, the use of so-called low-level evidence, such as small case and laboratory studies and expert opinion, in informing high-caliber athletes would still be necessary. The second caveat is that in this paper, I remain agnostic with respect to the general success of EBM. The argument at hand is directed at the discussion that concerns the epistemic challenges of giving advice to elite athletes. Even though many of these challenges are similar to the ones that emerge in clinical practice, I do not claim that the argument I make in this article applies to the clinical context.[2] Establishing this would require writing a lengthier article than is possible here.

In the next section, I give the reader a brief introduction to the reasoning that underlies evidence-based approaches in medicine and other fields. The aim of this section is to offer an overview of evidence-based thinking and its criticism. After this preface, I move on to exploring the epistemic landscape of sport nutrition. In Section 3, I describe the challenges that nutrition experts face when they advise athletes at the Olympic or professional level. I show that studies that could be labelled as high-quality according to the EBM standards are often practically impossible to conduct in sport nutrition. Moreover, even if evidence from such studies was available, the applicability of this evidence to practical planning of nutrition protocols would be limited. Consequently, amalgamating evidence from multiple sources is necessary in the practice of sport nutrition. In Section 4, I suggest that giving expert advice in elite sport nutrition features casuistic, or case-based, reasoning. Conclusions follow in Section 5.

2. Evidence-Based Practice

How should we determine the most effective treatment for depression? What is the best way to manage staff in small IT companies? On what basis should officials decide what programs to create for reducing the rates of domestic violence? According to evidence-based approaches, relying on expert opinion or tradition when answering questions like these comes with the risk of producing suboptimal outcomes. Instead, decision-making in medicine, management, policy, and other fields should be based on guidelines drawing from the best available scientific evidence—preferably evidence from RCTs. Evidence-based thinking originates from clinical medicine, where evidence-based medicine (EBM) was presented as a "new paradigm" in the 1990s [5]. The aim of EBM has been to standardize patient care and to avoid the supposedly negative influence of subjective judgments on clinical practice. In this way, EBM is believed to improve the objectivity and quality of patient care. As Sackett et al. [6] (p. 71) formulated, the central idea of EBM is "the conscientious, explicit, and judicious use of current best evidence in making decisions about the care of individual patients".

Evidence hierarchies, which describe the assumed strength and reliability of different types of evidence, have a central role in EBM. Evidence hierarchies typically place systematic reviews and meta-analyses on top, followed by RCTs, observational studies, case reports, and expert opinion at the

---

[1] In common parlance, "Casuistry" is often used to refer to faulty reasoning. In this paper, however, I use the term to refer to case-based reasoning.
[2] I thank an anonymous reviewer for pointing out the importance of making this clarification.

bottom of the hierarchy. According to Guyatt et al. [7] (p. 2420), "Evidence-based medicine de-emphasizes intuition, unsystematic clinical experience, and pathophysiological rationale as sufficient grounds for clinical decision making and stresses the examination of evidence from clinical research". The justification for this ordering is that evidence from double-blinded and randomized RCTs is taken to be less vulnerable to various biases than observational studies, case studies, physiological rationale, and expert opinion. Consequently, these lower-levels of evidence do not form a trustworthy basis for action [8].

According to the proponents of EBM, the so-called gold standard status of RCTs is justified because this method guarantees better internal validity than other methods. In other words, if a correctly conducted and well-designed RCT concludes that an intervention has an effect, we can believe that a causal relation really exists, and the observed effect is not due to confounding. Randomization and blinding are central tools for reaching internal validity. Randomization means that the trial subjects are randomly divided into two (or more) groups. One of the groups is the study group that receives the treatment, while the other gets a placebo or a control treatment. Randomization is supposed to make sure that the groups are as similar to each other as possible. If randomization succeeds perfectly, the only difference between the groups is that one of them gets the treatment and the other either placebo or a control treatment. Consequently, the difference in the outcomes of the groups can be explained by the exposure. Successful blinding, in turn, means that the participants, doctors and other involved parties do not know which participants belong to the treatment group. The aim is to reduce biases and placebo effect that could have an influence on the outcomes of the trial. Another benefit of RCTs is that they are believed to be able to detect small effects—if designed well [5,8].

In recent years, the practices and underlying assumptions of EBM have become a popular target for criticism by philosophers of medicine. Especially the gold standard status of RCTs has been attacked by numerous authors who claim that the method does not control for biases in the way claimed by the proponents of EBM. For example, Worrall [9] has argued that randomization cannot be perfect in practice and, consequently, that confounding cannot be ruled out even in RCTs. Bias can be caused by numerous factors, many of which are unknown, and in practice, it is impossible to make sure that there are no differences between the treatment and control group. Consequently, Worrall holds that it is unjustified to label RCTs prima facie more reliable than well-designed observational studies. In turn, Cartwright [10] has focused on the extrapolability of studies and shown that achieving external validity is a challenge for RCTs. Her work has demonstrated that it can be difficult, in practice, to apply the results from RCTs to new populations and contexts. Howick [8] has argued that blinding is not necessary except in studies that measure outcomes subjectively (e.g., pain, patient satisfaction). He and Kirsch [11] also claimed that in trials with large effect sizes, blinding is often broken; for example, in trials studying the efficacy of selective serotonin reuptake inhibitors—a type of antidepressant—the presence or absence of side effects often tells the participants whether they belong to the treatment group or not. Stegenga [12] has shown that conducting RCTs and meta-analyses requires multiple judgments, which means that subjectivity, and hence possible biases, cannot be avoided even in these methods that are situated high in the evidence hierarchy. Finally, Osimani [13] and Vandenbroucke [14] both argued that a single evidence hierarchy is not suitable for all needs. Even if it was the case that RCTs provided the most reliable evidence on the efficacy of medical interventions, they are not the best method for finding out about whether an intervention has unwanted side effects. This is because RCTs are designed to detect effects that are expected to exist and their power and scope in detecting unexpected effects is limited. Contrarily, observational studies and case reports can be valuable in gathering evidence of unexpected and small effects [14].

The gist of the aforementioned criticisms of EBM is that RCTs are no panacea for producing bias-free knowledge that could be used for clinical decision-making. Moreover, the abovementioned authors criticize the use of one evidence hierarchy as a tool for assessing the strength of evidence for all purposes. Depending on the epistemological demands of the situation (for example, detecting expected effects of a drug vs. gathering information on the potential unexpected harms of a treatment), different methods should be preferred.

Despite the criticism they have faced, the tenets of EBM have spread to other fields outside clinical medicine. For example, there are now movements such as evidence-based nursing [15], evidence-based management [16], and evidence-based public health [17]. However, transferring the standards of evidence from the clinical context to another raises further issues beyond those discussed with respect to EBM. For instance, Parkhurst and Abeysinghe [18] criticized applying the EBM standards of evidence in policy making. In evidence-based policy, the principle is that evidence produced by "rigorous evaluations—such as randomized controlled trials and quasi-experimental studies" [19] should be used for planning government-funded programs and other policy measures. The use of data and research is hoped to increase the effectiveness of chosen measures, for example, to help to find the best means of HIV prevention in a certain area. Yet, Parkhurst and Abeysinghe [18] argue that applying the EBM principles in policy-making has additional problems to the ones discussed in the medical context. For instance, health policy decisions include more than the evaluation of effectiveness of the suggested intervention(s). Instead, values such as individual autonomy and social acceptability must have an influence on decisions. Yet RCTs cannot inform us about such values and the role they could play in a policy decision. Parkhurst and Abeysinghe [18] (p. 669) note: "Prioritizing evidence from experimental methods serves to obscure, rather than remove, political considerations—imposing a de facto political position that holds clinical outcomes of morbidity and mortality reduction (i.e., those things conducive to RCT evidence) above other social values". It is likely that some promising public health interventions cannot be tested by using RCTs, and, thus, would not be considered as possible options in evidence-based policy making.

Nutrition science and policy are other fields that are often evaluated and criticized on the basis of EBM standards. According to some critics, the evidence base of many nutrition policies is weak; for example, policies that recommend limiting sugar intake are typically based on observational studies, which means that our trust in the effectiveness of these policies should be low [20]. In a recent paper [21], I questioned this argumentation strategy and argued that it is problematic to criticize nutrition policies and population-level dietary guidelines for not being based on RCTs. Conducting sound RCTs on topics relevant for issuing guidelines is often difficult or even impossible for practical, ethical, and theoretical reasons. An important goal of the Dietary Guidelines for Americans and other population-level guidelines is to reduce the risk of chronic diseases. Given that many chronic diseases take years or even decades to develop, carrying out RCTs assessing how different dietary patterns affect the risks of these diseases would be impossible in practice. Thus, it is not fruitful to use standards originating from EBM for evaluating evidence in this context if relevant RCTs simply are not available. Given the non-epistemic goals of the guidelines, especially improving population health and preventing chronic diseases, the standards of acceptable evidence have to be adapted to the different practical, ethical, and theoretical constraints of the situation.

3. Epistemic Challenges of Sport Nutrition Practice

Optimizing the intake of nutrients, energy, and fluid is essential for high-caliber athletes, whose results, and livelihood, can be dependent on the fractions of seconds or few millimeters that make the difference between winning and coming second in a competition. Thus, even small changes in dietary habits or supplement intake can be critical. Athletes are interested in the best way to load carbohydrates before competitions, how hydration during the competition should be managed, and which permitted supplements could be used for improving their performance. In deciding how a particular athlete should eat and drink, the nutrition coach is faced with a challenge.

Until recently, practices in sport nutrition were usually based on trial and error by different athletes and coaches. The role of scientists was to explain the observations post hoc by, for instance, searching for underlying biological mechanisms causing the effects of dietary patterns or supplements [22,23]. As Burke and Hawley [2] noted, basic sport nutrition science has advanced when the success of athletes has sparked interest in analyzing their training and diet habits in more detail. Lately, the influence of science on practice has become more important, and the current guidelines [24] and advice for elite athletes' nutrition strive to be science-based instead of experience-based. However, nutrition advice for elite athletes seldom qualifies as being based on high-quality evidence according to the usual EBM standards of evidence [2]. For example, in a review of studies on sports drink *Lucozade*, Heneghan et al. [3] (p. 1) stated: "If you apply evidence based methods, 40 years of sports drink research does not seemingly add up to much[.]" More broadly, most available evidence on the efficacy of performance supplements is still anecdotal or originates from laboratory studies [22]. Consequently, especially epidemiologically trained scientists have questioned the scientific justification of elite sport nutrition advice [3,22].

Sport nutrition experts acknowledge that RCTs are rarely available for testing the effectiveness of different nutrition practices. Sport nutrition, of course, faces the same challenges as nutrition science in general, namely that designing RCTs on the effects of nutrition is complicated because diet is a complex exposure. It can be difficult to isolate individual compounds in a way that is fitting for the RCT design [25]. This makes it difficult to test the efficacy of nutrition patterns and supplements. For instance, the effectivity of caffeine partly depends on the intake of carbohydrates and bicarbonate supplements [2]. Given the number of different combinations and permutations of possible supplements and nutrition strategies, overall effects of many nutrition patterns are not known [2]. This is a problem, especially because many athletes use a number of supplements at the same time. Athletes use caffeine, creatine, beta-alanine, bicarbonate, beetroot juice, and phosphate, for instance, in a number of combinations. Yet, there is very little evidence of the efficacy of these supplements when used together [22].

Another reason for the unattainability of relevant RCTs is rather simple: The lack of potential subjects. Detecting small effects requires large sample sizes. However, the population of elite athletes is, by definition, small. Professional and Olympic-level athletes are also usually unable or unwilling to participate in trials for epistemic purposes because doing so might negatively impact their preparations and endanger their chances of succeeding in competitions. Small, underpowered RCTs cannot offer information on the small beneficial changes in performance that an intervention could provide [22]. This means that evidence that would be of value to athletes is often practically impossible to acquire via RCTs.

One could try to argue that even though elite athletes are not available as trial subjects, elite sport nutrition coaches could base their practice on RCTs performed on well-trained but subelite populations. However, the extrapolability of results from these studies to an elite population is questionable: The training routines of Olympic-level athletes are likely to be more strenuous, and it is not unlikely that such athletes have physiological traits that other populations lack. These differences may cause variation in the responses to selected nutrition practices. For instance, the response to beetroot juice supplementation appears to be less noticeable in an elite population as compared to subelite athletes [2]. This difference in response may be explained by elite and subelite athletes having different composition of muscle fiber and the effects that intensive training has had on their physiology [2]. Despite observed differences in response, few studies have assessed how known characteristics such as age, sex or training status influence the efficacy of nutritional supplements [22]. A further issue related to extrapolability of the studies is that the existing studies are often conducted on male populations, while men and women differ in many ways that are relevant to sport nutrition [22].

In addition to the lack of suitable and willing subjects, the availability of applicable RCTs in elite athlete sport nutrition is limited by the fact that the needs of athletes competing in different sports vary considerably. Modern sport nutrition emphasizes the importance of personalizing nutritional plans to fit the needs of individual athletes. While earlier dietary guidelines used to promote similar dietary patterns to athletes in all sports, the different requirements of different sports are now recognized [24]. Different sports set different metabolic demands, as do athletes' competition goals and periodization of training. For instance, in some sports, athletes take part in series of heats through which they may qualify for finals (for example, in judo), and in some sports, they may compete in multiple events (for example, a swimmer can take part in several events for different distances and strokes) [22].

Weight-division sports require weight-cutting, i.e., athletes dehydrate themselves before competitions in order to qualify in a lower weight class. Moreover, the rules and cultural norms of sports pose limits to how athletes can take care of hydration or refueling of energy during the events. For example, in basketball and ice hockey, athletes can drink during substitution, while in football, drinking during each half is more difficult [2]. This variation between the requirements of and the acceptable practices in different sports means that it is difficult to extrapolate results from a study evaluating a nutritional strategy in a certain sport to other contexts.

In addition, variation between individuals is considerable, for example, with respect to the need for additional fluids to combat dehydration. For instance, according to Shirreffs at al. [26], sweat loss and drinking habits of football players varied considerably when doing the same exercises. Moreover, what nutritional strategy an athlete should choose does not only depend on which sport they are competing in but also on where and when the competition is taking place. Environmental conditions (e.g., temperature, altitude) of events vary, and the need of hydration and the effectiveness of performance supplements can differ accordingly [22]. Consequently, the right strategy for an athlete can change from competition to competition depending on external conditions.

An interesting example of how timing of a competition can pose added challenges to designing an athlete's diet is planning nutrition protocols for elite athletes who practice Sawm, i.e., fasting during Ramadan. Muslims should not eat or drink between sunrise and sunset during the 30 days of the ninth month of the Islamic calendar. Yet many Muslim athletes take part in competitions or at least continue training at this time. While in most Muslim countries, competitions are organized after sunset during Ramadan, in international events, this is not the case [27,28]. For instance, in 2012, the Olympic Games and Ramadan coincided. Consequently, many Muslim athletes could not follow their usual nutrition and hydration routines but had to adapt their practices to the special circumstances.

What all this means is that existing studies on the effectiveness of a certain nutrition strategy may be of little practical use for coaches and athletes. RCTs in sport nutrition typically look into questions such as "Will a supplement X improve performance in marathon running?" However, what an actual marathon runner or their coach would like to know is whether supplement X will improve their performance in running a marathon in 35 degrees heat in city C if they also take another supplement Y. Given the complexity of the question, acquiring relevant evidence from an RCT can be practically impossible [2,23]. As Burke and Peeling [22] (p. 160) note, "generic solutions my not always apply to specific scenarios".

The epistemic challenge of giving nutrition advice to elite athletes boils down to two issues: The unavailability of appropriate evidence from RCTs and the application of the available evidence to the particular case at hand. The feasibility of RCTs that could successfully inform elite athletes' dietary practices is highly questionable. Trials performed on elite populations would likely be underpowered, and the extrapolability of existing RCTs (performed on subelite populations) is low. Given the specificity of the situations where advice on how to improve performance is needed, studies that would allow direct application usually simply are not available. Consequently, experts in elite sports cannot rely on guidelines that would satisfy the EBM standards of reliable evidence.

4. Elite Sport Nutrition Advice as A Form of Casuistry

If evidence-based practice is impossible in elite sport nutrition, it seems natural to question what nutrition coaches, the assumed experts, are actually doing. Are they just charlatans or does their practice have some kind of legitimate scientific justification? According to Burke and Hawley [2], those who criticize practices in sport science for the lack of high-quality evidence have failed to acknowledge that what is needed for advising elite athletes is very context-specific knowledge. Even if RCT evidence was available, sport nutrition experts would have to take into consideration a number of factors that might limit its applicability to the circumstances of a particular athlete. Thus, "[t]he practical implementation of nutrition strategies by athletes in real-world settings confounds the establishment of an evidence base by traditional research methods and the development of generalizable (and uncontroversial) guidelines" [2] (p. 785). There is a tension between giving the best possible advice to athletes in their particular circumstances and the general, universal statements of RCTs and meta-analyses. In this section, I suggest that in order to understand how this tension could be solved, the practices of elite sport nutrition coaches can be perceived as a form of casuistry, i.e., reasoning that utilizes multiple sources of evidence and stresses the importance of paying attention to the circumstances of individual cases.

In order to understand the practice of casuistry in nutrition sport advice, it is important to grasp how the aim of this action differs from the aims of sport nutrition scientists. Unlike nutrition epidemiologists, practicing nutrition coaches are less interested in acquiring new knowledge concerning generalizable regularities and universal rules than solving particular cases. They are interested in particular bodies, while scientists typically are interested in establishing claims that apply to the universal abstract body [29]. However, this does not mean that the casuistic practice has no bearing on the development of scientific theories. I address this point in the end of this section.

Historically, casuistic reasoning has been practiced in law and theology, for instance. Currently, it is often discussed in the ethical context, where it can be defined as a stance that moral theories, such as utilitarianism or deontological ethics, cannot guide action in particular cases. This is because these theories are too general [30]. Instead, decisions concerning new cases should be made by comparing them to previous, already agreed upon cases in light of available information. Especially in bioethics, researchers in the latter half of the last century had to take seriously the challenge that individual cases pose to ethical experts instead of focusing on metaethics and building universal ethical theories [31]. New medical technologies and research created situations where interpreting and applying abstract ethical theories was essential, as well as taking into consideration the context, including institutional and social surroundings, of the case.

The need for casuistry arises in situations where there is a demand to act yet either no appropriate guidelines or principles that could be followed or there is a conflict between the existing protocols. For example, in clinical practice, doctors have to consider how treatment guidelines could be applied to best support the needs of an individual patient. According to the principles of EBM, evidence from clinical trials should guide decision making. However, as Tonelli [32] argues, in practice, a pathophysiological rationale or previous clinical experience can sometimes overrule this evidence. For instance, sometimes, patients' comorbidities prohibit carrying out the procedures recommended in the guidelines. Furthermore, clinical decision making requires taking into account patient values and goals, as well as societal, legal, and ethical norms. Because of this, guidelines cannot be applied similarly in all cases.

According to Tonelli [32], the problem of EBM is that clinical guidelines are based on studies conducted on populations and consequently best apply to average cases. Yet at the clinic, a doctor has to make decisions concerning individuals who can differ considerably from the average. Consequently, guidelines based on RCTs cannot determine clinical decisions. Applying clinical, evidence-based guidelines requires what Tonelli calls "practical wisdom":

> "[C]asuistic (case-based) approach to clinical decision making necessitates an understanding the meaningful ways in which the patient-at-hand differs from similar patients, remembered, heard or read about ... While scientific knowledge, whether basic or applied, informs the process, that knowledge alone is far from sufficient to allow for optimal clinical judgment."
> [32] (pp. 387–388)

When deciding how to act, a casuist must be aware about the circumstances of the case and the maxims applying to it. For instance, in a clinical context, circumstances include the particular nature of a patient's illness, their personal wishes and values, treatments that are available in the hospital in question, and local laws and regulations. The maxims include the Hippocratic Oath, principles such as "do not kill" and "relieve pain", and existing clinical treatment guidelines. Depending on the circumstances, different maxims receive more weight [31]. According to casuistry, no general rule or maxim can be said to be applicable in all cases. Instead, it is important to recognize in which cases rules apply, in which not, and how these cases differ from each other. In this way, a casuist can gather information concerning the applicability of the rules and about how different circumstances influence the applicability of different rules. "Successful casuistic practice depends on knowing which similarities are essential or relevant and which merely accidental" [30] (p. 513). There is no fixed set of rules for deciding when cases are similar enough or which aspects are relevant for evaluating similarity. Instead, this activity requires judgments, which is in conflict with the tenets of EBM. However, judgments do not have to be arbitrary. Rather, they are informed by experience and theory and can thus be criticized by other members of the community [33,34]. For example, clinicians have to know how alike their patient is to an average patient in the trials that treatment guidelines are based on and how the potential differences would affect treatment decisions. This may require not only knowledge of basic sciences such as biochemistry, genetics or pharmacology, but also of the cultural background or living conditions of the patient. By discussing with their colleagues, they can receive criticism for their judgments and, when needed, correct them accordingly.

In this way, casuistry requires combining different sources of information: "The ultimate view of the case and its appropriate resolution comes, not from a single principle, nor from a dominant theory, but from the converging impression made by all of the relevant facts and arguments that appear in each of those spaces" [31] (p. 245). In a clinical context, this means that also so-called lower-level evidence is needed for decision-making. By offering information on the potential differences between individuals and thus guiding clinical practice, evidence from laboratory studies and case reports can help to bridge the gap between clinical studies and the care of an individual patient. Clinical experience, in turn, is needed for comparing patients with previous cases.

In the same way as a clinician, a sport nutrition coach is focused on one individual. Casuistry involves recognizing the needs of individual athletes as well as how they differ from the populations on which the available studies have been conducted. Instead of established guidelines based on high-quality studies that could be directly applied to advise individual athletes, sport nutrition experts have to draw from available randomized controlled trials (which often are conducted on subelite populations), observational studies, biomechanical and chemical knowledge, as well as their knowledge concerning other athletes and the previous experiences of the given athlete. In other words, in sport nutrition practice, developing successful dietary plans requires combining evidence from multiple sources, many of which are labelled as low-quality in EBM. Especially the role of evidence from case reports and laboratory studies is often substantial in designing elite athletes' nutrition strategies. For example, according to Burke and Peeling [22], despite the lack of evidence from RCTs, integrating several performance supplements into an athlete's diet can be managed if the coach uses evidence from so-called low-level studies, especially single-case and small-group observations. Experts also use mechanistic reasoning concerning the genetic differences between individuals to explain why individuals react differently to performance supplements. Mechanistic and laboratory evidence thus helps experts to bridge the gap from available studies to new practical cases. Moreover, the role of experience and judgment is crucial in amalgamating heterogeneous evidence and planning nutrition protocols [22].

The fact that sport nutrition coaches, clinicians, and other casuists are focused on solving individual cases does not mean that their practice could not be relevant to formulating more general-level rules or theories. According to casuistry, the development of general rules or theory often follows the resolution of particular cases [31,35]. Evaluation and comparison of cases in which general rules seem to apply to cases in which rules are not applicable can help researchers to develop hypotheses regarding the underlying causal mechanisms at play. This is what has happened in sport nutrition. According to Burke and Hawley [2], the experiences of nutrition coaches and athletes are important for developing sport nutrition and sport nutrition guidelines further, and comparing cases can help in observing differences that can inform future research and give nutrition and sport scientists means to develop new testable hypotheses [35]. In this way, solving individual cases, i.e., advising individual athletes, can contribute to establishing population-level regularities in sport nutrition.

5. Conclusions

I have shown that EBM standards of evidence, which emphasize the importance of basing decisions on population-level studies and especially RCTs, are ill-suited for evaluating the practices in elite sport nutrition. Relevant RCT-level evidence is often not available for sport nutrition coaches, and even if there were RCTs, they are usually conducted on populations that differ in relevant ways from high-caliber athletes. Athletes need very context-specific information on how to carry out the intake of energy, fluid, and supplements, and it is unlikely that an athlete whose dietary protocol was based on RCTs only would succeed. Consequently, sport nutrition experts have to combine information from multiple sources, including studies that are ranked low in the EBM evidence hierarchy and anecdotal experience.

The case of elite sport nutrition demonstrates how important it is to take into consideration the goals of an action when assessing how standards of evidence should be set. The goal of a sport nutrition coach is to advise a particular individual in particular circumstances. RCTs, even if they were the best source of evidence for establishing that population-level regularities exist, are insufficient for guiding this practice. This implies that we need a pluralistic and contextual understanding of what constitutes good evidence.

Regarding the practice of elite sport nutrition coaches as a form of casuistry can promote understanding the relation that this activity has to more general-level sport science and nutrition theories. Especially, it can help in perceiving how and why the practices of coaches and athletes can inform scientists who are interested in examining population-level regularities using epidemiological methods. Thus, observations concerning potentially relevant differences between athletes and circumstances can spark new research. Moreover, "bench" or basic science has a central role in helping elite athletes' nutrition experts to bridge the gap between existing population-level evidence and their client. Additionally, the progress of precision medicine can deliver methods to serve the needs of elite athletes.[3] Increased understanding of how differences in genetic makeup and environmental factors influence responsiveness to treatments has potential to help nutrition coaches plan more individualized, science-based nutrition protocols. This suggests that close cooperation between scientists, coaches, and athletes is needed for sport nutrition to advance as a science and a practice.

Finally, I want to mention a prospect for evidence-based elite athletes' nutrition, namely N-of-1 trials.[4] In N-of-1 trial design, both the intervention and the control treatment are given to a single subject. The order in which the subject gets the intervention and the control can be either randomly allocated or decided by the researcher. As the aim of these trials is to find the best treatment for individuals [36], they have potential to serve as a source of evidence for designing optimal nutrition plans for athletes. Even though RCTs and systematic reviews of multiple RCTs are typically considered to deliver the most reliable evidence, N-of-1 trials have at least once been placed on the top of evidence hierarchy [37]. However, they are often ignored in EBM literature and philosophy of medicine. Utilizing this trial design could bring the practice of elite sport nutrition advice closer to satisfying the evidence-based ideal by reducing the need for judgments.

Funding: This research was funded by the Deutsche Forschungsgemeinschaft (DFG, German Research Foundation)—Project 254954344/GRK2073.

Acknowledgments: I am grateful to two reviewers for their constructive criticism and comments. I would like to thank Stefano Canali, Sebastian Dorny, Anna Höhl, David Hopf, Daria Jadreškić, Anja Pichl, Rose Trappes, and the participants of the workshop "Epistemic Trust in the Epistemology of Expert Testimony" in Erlangen, March 2019, for their helpful comments.

Conflicts of Interest: The author declares no conflict of interest.

---

[3] I thank an anonymous reviewer for pointing this out.
[4] I thank an anonymous reviewer for bringing up this possibility.

References

1. Peeling, P.; Binnie, M.J.; Goods, P.S.; Sim, M.; Burke, L.M. Evidence-based supplements for the enhancement of athletic performance. *Int. J. Sport Nutr. Exerc. Metab.* **2018**, *28*, 178–187. [CrossRef] [PubMed]
2. Burke, L.M.; Hawley, J.A. Swifter, higher, stronger: What's on the menu? *Science* **2018**, *362*, 781–787. [CrossRef] [PubMed]
3. Heneghan, C.; Perera, R.; Nunan, D.; Mahtani, K.; Gill, P. Forty years of sports performance research and little insight gained. *BMJ* **2012**, *345*, e4797. [CrossRef]
4. Aschwanden, C. Sport Science Is Finally Talking about Its Methodology Problem. 2019. Available online: https://fivethirtyeight.com/features/sports-science-is-finally-talking-about-its-methodology-problems/ (accessed on 3 April 2019).
5. Solomon, M. Just a paradigm: evidence-based medicine in epistemological context. *Eur. J. Philos. Sci.* **2011**, *1*, 451–466. [CrossRef]
6. Sackett, D.L.; Rosenberg, W.M.; Gray, J.M.; Haynes, R.B.; Richardson, W.S. Evidence based medicine: What it is and what it isn't. *BMJ* **1996**, *312*, 71–72. [CrossRef] [PubMed]
7. Guyatt, G.; Cairns, J.; Churchill, D.; Cook, D.; Haynes, B.; Hirsh, J.; Irvine, J.; Levine, M.; Levine, M.; Nishikawa, J.; Sackett, D. Evidence-based medicine: A new approach to teaching the practice of medicine. *JAMA* **1992**, *268*, 2420–2425. [CrossRef]
8. Howick, J. *The Philosophy of Evidence-based Medicine*; John Wiley & Sons: Chichester, UK, 2011; ISBN 978-1405196673.
9. Worrall, J. What evidence in evidence-based medicine? *Philos. Sci.* **2002**, *69*, S316–S330. [CrossRef]
10. Cartwright, N. Are RCTs the gold standard? *BioSocieties* **2007**, *2*, 11–20. [CrossRef]
11. Kirsch, I. Antidepressants and the placebo effect. *Z. Für Psychol.* **2014**, *222*, 128–134. [CrossRef] [PubMed]
12. Stegenga, J. *Medical Nihilism*; Oxford University Press: Oxford, UK, 2018; ISBN 9780198747048.
13. Osimani, B. Until RCT proven? On the asymmetry of evidence requirements for risk assessment. *J. Eval. Clin. Pract.* **2013**, *19*, 454–462. [CrossRef] [PubMed]
14. Vandenbroucke, J.P. Observational research, randomised trials, and two views of medical science. *PLoS Med.* **2008**, *5*, e67. [CrossRef] [PubMed]
15. Melnyk, B.M.; Fineout-Overholt, E. (Eds.) *Evidence-based Practice in Nursing & Healthcare: A Guide to Best Practice*; Lippincott Williams & Wilkins: Philadelphia, PA, USA, 2011; ISBN 1605477788.
16. Barends, E.; Rousseau, D.M. *Evidence-based Management: How to Use Evidence to Make Better Organizational Decisions*; Kogan Page Publishers: New York, NY, USA, 2018; ISBN 0749483741.
17. Brownson, R.C.; Baker, E.A.; Deshpande, A.D.; Gillespie, K.N. *Evidence-based Public Health*, 3rd ed.; Oxford University Press: Oxford, UK, 2017; ISBN 9780190620936.
18. Parkhurst, J.O.; Abeysinghe, S. What constitutes "good" evidence for public health and social policy-making? From hierarchies to appropriateness. *Soc. Epistemol.* **2016**, *30*, 665–679. [CrossRef]
19. Principles of Evidence-based Policymaking. Available online: https://www.evidencecollaborative.org/principles-evidence-based-policymaking (accessed on 3 April 2019).
20. Erickson, J.; Sadeghirad, B.; Lytvyn, L.; Slavin, J.; Johnston, B.C. The scientific basis of guideline recommendations on sugar intake: A systematic review. *Ann. Intern. Med.* **2017**, *166*, 257–267. [CrossRef] [PubMed]
21. Jukola, S. On the evidentiary standards for nutrition advice. *Stud. Hist. Philos. Sci. Part C Stud. Hist. Philos. Biol. Biomed. Sci.* **2019**, *73*, 1–9. [CrossRef]
22. Burke, L.M.; Peeling, P. Methodologies for investigating performance changes with supplement use. *Int. J. Sport Nutr. Exerc. Metab.* **2018**, *28*, 159–169. [CrossRef] [PubMed]
23. Hawley, J.A.; Lundby, C.; Cotter, J.D.; Burke, L.M. Maximizing cellular adaptation to endurance exercise in skeletal muscle. *Cell Metab.* **2018**, *27*, 962–976. [CrossRef] [PubMed]
24. Thomas, D.T.; Erdman, K.A.; Burke, L.M. American College of Sports Medicine Joint Position Statement. Nutrition and Athletic Performance. *Med. Sci. Sports Exerc.* **2016**, *48*, 543–568. [PubMed]
25. Satija, A.; Yu, E.; Willett, W.C.; Hu, F.B. Understanding nutritional epidemiology and its role in policy. *Adv. Nutr.* **2015**, *6*, 5–18. [CrossRef] [PubMed]
26. Shirreffs, S.M.; Sawka, M.N.; Stone, M. Water and electrolyte needs for football training and match-play. *J. Sports Sci.* **2006**, *24*, 699–707. [CrossRef]

27. Fallah, S.J. Ramadan fasting and exercise performance. *Asian J. Sports Med.* **2010**, *1*, 130.
28. Maughan, R.J.; Zerguini, Y.; Chalabi, H.; Dvorak, J. Achieving optimum sports performance during Ramadan: Some practical recommendations. *J. Sports Sci.* **2012**, *30*, S109–S117. [CrossRef] [PubMed]
29. Huovila, J.; Saikkonen, S. Casuistic Reasoning in Expert Narratives on Healthy Eating. *Sci. Cult.* **2018**, *27*, 375–397. [CrossRef]
30. Kuczewski, M. Casuistry and principlism: The convergence of method in biomedical ethics. *Theor. Med. Bioeth.* **1998**, *19*, 509–524. [CrossRef] [PubMed]
31. Jonsen, A.R. Casuistry as methodology in clinical ethics. *Theor. Med.* **1991**, *12*, 295–307. [CrossRef]
32. Tonelli, M.R. The challenge of evidence in clinical medicine. *J. Eval. Clin. Pract.* **2010**, *16*, 384–389. [CrossRef] [PubMed]
33. Arras, J.D. Getting down to cases: The revival of casuistry in bioethics. *J. Med. Philos.* **1991**, *16*, 29–51. [CrossRef]
34. Longino, H. *The Fate of Knowledge*; Princeton University Press: Princeton, NJ, USA, 2002; ISBN 0691088764.
35. Ankeny, R.A. The overlooked role of cases in causal attribution in medicine. *Philos. Sci.* **2014**, *81*, 999–1011. [CrossRef]
36. Lillie, E.O.; Patay, B.; Diamant, J.; Issell, B.; Topol, E.J.; Schork, N.J. The n-of-1 clinical trial: The ultimate strategy for individualizing medicine? *Pers. Med.* **2011**, *8*, 161–173. [CrossRef]
37. Guyatt, G.; Haynes, B.; Jaesche, R. The philosophy of evidence-based medicine. In *Users' Guides to the Medical Literature: A Manual for Evidence-Based Clinical Practice*, 2nd ed.; Guyatt, G., Rennie, D., Maede, M., Cook, D., Eds.; AMA Press: New York, NY, USA, 2008; pp. 9–16, ISBN 0-07-159035-8.

 © 2019 by the author. Licensee MDPI, Basel, Switzerland. This article is an open access article distributed under the terms and conditions of the Creative Commons Attribution (CC BY) license (http://creativecommons.org/licenses/by/4.0/).

Article

Unnatural Technology in a "Natural" Practice? Human Nature and Performance-Enhancing Technology in Sport

Francisco Javier Lopez Frias

Kinesiology Department and Rock Ethics Institute, The Pennsylvania State University, University Park, PA 16801, USA; fjl13@psu.edu

Received: 15 April 2019; Accepted: 20 June 2019; Published: 26 June 2019

Abstract: (1) Background: The World Anti-Doping Agency (WADA) utilizes three criteria to include a technology in the List of Banned Substances and Methods—performance enhancement, health, and the spirit of sport. The latter is arguably the most fundamental one, as WADA justifies the anti-doping mission by appealing to it. (2) Method: Given the interrelationship among the notions of "human nature," "natural talent," and "sport," I investigate what view of human nature underpins the "spirit of sport" criterion. To do so, I focus on both WADA's official documents and scholarly formulations of the spirit of sport (that align with that of WADA). (3) Results: I show that the value attributed to excellence and effort in WADA's formulation of the "spirit of sport" criterion has its roots in the notion of human nature of the work ethic that resulted from the secularization of the Protestant ethic. (4) Conclusion: Drawing on my analysis of the "spirit of sport" criterion, I pose critical questions concerning the justification of WADA's anti-doping campaign and a tentative solution to move forward in the debate.

Keywords: sport ethics; technology; the spirit of sport; excellence; anti-doping; nature

1. Introduction: Naturalness, Perfectibility, and Anti-Doping. Three Strongly Related Concepts

In *Defining Reality: Definitions and the politics of meaning*, Edward Schiappa [1] (p. 21) argues that concepts are like "road maps" that help to navigate reality by presenting it in a specific way. Concepts strongly influence how individuals experience and deal with the world. Thus, despite often being regarded as a purely theoretical task, the tasks of clarifying and defining concepts have tremendous practical consequences. In Schiappa's words, "the act of defining [has] ethical and normative ramifications" [1] (p. 3). Definitions guide humans' action in two ways: Individually and collectively. From an individual standpoint, they serve to categorize objects and phenomena in the world and know what to expect from them (e.g., the category "fire" includes the aspect of being harmful). Collectively speaking, concepts provide shared understandings that enable communication and facilitate social cooperation.

Given the practical implications of definitions, it could be argued that the more foundational the concept, the higher its practical and theoretical impact. One such foundational concept is "human nature." By analyzing the different uses of the concept of "the natural" in public debates, the Nuffield Council on Bioethics' analysis paper, "(un)naturalness," states that the concept has become a rhetorical tool that acts as a placeholder for a range of values and concerns that are meaningful and important to people [2]. Thus, the definition of "the natural" has significant theoretical and practical ramifications. Its implications can be observed in the medical practice, where the concept of "human nature" heavily influences those of "health" and "medicine." In shamanic culture, for instance, the body is characterized as a recipient of energy, a healthy state is determined by the correct flow of energy throughout the body, and medicine is the art to secure and restore the body's energy flow. In modern society, where human nature is defined materialistically by appealing to a series of biological elements (i.e., heart, lungs, veins, genes, and neurons) and functions (i.e., respiration, blood flow, digestion, and neuronal activity), health is regarded as the natural functioning of the body, and medicine as the art of restoring humans' bodily functioning to its natural levels.

Similarly, in the debate on the ethics of performance-enhancing technology, the notion of "the natural" informs the concept of "sport," which, in turn, determines how sports are regulated to protect and promote their essential values. For instance, Sigmund Loland and Mike McNamee identify two views of human nature (and sport) in the debate, namely: Restrictive and permissive, and argue that, "The dominant or official public sport policy response ... is [the] restrictive one" [3] (p. 117). Proponents of the "permissive" view of sport take the defining character of sport to be the empowerment of individuals as autonomous and responsible agents [4]. In a more extreme version of this approach, sport is regarded as an arena for humans to push human limits further [5,6]. Thus, in these conceptions of sport, the exercise of freedom is the defining trait of human nature. They build upon the idea that to be human is to exercise freedom. From an ethical standpoint, actions that protect and foster freedom are accepted. In contrast, those that limit the exercise of freedom are condemned. Permissive sport philosophers, therefore, advocate for relaxing or, in some cases, removing the ban on doping because it limits athletes' freedom and possibilities to enhance themselves.

From a restrictive perspective, sport, "is a sphere of ethically admirable human excellence" [3] (p. 117). Restrictive approaches to sport draw on a teleological Aristotelian understanding of human nature grounded in the principle that all entities are, by nature, oriented towards a goal or purpose, namely, the actualization of their potentialities. For instance, a seed has the potential to develop into a plant. From an ethical perspective, in teleological accounts of human nature, the actualization of potentialities and moral value are intertwined. Thus, a seed is good when it becomes a plant and bad when it fails to do so. The same logic applies to human beings. Humans, as natural beings, also gravitate towards the goal of actualizing their potential. Ethically speaking, the realization of their natural potentialities leads to good action or, more broadly speaking, good life.

In Loland and McNamee's words, the search for "perfectibility" defines humans. Human activities, including sport, are "exponent[s] of human excellence [or perfectibility]" [3] (p. 118). In alignment with this, they argue that what helps humans develop their potential is morally acceptable, whereas what undermines it is condemnable. Therefore, they consider doping to be morally wrong because it provides a shortcut to the development of physical talents. That is to say, doping allows athletes to perform better by bypassing the natural and virtuous way of developing their talents. Doped athletes, thus, might achieve higher levels of performance, but they are not excellent. For such higher levels have been reached through corrupt means. As it was stated above, the restrictive approach to human nature and sport underpins anti-doping policy. For instance, the World-Anti Doping Agency (WADA) justifies its mission based on the preservation of sport as a "pursuit of human excellence through the dedicated perfection of each person's natural talents" [7] (p. 14)[1]. Hence, an analysis of the notion of human nature at the root of WADA's mission is critical to understand anti-doping more fully.

In this article, following the methodology deployed in the Nuffield Council of Bioethics' analysis paper mentioned above, I explore the public debate on doping in order to locate the values at the core of the restrictive view of human nature and sport. To do so, I examine WADA's justification of anti-doping (Section 2). Then, I analyze the work of philosophers who have assisted WADA in formulating it (Section 3). After having identified the worldview that grounds the justification for anti-doping, I explore the connections and similarities between the anti-doping movement and the work ethic that resulted from the secularization of the Protestant ethic (Section 4). Next, I pose critical questions regarding the Protestant, work-based philosophical notion of human nature underpinning

---

[1] It must be noted that by "sport" here I mean professional, elite-level sport. For this is the type of sport most affected by WADA's anti-doping regulation.

the anti-doping initiative and briefly propose a tentative way to move forward in the debate (Section 5). I conclude with a summary of the main points made throughout the article (Section 6).

2. The View of the Spirit of Sport at the Heart of WADA

The concept of the "spirit of sport" is central in anti-doping policy. To evaluate the inclusion of a substance or method within the *List of Prohibited Substances and Methods* (*List*), WADA draws on the following three criteria:

> 4.3.1.1 Medical or other scientific evidence, pharmacological effect or experience that the substance or method, alone or in combination with other substances or methods, has the potential to enhance or enhances sport performance;

> 4.3.1.2 Medical or other scientific evidence, pharmacological effect or experience that the use of the substance or method represents an actual or potential health risk to the Athlete;

> 4.3.1.3 WADA's determination that the Use of the substance or method violates the spirit of sport. [7] (p. 30)

For a substance or method to be included on the *List*, it must meet at least two of the criteria above. However, it could be argued that the "spirit of sport" criterion is more fundamental than the other two. For, in the *World Anti-Doping Code* (*Code*), it is declared that, "Doping [must be fought because it] is fundamentally contrary to the spirit of sport." [7] (p. 14). Thus, WADA not only locates the spirit of sport at the heart of anti-doping but also utilizes it to justify the anti-doping campaign. In the *Code*, the spirit of sport is referred to as "what is intrinsically valuable about sport" [7] (p. 14) and further characterized as follows:

- "the pursuit of human *excellence* through the dedicated *perfection* of each person's *natural talents*;"
- "it is the essence of Olympism;"
- "how we play true;"
- "the celebration of the human spirit, body and mind," and;
- "reflected in values we find in and through sport, including: Ethics, fair play and honesty; Health; *Excellence* in performance; Character and education; Fun and joy; Teamwork; *Dedication and commitment*; Respect for rules and laws; Respect for self and other Participants; Courage; [and] Community and solidarity." [7] (p. 14, my emphasis).

The characterizations of the "spirit of sport" principle above indicate that the anti-doping movement pivots around the terms "natural," "talent," excellence," "perfection," and "commitment (effort)." Ultimately, WADA's attempt to pin down the nature of the spirit of sport is an effort to respond to the classic sport philosophical questions "What is sport?" and "What is the meaning of sport?"[2]. The *Olympic Charter*, which is cited in the *Code* as an illustration of the spirit of sport, contains answers to those questions:

> Olympism is a philosophy of life, exalting [(or perfecting)] and combining in a balanced whole the *qualities* [(or natural talents)] *of body, will and mind*. Blending sport with culture and education, Olympism seeks to create a way of life based on the joy of *effort*, the educational value of good example, social responsibility and respect for universal fundamental ethical principles. [8] (p. 11, my emphasis)

---

[2] Or, better said, "What is the significance of competitive sport?" For the anti-doping campaign centers on controlling the use of banned substances in elite-level sport competitions. Only in the last decade, the use of performance-enhancing technology has been regarded as a public health problem and tackled at the amateur and non-competitive level in some countries.

In Olympism, providing individuals with the experience of joy in the effort to perfect natural talents is the primary function of sport. As WADA resulted from a 50/50 effort between the International Olympic Committee (IOC) and national governments, the Olympic ideals substantially shaped anti-doping. Sport officials and athletes who sympathize with WADA's anti-doping campaign usually appeal to effort to justify the ban on performance-enhancing technology. For instance, swimmer Matt Dunn, who was appointed as member of WADA's Athlete Committee in 2011, argues that, "Some sportsmen and women take drugs to try and cheat their way on to an Olympic team or to a medal at the Games, rather than relying on *hard work* and *natural talent*" [9]. Likewise, in an interview published in WADA's website, Olympic medalist Koji Murofushi, argues, "there are no short cuts in life" [10]. For him, success in the sport arena must be achieved through natural talent and many hours of hard work.

For anti-doping advocates, the ban on performance-enhancing technology is justified because it protects the nature of sport by ensuring that sport performance results from effort in cultivating natural talent. Effortless performances are viewed with suspicion. However, the mere appeal to effort and talent is insufficient to justify the anti-doping campaign. The value of both effort and natural talent must be clarified and specified. Why are both elements so significant in elite competitive sport? More importantly for the topic discussed in this article, what confers moral value to effort and natural talent? To tackle these issues, in the next section, I will examine philosophical views of sport, with a significant presence in public discourse, that justify the value of effort and natural talent in competitive sport.

3. Scholarly Interpretations of the "Spirit of Sport" Principle: Superior Inborn Talents and Work Ethics

The value of effort and natural talent in sport is pivotal in the work of sport philosophers Thomas H. Murray [11], Michael J. McNamee [12], and Sigmund Loland [13], who have shaped the public debate on doping through their collaboration with WADA and scholarly work. For instance, the three philosophers are listed as the experts on sport enhancement of The Hastings Center [14] and McNamee and Loland serve in the WADA Ethics Panel [15]. To be fair, these authors also consider other normative elements related to anti-doping, such as the right to privacy, equality, and physical integrity [3,16]. However, for the purposes of this paper, I focus on their analysis of the spirit of sport, that is, the normative elements intrinsic to sport that must be protected and promoted.

For Murray, "The glory of sport is learning what we can do with the natural talents we have, perfecting them through admirable, persistent effort" [11] (p. 26). His characterization of sport places natural talent, excellence (perfection), and effort at the center of what sport is about, conferring more magnitude to the latter by referring to it as "admirable." Along these lines, in *Good sport: Why our games matter and how doping undermines them*, he argues that the meaning of sport is "the celebration of the variety of human talents" [16] (p. 13). That is to say, paraphrasing the title of his book, our games matter because they are sites for the cultivation of talent through effort. To explore the interrelationship among talent, effort, and ethical value in Murray's characterization of sport, the concepts of "talent" and "variety" must be analyzed in depth. With regard to the former, Murray claims that rules in sport are intended to restrict the participants' action to bring to light specific human talents. For instance, soccer rules forbid the use of hands to find out how talented people are at controlling a ball using any part of their body, the feet mostly, other than their hands. Similarly, to display people's speed and endurance talents, the rules of foot racing require to complete the track by running, barring wheeled or motorized means of transportation.

According to Murray, the concept of "variety," or "difference," plays a crucial role in three aspects of sport. First, different sports test various types of talents. For example, participants in a 100 m race test their talents for foot racing and speed, whereas participants in a car race test their driving and strategic thinking talents. However, sports are not tests of abilities only but also contests [17]. Sports involve competition. Participants confront each other to compare their performance and determine who is most talented. Competition, according to Murray, makes sport more engaging and becomes the second aspect of sport in which, he claims, difference plays a key role. Determining who is best is only possible if the exercise of natural talent generates different performance levels. For instance, if all participants in a foot race run at the same pace and crossed the finish line at the same time, the contest would fail to determine who is best, becoming less interesting. Third, sport rules discriminate among various ways to perfect human talents. For example, utilizing tactical innovations is accepted, whereas using pieces of equipment to which some participants have exclusive access is not.

In sum, ethical analyses of sport, according to Murray, must consist in examining "what ought to make a difference" in sport [16] (p. 62) by considering: (a) The talents tested in the game (nature of sport); (b) the way the competition determines who is best (nature of the competition); and (c) the means to develop talent (nature of sport performance). Anti-doping regulation mostly focuses on (c). Thus, Murray argues, "What we care about in sport is the combination of *natural talents, dedication and discipline* to perfect those talents, and the *courage* to test yourself against an external standard" [16] (p. 21, my emphasis)[3]. That is to say, differences tested in sport must result from the participants' "superior gifts and work ethics" [16] (p. 63). In his view, talent and work give meaning to sport. To support his "talentocratic" view of sport based on "the virtuous perfection of natural talent" [18] (p. 83), Murray argues that,

> We want interesting contests, and we want athletes to be able to compete on a level playing field that is roughly level except for natural gifts, honed by dedication, that athletes bring to the competition. [16] (p. 24)

For him, sport acquires significance based on what "we"[4] want it to be. "We" collectively determine the meaning of sport. To illustrate this point, he refers to the ban on polyurethane, full-body suits in swimming. When athletes started using such swimsuits, the number of records broken increased significantly. This alerted International Swimming Federation (FINA) officials, who, after investigating the performance-enhancing effects of the suits, banned them on the basis that they, in Murray's words, "threatened to change the meaning of the sport [by] rewarding muscled, stocky athletes who paddled on top of the water rather than sleek bodies slicing through it. The new swimsuits threatened to alter what swimming valued" [16] (p. 44). I take the phrase "what swimming valued" to mean "what the swimming community values." That is to say, in Murray's view, people's admiration for the exhibition of a specific set of natural talents confers value to the sport: "The achievement of athletes ... find their meaning and value in the celebration of whatever natural talents those persons bring to their sport" [16] (p. 56).

Performance-enhancing technology, like revolutionary swimsuits, poses a threat to what people value from sport. It undermines what they admire and celebrate by playing down the effort to develop natural talents. In alignment with this, Murray argues, "people who play and love sport are uncomfortable with the use of performance-enhancing drugs [is that] the size of one's medicine cabinet doesn't fit into the picture [of] what we admire about athletic excellence." [16] (p. 52). Differences in sport performance, according to him, should not be the result of taking drugs because sports are not intended to test the effectiveness of drugs.

Loland and McNamee further elaborate on Murray's view of sport by linking the perfection of natural athletic talent to the cultivation of moral excellence. For them, unlike for Murray, sport does not acquire value mostly from the meaning that individuals attribute to it. Instead, it becomes valuable as a site for forging moral excellence. Thus, they argue:

---

[3] This aligns with Pieter Bonte's claim that appeals to the "spirit of sport" principle to morally evaluate differences in sport performance based on (a) the origin of sport performance (natural); (b) the processes by which performance is perfected (dedication and discipline); and (c) its outcome (individuals' own performance) [18].

[4] A clarification of what the term "we" stands for is needed. I take it to refer to the sporting community. However, this is still problematic for two reasons. First, it remains unclear who the members of such community are. Second, if as Murray argues, sport is a social good, then all members of a society, regardless of whether they are involved in sport, must be regarded as members of the sporting community. An in-depth investigation of who counts as a member of a practice community can be found in William J. Morgan's *Leftist Theories of Sport* [19].

Sport is a cultural practice in which human capabilities of particular performances are measured, compared, and ranked ... More generally, developing these capabilities is considered to lead towards moral development of the individual. [3] (p. 117)

A fundamental assumption in Loland and McNamee's "neo-Aristotelian" view, as they refer to it [3], is that dedication to the development of athletic excellence is connected to that of moral excellence. Drawing on the claim that sport can build character, they argue that the ethical assessment of performance-enhancing technology must focus on how such technology affects the promotion of excellence. For them, "enhancement and performance development has to take place in particular ways to enable development of virtue" [3] (p. 118). Thus, from their perspective, performance enhancement is morally problematic when it hinders the acquisition and development of virtue. In particular, when it undermines the importance of training and effort in perfecting athletic talent. Loland and McNamee acknowledge that the claim that training and effort lead to human excellence is, at the very least, controversial. Thus, they devote a significant part of their work to elaborate on it [20–22].

In "Performance-enhancing drugs, sport, and the ideal of natural athletic performance" [23] (p. 4), Loland builds upon Richard Norman's view of "nature" as a background of limitations that are not a matter of choice to argue that achievement in sport "gains significance" against constraints coming from two sources: Humans' bodily configuration and the logic of games. Such constraints, Loland points out, are absolute. That is to say, they are not matters of human choice, but *given*. Drawing on David C. Malloy and his collaborators' notion of "physiological authenticity" [24] (p. 294), Loland argues that humans share a, "phenotypic plasticity of the human organism as developed in evolution" [25] (p. 10). This phenotypic plasticity is essential to the cultivation of physical talent. For it is the basis of the processes "within the individual" that make enhancing performance possible [25] (p. 10). For instance, through training, athletes tackle and benefit from such processes by "expos[ing] the human organism to environmental stress, resulting in response and adaptation patterns from the molecular to the systemic level" [25] (p. 10). Performance-enhancing technologies, Loland points out, affect the body very differently. They "bypass human experience to work their biological 'magic' directly" (President's Council on Bioethics, 2003, 130 cit. in Loland, 2018, 12) by "produc[ing] a beneficial physiological effect in an athlete without invoking the complex organismal reaction described for the training stress response" [20].

Acknowledging that biological processes per se lack ethical value, Loland claims that bypassing the natural adaptation processes of the body eliminates, or negatively affects, valuable elements of sport performance. That is to say, despite being ethically neutral, biological processes are vital to the moral evaluation of sport performance. In particular, they provide a set of biological constraints that individuals must accept in order to exert their agency and effort. Thus, Loland argues that the removal of biological constraints threatens "athlete autonomy [and sport], as a measure of athletic effort and performance, loses its significance" [26] (p. 74). Agency and effort give value to sport. Performance-enhancing technology is morally problematic as it shifts the locus of performance from athletes to the technology on which they rely[5]. In Loland's words, "PEDs exert their performance-enhancing effect without real athlete insight and control" [28] (p. W2). Technology removes effort and, in turn, negatively affects the merit in athletic achievement. The concept of "merit" is key in Loland's assessment of performance-enhancing technology, for it connects biological constraints to those related to game play.

Loland, in alignment with Murray, regards sports as meritocratic activities intended to measure, compare, and rank participants based on "rule-defined abilities and skills" [25] (p. 10). Game rules

---

[5] This position is widespread in the sporting community. For instance, the Lugano Charter issued by the Union Cycliste Internationale (UCI) declares that the technical aspects of bicycles must be controlled so that "[t]he performance achieved [does not depend] more on the form of the man-machine ensemble than the physical qualities of the rider, [which] goes against the very meaning of cycle sport" [27]. In cycling, as stated in the Charter, "The bicycle serves to express the effort of the cyclist, but there is more to it than that" [27].

limit the participants' scope of action to promote the cultivation of specific skills. In doing so, they set constraints that, like the biological ones, give significance to the practice. Better said, the obstacles to be overcome through sport-specific skills confer meaning to the practice. For instance, the rules of soccer limit the scope of skills exercised in the game to favor kicking, teamwork, and strategic thinking. Thus, soccer players engage in the sport for the sake of experiencing the development and exercise of such skills.

Elaborating on the centrality of skill exhibition in sport, Loland points out that rules emphasize the role skills play in the game by eliminating, or at least minimizing, the influence of factors over which participants have no control. Good games are those whose outcome is decided based on skillful performance for which individuals are responsible. To put it differently, for Loland, participants deserve to be recognized as better competitors than their opponents only when their performance results from their effort. According to Loland, athletes whose performance results from the use of performance-enhancing technology, "can no longer be identified clearly with the upper (and often decisive) edge of their performance" [25] (p. 12). If athletes cannot be identified with their superior performance, then they do not deserve to take credit for it.

In sum, for Loland, performance-enhancing technology is detrimental to sport because it bypasses the effort exerted to overcome artificial obstacles in the game and biological constraints evolutionary developed. In other words, sport is valuable as a site to exert effort to develop inborn talents and overcome challenges. Effort is the normative cornerstone of competitive sport. Thus, Loland claims, "elite sport ... is better conceived of as a moral testing ground. Athletes are challenged not only on their sporting abilities and skills, but on their values" [25] (p. 12). Engagement in sports is valuable for its role in helping individuals hone excellences and build character. Differently put, sports are valuable as a means to acquire (physical and moral) excellence.

4. What Concept of Human Nature Underpins WADA's "Spirit of Sport" Criterion? Protestantism, Anti-Doping, and Human Nature

Sport historians and sport philosophers argue that the value attached to effort in sport emerged within a specific view of the world, namely, that of the Protestant ethic and, in turn, modern capitalism[6]. For instance, Verner Møller, drawing on Max Weber's [30] analysis of modernity, argues that the emphasis on effort and work that characterizes modern sport has its origin in the Protestant notion of "calling" or "vocation" [31] (p. 104). The Protestant approach to life is built upon the idea that individuals' fate, that is, whether they will obtain salvation, is decided from birth. Despite this, they search for signs that indicate "whether [they are] saved or dammed" [32] (p. 524). Good works are such signs. Through them, Protestants acquire evidence and assurance of salvation.

Luther and Calvin connect the effort to do good works to the notion of "calling" or "vocation." They regard good works as duties that God has appointed to humans. For instance, Luther states, "The Gospel ... requires that ... each according to his own calling, manifest Christian love and genuine good works in his station of life" [33] (p. 145), and Calvin says, "every one should be contented with his calling, and pursue it, instead of seeking to betake himself to anything else. A calling in Scripture means a lawful mode of life" [34].

Each individual has their own line of life, that is, specific duties pertaining to their calling. Thus, doing good works involves fulfilling the duties that God has appointed to them. This does not imply that individuals are fully determined to stick to a specific role in life. Rather, they are free to choose their own path, as long as it involves fulfilling the duties attached to the calling, namely: Serving God and engaging in productive enterprises with diligence. In alignment with this, Calvin states:

---

[6] Despite the strong connection between Protestant ethic and the ethos of modern sport, Allen Guttmann, in his seminal analysis of the origins of modern sports, *From ritual to record. The nature of modern sports*, argues that, the emergence of modern sports represents neither the triumph of capitalism nor the rise of Protestantism but rather the slow development of an empirical, experimental, mathematical *Weltanschauung* [(worldview)] [29] (p. 85).

Farther, he calls every one to this rule also—that they bear in mind what is suitable to their calling. He does not, therefore, impose upon any one the necessity of continuing in the kind of life which he has once taken up, but rather condemns that restlessness, which prevents an individual from remaining in his condition with a peaceable mind and he exhorts, that every one stick by his trade. [34]

The emphasis on fulfilling the duties of one's calling or vocation leads to the glorification of work, the virtues related to it, and, especially, its outcomes (i.e., production, wealth, ownership, and profit). This is illustrated by Thomas Carlyle's dictum, "The latest Gospel in this world is, 'know thy work and do it'" [35] (p. 244). Individuals must take their calling seriously and work with diligence to fulfill their duties. In turn, unproductive behavior that distracts individuals from working or, in Steven J. Overman's words, "from serious and useful activities" [36] (p. 30) is vilified. Therefore, any activity engaged in for the sake of enjoyment, with no further purpose or higher goal, is condemned and regarded as trivial, non-serious, or "time-wasting." Trivial activities are related to idleness, play, and pleasure, which are accepted only when subordinated to social labor or the achievement of a higher purpose.

Sport, from a Puritan perspective, is embraced as preparation for labor or, like in Victorian English schools, as a means to build people's character. In his study on Puritanism and sport, Heinz Mayer argues, "Puritanism regarded sport as a help in shaping one's life, in conserving health, in developing and forming character" [37]. Along these lines, in his seminal autobiography, C. L. R. James explains how his engagement in cricket affected his character in the following way: "almost entirely by my own efforts, I mastered thoroughly the principles of cricket... and attained a mastery over my own character which would have done credit to my mother and Aunt Judith" [38] (pp. 23–24). Understanding the reference to his mother and aunt is crucial here. Throughout the book, both are portrayed, especially his aunt, as living illustrations of the Protestant ethic.

Protestants see life as a series of "problems to be solved" [36] (p. 22) in order to become successful through, among other activities, profit-making and ownership. To do so, they must embody an "innerworldly ascetic" attitude consisting in self-discipline. This explains why the Protestant attitude favored the development and triumph of capitalism. For not only did it turned profit-making and economic (instrumental) rationality into the main drivers of people's action, but also into means for acquiring social status and affirming human worth. Devotion to work, productivity, and human worth are intertwined in the Protestant ethic. In Overman's words, "The spirit of capitalism didn't imply a greater love of money; its real import was in the drive to acquire money and the moral value attached to its acquisition" [36] (p. 49). The devotion to work in order to become successful, not the enjoyment of the outcome of work, defines Protestantism. Thus, Protestants demand abstinence and self-cultivation and condemn gratification pursued for its own sake. The following claim by the main character in George Santayana's novel, *The Last Puritan*, perfectly illustrates Protestants' attitude towards pleasure and gratification: "I hate pleasure. I hate what is called having a good time" [39] (p. 371).

In the historic progress of modern society, the main elements of the Protestant ethic became secularized. Religious motivation and practices receded to the background. Mundane concerns superseded supernatural preoccupations. However, the Protestant ascetic way of life persevered through secular practices and motivation inherent to the modern work ethic that prevails in today's capitalist society. Labor is one such activity; sport is another. In the factory and sport field, work and effort remain to be regarded as the primary sources of value. Moreover, work and sport have become characterized by the same elements at defining the Protestant ethic, to wit: Self-reliance, compulsive behavior towards work, perfectionism, a sense of responsibility for improving one's skills, excelling, overcoming obstacles, delayed gratification, striving, and competing [36] (p. 57). Interestingly, sport winded up becoming a better site for cultivating the work ethic, as technological progress increasingly resulted in the automatization of laborious manual tasks, reducing the level of difficulty found in labor activities. As Overman argues,

> Sport provided a counterweight to the existential impoverishment of work. [T]hrough the natural motions of sport, the stifled artisan was able to rediscover activities in which he could compete against himself, manipulate innate forces, and actively execute the craftsman-like skills inherent to traditional work. [36] (pp. 133–134)

Sport became the new outlet of the Protestant spirit. The Protestant view of human nature as something given that must be accepted and improved through effort and work to become successful underpins the restrictive view of sport that characterizes sport in terms of struggle for excellence, overcoming obstacles, suffering, discipline, and skill development. Baron Pierre de Coubertin's formulation of Olympism as a "philosophy of life" [8] (p. 13) focused on the cultivation of excellence to achieve a higher purpose (i.e., harmonious development of humankind and peace). This facilitated the transformation of the values inherent to the modern work ethic into concepts to think about and conceptualize modern sport. Furthermore, given the role the IOC played in the creation of WADA, it is apparent that the work-related ethical principles underpinning Olympism have shaped the doping public debate and anti-doping policy significantly.

In sum, like the IOC and WADA, Murray's, Loland's, and McNamee's view of sport and human nature revolve around the values inherent to the modern work ethic. As it has been shown in Sections 2 and 3, the three philosophers above emphasize the need to eliminate luck and chance to favor skill development and effort through training. They also regard technological means that undermine the role of effort and work as morally dubious. Such technologies are undesirable shortcuts and signs of the weakness of the will and lack of moral fiber [31] (p. 105). Moreover, they ground the normative value of sport in higher goals such as building character and promoting social goods. Therefore, the work ethic and its notion of human nature have had a strong influence on the views of sport held by WADA and the philosophers who have been instrumental in justifying the anti-doping movement. Their view of what is natural in sport is connected to the protection of the value of the athletes' effort to become successful through the acceptance of what has been given to them.

5. Challenging the "Effort-Based" View of Sport Underpinning WADA's Justification of Anti-Doping

In this section, I will pose critical questions that proponents of the restrictive view of sport at the heart of anti-doping must address to strengthen their position.

5.1. Why are Hard Work, Effort, and Excellence the Normative Cornerstones of Sport and Anti-Doping?

The restrictive view of sport builds upon a view of human nature founded on the value of work. However, as R. Scott Kretchmar argues [40] (p. 46), pluralism, instead of monism, seems to best capture the debate on the nature of sport. According to him, there are multiple interpretations of human nature and sport, including elite-level sport. In particular, the notions of sport vary depending on the degree to which they embody the following six aspects: (a) Achievement, (b) serendipity, (c) knowledge, (d) aesthetic value, (e) authenticity, and (f) community. For Kretchmar, these aspects of sport "are not free standing species or types of sport [but rather] normative emphases that can be realized in [sports]" [40] (p. 86). That is to say, multiple types of sport can be built upon one or several of them. Analyzing each of the aspects is beyond the scope of this paper. Nevertheless, I will offer several examples of how sport practices might be modulated differently depending on the emphasis placed on some aspects.

Consider first high school sport, which I regard as a version of sport that embodies most of, if not all, the aspects. As described in the National Federation of State High School Associations (NFHS) Mission Statement, sport at the high-school level,

> enriches the educational experience; encourages academic achievement; promotes respect, integrity and sportsmanship; prepares for the future in a global community; develops leadership and life skills; fosters the inclusion of diverse populations; promotes healthy

lifestyles and safe competition; encourages positive school/community culture; and should be fun. [41]

Drawing on Kretchmar's six aspects of sport [42], high-school sport is an arena for (a) seeking temporary relief from everyday life obligations by presenting individuals with interesting artificial problems to be overcome (serendipity); (b) finding out who one is by testing one's abilities (knowledge); (c) experiencing uncertainty and pleasure experiences derived from overcoming challenges and testing one's skills (aesthetic); and (d) engaging in a cooperative enterprise with others and realizing that individuals are always inextricably tied to others (community).

Similar statements can be found in governing bodies that regulate elite-level sport. For instance, for the National Collegiate Athletic Association (NCAA), the core values to be embodied by college sports are: pursuit of athletic and academic excellence, enhancing the sense of community, ethical leadership, and respect for the others. Likewise, since June 2007, the Fédération Internationale de Football Association's (FIFA) motto has become "For the Game. For the World." These goals significantly differ from, and often clash with, other goals pursued by most elite-level, professional sporting institutions. For instance, the Chicago Bulls Mission Statement states:

> The Chicago Bulls organization is a sports entertainment company dedicated to winning NBA Championships, growing new basketball fans, and providing superior entertainment, value and service. [43]

Professional sport seen in this way is primarily built upon the achievement principle, that is, upon the pursuit of victory and financial success. This aligns with the most widespread view of professional sport as a meritocratic activity whose main goal is to strive for (and ultimately achieve) victory.

Yet, even among those who understand sport merely based on the achievement principle, there is disagreement about the nature of sport. For instance, in soccer, there are two opposing views on what the sport is about and, more importantly, how it should be played. One view defines soccer based on the deployment of passing skills to control the pace of the game (through possession) and score in a highly aesthetically pleasing way. This play style is referred to as "*jogo bonito*" or "beautiful play style" [44]. The other view is more pragmatic. Regarding victory as the most important thing, proponents of pragmatic soccer rely on strategic thinking to control every aspect of the game and find the most effective, not the most beautiful, way to score. Defenders of this soccer style call it "humble play style" or "smart play style" [45]. In sum, at the very least, there are two conflicting views in professional soccer, that of the poets and that of the workers, and proponents of each of them claim theirs as the best interpretation of soccer.

Given the plurality of views and essential aspects of sport, it is worth asking why anti-doping is built around the principles of hard work and excellence instead of other valuable elements such as idleness, excitement, self-knowledge, or joy. Proponents of the work-based (restrictive) view of sport might provide the following answers. First, drawing on the philosophical theory of sport called "broad internalism" or "interpretivism," they might argue that the "protection and promotion of the excellences of sport" [46] through hard work understands professional, competitive sport in its best light. This, after all, is the type of sport governed by anti-doping regulations. Second, they might argue that work and effort are two of the main pillars of contemporary society. Thus, the key role both elements play in sport, especially at the professional level, is a reflection of the dominance of such principles in the larger society. This claim aligns with the conventionalist view of sport, which takes sports to be social practices created to fulfill basic social and psychological needs that change through time. In modern society, thus, such needs have to do with the feelings of fulfilment, self-realization, and well-being derived from the value modern individuals place in work.

Against these responses, it can be argued that thinking about the nature of sport in terms of excellence might not reflect the most prevalent view of sport nowadays, that is, the view that prioritizes victory. In a different vein, if the restrictive view of sport aims to criticize the view of sport most prevailing among professionals, they could deploy alternative, more critical views of sport. For instance, sport could be a more "revolutionary, critical, or utopian social practice" if its goal was to subvert and challenge the main driving forces in the contemporary society, that is, the dominance of the work ethic. Indeed, philosophers Peter Sloterdijk [47], Brian O'Connor [48], and Suits [49], among others, defend that ludic activities such as sport could be shaped to instill a post-work attitude towards life.

5.2. Could Anti-Doping be Grounded in an Assumption for Which Evidence is Less Ambiguous?

Despite being widely accepted (and utilized) in the sporting world, philosophers have questioned the claim that athletic excellence and moral character are connected, especially in the context of professional, competitive sport. For instance, Allan Bäck agrees that sport is a site for developing some sort of skills and abilities, which athletes might come to excel. However, he wonders what such excellences entail. According to him, most sport excellences (e.g., putting a ball in a hole or running a ball up and down a field) are confined within the limits of sport itself. Thus, he argues, such excellences "even if attained, may thereby, for many people, be restricted to this artificial setting with its artificial rules." [50] (p. 225).

Bäck appeals to historical and psychological evidence to strengthen his critique and cast doubt on the connection between sport excellence and moral character. While he agrees that sports might have had positive effects on moral character, the opposite is also the case, especially in professional sports. For instance, he argues that, throughout history, sport has helped promote and perpetuate violent, dangerous, corruptive, and discriminatory behaviors. This is specially the case, his argument goes on, when victory becomes too important, as in modern professional sports. There seem to be intrinsic negative moral elements to sport. Even if these were eliminated, so that sport only promoted positive moral aspects, Bäck remains skeptical about the connection between moral behavior *in sport* and *outside of it*.

Psychological evidence on the transference of habits and values acquired in sport into other areas and contexts of life motivates his skepticism [50] (p. 226). He argues that, "often skills acquired in one role or social setting do not in general transfer: a person trained in critical thinking problems may continue to commit the same fallacies in other areas of her life." [50] (p. 226). Sport, according to him, is especially vulnerable to this problem because of the artificial nature of sport activities. Moreover, doubts about sports' positive effect on moral character are raised by psychological studies on the nature of competition and sport. Studies in moral psychology and group dynamics show that people invested in sport operate within an "in-group and out-group" mental framework that blinds them to moral status of individuals that belong to or are connected to rival sporting communities [51]. Similarly, studies on moral character and personality based on quantitative methods, such as the MMPI (Minnesota Multiphasic Personality Index) and the JPI (Jackson Personality Inventory), conclude that athletes do worse on these scales than non-athletes.

Sport philosophers such as David Carr [52] and Russell Gough [53] play down the validity of empirical studies of moral development. They argue that, in order to operationalize and quantify moral development, psychologists reduce the complexity of ethical concepts. However, such a methodological simplification undermines the project of understanding moral behavior. Mike McNamee adopts a similar but more moderate approach [22]. He agrees with the core of Carr's and Gough's critique of moral psychology, but advocates for a different solution, namely, the collaboration between psychologists and philosophers to overcome the limitations identified. Thus, for him, the attempt to ground the connection between sport excellences and moral character in empirical evidence is not fundamentally flawed and doomed to fail but "yet to be revealed" [22] (p. 86), that is, requires further research. According to him, philosophical analyses of moral development and judgment suffice to provide good reasons for upholding to the connection between sport excellences and moral character.

While I agree with McNamee's claims, I wonder if anti-doping policy, which affects thousands of athletes, should appeal to a notion for which empirical evidence remains relatively scarce and "yet to be revealed." To be clear, my claim here is neither that sport has no pedagogical effect, nor that philosophy has no say in policymaking. Quite the contrary. Like McNamee, I think that philosophical reasons suffice to support claims regarding moral development and that sport has the potential to shape moral judgment, at least to some extent. My claim concerns the grounds of policymaking. A policy can perform its role satisfactorily if it is regarded as justified by those whose behavior is governed by the policy. Policies that are viewed as lacking justification result in dissension, opposition, disobedience, and, in some cases, violence.

As Giandomenico Majone [54] argues, the existence of multiple views (pluralism) is a major challenge for policy justification. In social practices where multiple views coexist, Majone posits, multiple policy evaluation criteria must be deployed. In his words, "multiple policy evaluation ... would recognize the legitimacy of the different perspectives [and would] contribute to the shared understanding of the multiple perspectives involved" [54] (p. 9). For this reason, given the limitations of the empirical evidence supporting the connection between sport and character development, anti-doping regulation must not appeal to such a connection until further evidence is provided. A regulation with profound implications in people's lives such as anti-doping (e.g., athletes can lose the career to which they have devoted their lives as a consequence of an anti-doping sanction) must be built upon a firmer and broader foundation. Such a foundation can be provided through concepts such as health, primary goods, consent, justice, and autonomy. Although the nature of these concepts might be difficult to pin down fully and completely, there is consensus in the contemporary society on their validity to support policies affecting everybody.

5.3. Are the Excellences Acquired Through Effort and Hard Work More Valuable than Those Resulting from other Aspects of Sport?

Even if empirical evidence supported the connection among athletic excellence, moral excellence, and normative value, devoting effort to refining natural talents would not be the only source of moral value in sport. Rather, the cultivation of aspects other than effort might also shape character positively. The restrictive view of sport does not capture the meaning of sport *in general*, but of a *particular* formulation of sport. For instance, according to Savulescu [55], taking risks to push human limits further is morally praiseworthy and leads to the development of moral virtues such as courage. In a different work [56], I referred to this view of sport as "posthumanist." This view, unlike the restrictive view of sport, builds upon a notion of human nature that denies the possibility of providing a clear-cut distinction between natural and artificial aspects. In this view, not only is technology inherent to human nature, but it realizes the aspect that best defines humans, namely: autonomy. Thus, doping is regarded as a means for exercising freedom [4]. This view conceives of the source of moral value in sport in relation to the notion of human nature and sport defined based on the exercise of freedom, not the effort in developing natural talents. Therefore, posthumanists might also argue that a source of value in sport is the cultivation of excellence and the forge of moral character but might interpret the latter in a significantly different way from those in the restrictive side.

Moreover, according to Sinclair A. MacRae, "defenders [of the view that excellence has normative value] would need to show both that excellence can function as a foundational or overarching goal and that it is an ethical value. However, neither of these claims is true" [57] (p. 292). For MacRae, excellence is neither a moral nor a prudential value but a perfectionist value that requires an objective standard of perfection. Therefore, if different views of sport, such as the posthumanist and the restrictivist, hold diverse standards of perfection, then rational agreement on what athletic excellence is would be difficult to achieve, if not impossible. With regard to rational disagreement, Alasdair MacIntyre [58] argues that each tradition holds its view of the good that can only be rationally accepted by those within the tradition, because they share a basic set of standards of rationality. As individuals only understand the notion of the good by being part of a particular tradition, MacIntyre argues that traditions and their standards are incommensurable with each other. Thus, rational discussion and agreement among them is uncommon. William J. Morgan draws on MacIntyre and, regarding the anti-doping debate, argues that there are other views of sport besides the work-based view that WADA holds [59] (p. 289). For instance, professionalism, whose advocates view sport as a meritocratic activity open to talent where the pursuit of victory plays a central role, and "transhumanist sport," which builds upon the notion that sport is a site for pushing the limits of human nature further by deploying technological means. A transhumanist, for example, as I have stated above, world regard a performance as excellent when an athlete sets a new record or standard within a sport (i.e., completing a marathon in under one hour).

5.4. A Consensus around a Common View of Sport?

In sum, given the plurality of conceptions of human nature and sport in the contemporary society, there is disagreement around the justification for anti-doping policy. If the view of human nature at the root of the different views of sport is the fundamental source of disagreement, I wonder if it would be possible to find, in Rawls' terms, an "overlapping consensus on a common minimal view of human nature or sport" [60]. Here I draw a parallel between the debate on the nature of sport and that of modern society. The coexistence of multiple worldviews is the defining mark of modern societies. Thus, pluralism and moral disagreement are the norm, not something to avoid and correct. The challenge modern ethical theories face is to create and organize social cooperation irrespective of people's individual conceptions of the good life, assuming that most people would not agree on what the good is. One possible solution to the problem of cooperation has been provided by Kantian-inspired "thin moral (or political) theories." Based on the fact all human beings share some feature/s in common, Kantian-inspired approaches claim that people have the potential to agree on a basic set of minimal ethical principles to arrange cooperation. Therefore, a possible solution to the doping debate might be to provide a Kantian-inspired thin moral theory of sport that focuses on features that all sport participants share in common in order to make cooperation possible by resolving the existing moral disagreement on the nature of sport. That is to say, contemporary sport philosophers should explore the possibility of providing a "shallow (or thin) model of sport" [61]. Indeed, Loland and McNamee might lead the way in this respect. In a recent paper, they wonder whether "references to 'the spirit of sport' [can] serve as basis for an overlapping consensus among all stakeholders in the anti-doping domain" [62] (p. 7), and offer an alternative formulation of the "spirit of sport" principle that might facilitate the achievement of such a type of consensus: "The purpose of anti-doping policy and practice is to preserve and promote the committed pursuit of athletic excellence in ways that respect the health of athletes and the integrity of sport competition" [62] (p. 11). Their formulation of the "spirit of sport" principle, however, still pivots around the concept of "excellence," which is problematic. Elsewhere, I explore an alternative to achieve overlapping consensus among different sport traditions [63]. Drawing on discourse ethics, I propose that philosophers should focus less on the specific content of sport regulations and more on the structure and conditions of the deliberative and decision-making practices whereby such regulations are discussed, formulated, and accepted. This focuses the sport philosophers' attention on the *real* debates around normative aspects of sport that take place within sport institutions and recommends philosophers to work with institutions in creating and structuring deliberative spaces for individuals to engage in rational discussion and collectively pursue rational consensus [64].

6. Conclusion: Anti-Doping, the Work Ethic, and the Natural

I have examined the "spirit of sport" criterion on which WADA relies to justify the ban on performance-enhancing technologies. By analyzing the connection between anti-doping and the notion of the "natural," I have identified the view of human nature that underpins the "spirit of sport" criterion. By reviewing WADA's official documents and scholarly works articulating the WADA's notion of the "spirit of sport," I have shown that WADA's justification for anti-doping has its roots in the notion of human nature of the work ethic that resulted from the secularization of the Protestant ethic. I have concluded by raising the following critical questions concerning the view of human nature and sport at the basis of WADA's justification of anti-doping:

- Why are hard work, effort, and excellence the normative cornerstones of sport and anti-doping?
- Could anti-doping be grounded in an assumption for which evidence is less ambiguous?

- Are the excellences acquired through effort and hard work more valuable than those resulting from other aspects of sport?

My tentative response to these questions has been that there is plurality of views of sport nowadays. Therefore, anti-doping must not be built upon any of them, but upon a "shallow (or thin) model of sport" that all sport participants can accept regardless of their specific view of human nature and sport. Providing such a model of sport is one of the main challenges that contemporary sport philosophers must face.

Funding: This research received no external funding.

Conflicts of Interest: The author declares no conflict of interest.

References

1. Schiappa, E. *Defining Reality: Definitions and the Politics of Meaning*; Southern Illinois University Press: Carbondale, IL, USA, 2003; ISBN 978-0-8093-2500-9.
2. Nuffield Council on Bioethics (Un)natural. *Ideas about Naturalness in Public and Political Debates about Science, Technology and Medicine*; Nuffield Council on Bioethics: London, UK, 2015.
3. Loland, S.; McNamee, M.J. Anti-doping, performance enhancement and 'the spirit of sport': A philosophical and ethical critique. In *Doping and Public Health*; Ahmadi, N., Ljungqvist, A., Svedsäter, G., Eds.; Routledge: London, UK, 2016; pp. 111–123.
4. Brown, W.M. Ethics, drugs, and sport. *J. Philos. Sport* **1980**, *7*, 15–23. [CrossRef]
5. Savulescu, J.; Foddy, B.; Clayton, M. Why we should allow performance enhancing drugs in sport. *Br. J. Sports Med.* **2004**, *38*, 666–670. [CrossRef]
6. Miah, A. *Genetically Modified Athletes: Biomedical Ethics, Gene Doping and Sport*; Routledge: New York, NY, USA, 2004; ISBN 1-134-42599-6.
7. World Anti-Doping Agency (WADA). World Anti-Doping Code 2015. Available online: https://www.wada-ama.org/sites/default/files/resources/files/wada-2015-world-anti-doping-code.pdf (accessed on 22 June 2019).
8. International Olympic Committee (IOC). Olympic Charter 2015. Available online: https://stillmed.olympic.org/Documents/olympic_charter_en.pdf (accessed on 22 June 2019).
9. Dunn: Dopers Must Stay Away from London 2012 (24 February 2012). Available online: https://www.wada-ama.org/en/media/news/2012-02/dunn-dopers-must-stay-away-from-london-2012 (accessed on 23 January 2019).
10. Koji Murofushi—Why the Spirit of Sport Must be Maintained (22 September 2014). Available online: https://www.wada-ama.org/en/media/news/2014-09/koji-murofushi-why-the-spirit-of-sport-must-be-maintained (accessed on 23 January 2019).
11. Murray, T.H. Ethics, enhancement, and sport. *Play True: Off. Publ. World Anti-Doping Agency* **2007**, 24–32.
12. McNamee, M.J. The Spirit of Sport and Anti Doping Policy: An Ideal Worth Fighting for. Available online: https://www.wada-ama.org/en/media/news/2013-02/the-spirit-of-sport-and-anti-doping-policy-an-ideal-worth-fighting-for (accessed on 23 January 2019).
13. Borry, P.; Caulfield, T.; Estivill, X.; Loland, S.; McNamee, M.; Knoppers, B.M. Geolocalisation of athletes for out-of-competition drug testing: Ethical considerations. Position statement by the WADA ethics panel. *Br. J. Sports Med.* **2018**, *52*, 456–459. [CrossRef]
14. Murray, T. Sports Enhancement. Available online: https://www.thehastingscenter.org/briefingbook/sports-enhancement/ (accessed on 23 January 2019).
15. WADA Ethics Panel. Available online: https://www.wada-ama.org/en/who-we-are/governance/wada-ethics-panel (accessed on 23 January 2019).
16. Murray, T.H. *Good Sport. Why Our Games Matter and How Doping Undermines Them*; Oxford University Press: New York, NY, USA, 2018; ISBN 978-0-19-068798-4.
17. Kretchmar, R.S. From test to contest: An analysis of two kinds of counterpoint in sport. *J. Philos. Sport* **1975**, *2*, 23–30. [CrossRef]
18. Bonte, P. Dignified doping: Truly unthinkable? An existentialist critique of "talentocracy" in sports. In *AthleticEnhancement, Human Nature and Ethics: Threats and Opportunities of Doping Technologies*; Tolleneer, J., Sterckx, S., Bonte, P., Eds.; Springer: Dordrecht, The Netherlands, 2013; pp. 59–86, ISBN 94-007-5101-X.

19. Morgan, W.J. *Leftist Theories of Sport: A Critique and Reconstruction*; University of Illinois Press: Champaign, IL, USA, 1994; ISBN 0-252-06361-9.
20. Loland, S.; Hoppeler, H. Justifying anti-doping: The fair opportunity principle and the biology of performance enhancement. *Eur. J. Sport Sci.* **2012**, *12*, 347–353. [CrossRef]
21. Loland, S. A well balanced life based on 'the joy of effort': Olympic hype or a meaningful ideal? *Sport Ethics Philos.* **2012**, *6*, 155–165. [CrossRef]
22. McNamee, M. *Sports, Virtues and Vices: Morality Plays*; Routledge: New York, NY, USA, 2008; ISBN 1-134-64978-9.
23. Norman, R. Interfering with nature. *J. Appl. Philos.* **1996**, *13*, 1–12. [CrossRef] [PubMed]
24. Malloy, D.C.; Kell, R.; Kelln, R. The spirit of sport, morality, and hypoxic tents: Logic and authenticity. *Appl. Physiol. Nutr. Metab.* **2007**, *32*, 289–296. [CrossRef] [PubMed]
25. Loland, S. Performance-enhancing drugs, sport, and the ideal of natural athletic performance. *Am. J. Bioeth.* **2018**, *18*, 8–15. [CrossRef]
26. Loland, S.; Caplan, A. Ethics of technologically constructed hypoxic environments in sport. *Scand. J. Med. Sci. Sports* **2008**, *18* (Suppl. 1), 70–75. [CrossRef]
27. UCI. The Lugano Charter 1996. Available online: http://62.50.72.82/imgArchive/Road/Equipment/The%20Lugano%20charter.pdf (accessed on 20 June 2019).
28. Loland, S. Response to open peer commentaries on "performance-enhancing drugs, sport, and the ideal of natural athletic performance". *Am. J. Bioeth.* **2018**, *18*, W1–W3. [CrossRef]
29. Guttmann, A. *From Ritual to Record: The Nature of Modern Sports*; Columbia University Press: New York, NY, USA, 1978; ISBN 978-0-231-08369-0.
30. Weber, M. *The Protestant Ethic and the Spirit of Capitalism*; Unwin Paperbacks: London, UK, 1985.
31. Møller, V. *The Ethics of Doping and Anti-Doping: Redeeming the Soul of Sport?* Routledge: London, UK, 2010; ISBN 978-0-415-48465-7.
32. Parsons, T. *The Structure of Social Action: A Study in Social Theory with Special Reference to a Group of Recent European Writers*; Amerind: New Delhi, India, 1974.
33. Gritsch, E.W.; Jenson, R.W. *Lutheranism: The Theological Movement and Its Confessional Writings*; Fortress Press: Philadelphia, PA, USA, 1976.
34. Calvin, J. *John Calvin's Bible Commentaries on St. Paul's First Epistle to the Corinthians*; Jazzybee Verlag: Altenmünster, Germany, 1989.
35. Carlyle, T. *Past and Present*; Chapman and Hall: London, UK, 1870.
36. Overman, S.J. *The Protestant Ethic and the Spirit of Sport: How Calvinism and Capitalism Shaped America's Games*; Mercer University Press: Macon, GA, USA, 2011; ISBN 978-0-88146-226-5.
37. Meyer, H. Puritanism and physical training: Ideological and political accents in the Christian interpretation of sport. *Int. Rev. Sports Soc.* **1973**, *8*, 37–52. [CrossRef]
38. James, C.L.R. *Beyond a Boundary*; Stanley Paul: London, UK, 1976.
39. Santayana, G. *The Last Puritan*; Scribner: New York, NY, USA, 1937.
40. Kretchmar, R.S. Simon on realism, fallibilism, and the power of reason. *J. Philos. Sport* **2016**, *43*, 41–49. [CrossRef]
41. National Federation of State High School Associations (NFHS). Mission Statement. Available online: https://www.nfhs.org/who-we-are/missionstatement (accessed on 4 March 2019).
42. Kretchmar, R.S. Pluralistic internalism. *J. Philos. Sport* **2015**, *42*, 83–100. [CrossRef]
43. Chicago Bulls Mission Statement. Available online: https://www.nba.com/bulls/news/mission_statement.html (accessed on 4 March 2019).
44. McLaughlin, D.W.; Torres, C.R. Sweet tension and its phenomenological description: Sport, intersubjectivity and horizon. *Sport Ethics Philos.* **2011**, *5*, 270–284. [CrossRef]
45. Wilson, J. *Inverting the Pyramid: A History of Football Tactics*; Orion: London, UK, 2008.
46. Russell, J.S. Are rules all an umpire has to work with? *J. Philos. Sport* **1999**, *26*, 27–49. [CrossRef]
47. Sloterdijk, P. Good-for-nothing returns home. Or the end of an alibi—And a theory of the end of art. In *The Aesthetic Imperative: Writings on Art*; Polity: Malden, MA, USA, 2017; pp. 100–112, ISBN 978-0-7456-9986-8.
48. O'Connor, B. *Idleness: A Philosophical Essay*; Oxford Princeton University Press: Princeton, NJ, USA, 2018; ISBN 978-0-691-16752-7.
49. Suits, B. *The Grasshopper: Games, Life, and Utopia*; D.R. Godine: Boston, MA, USA, 1978; ISBN 978-0-87923-840-7.

50. Bäck, A. The way to virtue in sport. *J. Philos. Sport* **2009**, *36*, 217–237. [CrossRef]
51. Lopez Frias, F.J. The psycho-biological bases of sports supporters' behaviour: The virtuous supporter. *Sport Ethics Philos.* **2012**, *6*, 423–438. [CrossRef]
52. Carr, D. What moral education significance has physical education? A question in need of disambiguation. In *Ethics and Sport*; McNamee, M., Parry, S.J., Eds.; Routledge: New York, NY, USA, 2016; pp. 119–133, ISBN 978-1-138-14197-1.
53. Gough, R. Moral development research in sports and its quest for objectivity. In *Ethics and Sport*; McNamee, M., Parry, S.J., Eds.; Routledge: New York, NY, USA, 2016; pp. 134–147, ISBN 978-1-138-14197-1.
54. Majone, G. *Evidence, Argument, and Persuasion in the Policy Process*; Yale University Press: New Haven, CT, USA, 1989; ISBN 978-0-300-04159-0.
55. Savulescu, J. Justice, fairness, and enhancement. *Ann. N. Y. Acad. Sci.* **2006**, *1093*, 321–338. [CrossRef] [PubMed]
56. Lopez Frias, F.J. Walking into the cyborg gym. Two conceptions of the cyborg athlete. *Teknokult. Rev. Cult. Digit. Mov. Soc.* **2018**, *15*, 105–117. [CrossRef]
57. MacRae, S.A. Toward a shallow interpretivist model of sport. *J. Philos. Sport* **2017**, *44*, 1–15. [CrossRef]
58. MacIntyre, A.C. *After Virtue: A Study in Moral Theory*; University of Notre Dame Press: Notre Dame, IN, USA, 1984.
59. Morgan, W.J. The normativity of sport: A historicist take on broad internalism. *J. Philos. Sport* **2016**, *43*, 27–39. [CrossRef]
60. Rawls, J. *Justice as Fairness: A Restatement*; The Belknap Press of Harvard University Press: Cambridge, UK; London, UK, 2001; ISBN 978-0-674-00510-5.
61. Lopez Frías, F.J. A critique of mutualism's combination of the Aristotelian and Kantian traditions. *J. Philos. Sport* **2018**, *45*, 161–176. [CrossRef]
62. Loland, S.; McNamee, M.J. The 'spirit of sport,' WADAs code review, and the search for an overlapping consensus. *Int. J. Sport Policy Polit.* **2019**, 1–13. [CrossRef]
63. Lopez Frías, F.J. Beyond Habermas, with Habermas: Adjudicating ethical issues in sport through a discourse ethics-based normative theory of sport. *Sport Ethics Philos.* **2019**, in press.
64. Read, D.; Skinner, J.; Lock, D.; Houlihan, D. Legitimacy driven change at the World Anti-Doping Agency. *Int. J. Sport Policy Polit.* **2018**, 1–13. [CrossRef]

© 2019 by the author. Licensee MDPI, Basel, Switzerland. This article is an open access article distributed under the terms and conditions of the Creative Commons Attribution (CC BY) license (http://creativecommons.org/licenses/by/4.0/).

Article

Chips and Showmanship: Running and Technology

Pam R. Sailors

Philosophy Department, Missouri State University, Springfield, MO 65809, USA; pamelasailors@missouristate.edu; Tel.: +1-417-836-6259

Received: 23 April 2019; Accepted: 1 June 2019; Published: 5 June 2019

Abstract: A brief review and classification of technology in general begins the paper, followed by an application of the classification to two specific marathon case studies: the 2018 Boston marathon and the 2017 Nike Breaking2 Project marathon. Then concepts from an array of sport philosophers are discussed to suggest an explanation for why each of the case studies strikes us as problematic. The conclusion provides a reasonable explanation for our misgivings, as well as an indication of how we might evaluate sporting endeavors in the face of increasing technological innovation.

Keywords: technology; running; fairness; competition

1. Introduction

This is a story of two marathons, one in objectively miserable conditions and the other in near-perfect ones. The influence of technology on the first was relatively light, while the other was engineered with cutting-edge technology. Yet, technology, in both cases, created controversy about the validity of the results. A brief review and classification of technology in general begins the paper, followed by an application of the classification to the two specific marathon case studies. Then I pull concepts from an array of sport philosophers to suggest an explanation for why each of the case studies strikes us as problematic. My hope is to provide a reasonable explanation for our misgivings, as well as an indication of how we might evaluate sporting endeavors in the face of increasing technological innovation.

2. Technology

Technology is vastly diverse, so adopting a classificatory scheme is helpful before making general claims. Butryn suggests five categories to distinguish sport technologies: self, landscape, implement, rehabilitative, and movement [1] (p. 112). Taking each in turn, self technologies make physical or psychological changes to athletes, so would include doping, genetic engineering, and sports psychological interventions. Landscape technologies involve the competitive area itself, e.g., innovative court and track surfaces. Implement technologies refer to sporting equipment, like bats and balls and shoes. Rehabilitative technologies are used to assist athletes in recovering from injury and strenuous training. And movement technologies are employed to evaluate and improve motions athletes undertake during their sports, like stride-length and cadence. To Butryn's list, Emily Ryall adds a sixth category, namely "*adjudication* technologies, e.g., Hawk-Eye, video replays" [2] (p. 56).

These categories are important because they open up distinctions between the types that allow us to avoid sweeping statements about the value of technology in general. For example, Butryn argues that self technologies are different from the other types because they change athletes internally, while the effects of the other technologies are external to athletes. For this reason, he suggests heightened caution is in order regarding the application of self technologies since they cyborgize sport, that is, decrease authentic human contribution to sport performance, while external technologies merely enhance human performance [1] (p. 113). To put it another way, self technologies may create "revenge effects," wherein a technological innovation designed to improve performance results in the occurrence of some unexpected problem that didn't exist before the technology [3]. Of course, revenge effects are not limited to self technologies, as illustrated in the first case study below.

3. Case Studies

3.1. Boston 2018

The 2018 Boston marathon took place in unusually foul weather conditions—30 mph head and cross winds, steady driving rain, and temperatures in the 40s (5–7 C). As is standard practice at Boston and some of the other large marathons, the elite women began the race first. Twenty-eight minutes later, the elite men started, followed almost immediately by the faster non-elite runners in the main pack. The forty-six elite women started slowly because of the gusty winds and pouring rains, but the professionals started to break away shortly after the first mile. Long before the women reached the midpoint of the race, the runners had spread out and most were running alone. This is significant because it meant that none of these runners was able to tuck into a pack to avoid the full brunt of the wind and rain, resulting in a struggle that added an average of about fifteen minutes to the best times of the professional women. One of the non-professional elite runners who finished in the top ten estimated her finishing time would have been roughly five minutes faster if she had started in the first corral behind the elite men. Overall, the winning times were the slowest since the 1970s.

Most unusually, the women's top finishers list changed long after all the elites had crossed the line because three of the women who started the race in the first corral behind the elite men had cumulative times to fast enough to place them in the top fifteen. Exact calculation of each runner's finishing time was made possible by chip timing, an example of an overlap of implement and adjudication technology. Chip timing involves tiny transponders attached to runners' shoelaces or, more commonly now, embedded in the race numbers they pin to their shirts. The transponders contain coils that are triggered by electromagnetic waves emitted by mats at the starting line, key points along the course, and the finish line. When a coil is triggered, it generates an electrical signal, sending to a computer the exact time and identity of the runner crossing the mat. This innovation was introduced to solve the problem created in large races when runners back in the pack were unable even to cross the starting line until minutes (or, in very large races, even hours) after the race officially began. With chip timing, one's "gun time" is the official beginning of the race, while one's "chip/net time" is the time it takes that individual runner to travel from the starting line to the finish line. This is an example of a "regenerating effect," wherein an attempt to solve one problem multiplies the number of problems [4] (p. 211). Solving the problem of establishing an exact time for each runner created the problem of determining how to rank and reward the top finishers in the women's race. The official policy of the Boston Athletic Association (B.A.A.) is that only women in the Elite Women's Start (EWS) are eligible for prize money, but the organization, after public criticism, eventually awarded prize money to all the women whose net times placed them in money positions.[1]

In order to evaluate the rectitude of this decision, it's important to understand the rationale behind starting the elite women almost half an hour ahead of everyone else. According to T.K. Skenderian, one of the members of the B.A.A.: "As opposed to starting men and women at the same time, and ultimately having the female competitors lose each other among packs of men (and potentially receive pacing assistance), the EWS allows athletes to compete without obstruction." Instituted "to highlight head-to-head racing and competition," the EWS "gives the fastest women the chance to race each other openly" [5]. However, not just anyone can line up with the elite women; getting into the EWS requires having run a qualifying time at a previous marathon. None of the women who started in the first

---

[1] The B.A.A. clarified its rules in 2019, emphasizing that only those starting in the EWS will be eligible for prize money going forward. As well, the organization changed its practice of allowing the first wave to start immediately following the elite men; now there is a two-minute hold between the elite men's start and the first wave. While this change was met with fierce criticism from sub-elite men, it did have the fortunate effect of treating men and women consistently and equitably.

corral had run fast enough to qualify, so they cannot be accused of seeking an unfair advantage. Still, they certainly were advantaged by being surrounded by others who could help them through the adverse weather. As well, the women in the EWS were disadvantaged by not being aware of how well the women who started half an hour later were running. As one of the women who was in the EWS put it, "In Boston, the race was strategic to overcome the elements (as any race is regardless of the tough conditions). Why would you run harder if you think you are in first place? You can only race those that you are lined up with. The flow of a race goes up and down based on who wants to press/make a move. It's about strategy" [6]. So this case offers an example of a way in which the use of technology creates a problem, namely, identifying the winner(s) of a race. I will say more about this later, but it also raises the question of identifying the essential characteristics of competition more generally. What make a race a race? Were the women in the EWS in the same race as the women in the first corral? I'll return to these questions, but, first, I consider another marathon in which technology played a huge role, complicating the evaluation of the participants' running performance.

3.2. Monza 2017

The marathon world record hovered just over two hours for several years, dropping a few seconds here and a few more there, approaching but never dropping below the two hour mark. (At the time of this writing, the official record is 2:01:39.) The Nike Breaking2 Project aimed to change that and spent more than two years and an incalculable amount of money in the attempt, employing a team of experts to determine how best to apply technology to the quest. Three world-class athletes—Lelisa Desisa, Eliud Kipchoge, and Zersenay Tadese—were selected based on previous accomplishments to train for completing a marathon in less than two hours in an event technologically-engineered to be as close to perfect as possible. Each of the previously-discussed categories of technology were represented, thus the categories offer a useful structure for examining the event.

Self technologies were employed in workouts designed to make psychological changes to the athletes through brain endurance techniques, using positive self-talk and intentionally monotonous training. The idea here is that training the brain to continue to focus through monotony prevents the mental fatigue that leads to the false perception that one has reached one's physical limits. Landscape technologies were used in the decision to hold the event in Monza, an oxygen-dense location situated only 600 feet above sea level. Further the race was run on a near-flat one-and-a-half mile auto racing track, requiring the psychological training for monotony just noted. Weather stations sent continuous data regarding temperature, humidity, and wind. Instead of scheduling the event for a particular day, the Nike team determined a three-day window in which conditions were calculated to be most favorable. Adjudication technology was also a part of the attempt, as timing mats provided pace feedback to the athletes and scientific team every 200 m [7] (p. 202).

Rehabilitative technologies were employed throughout the training, perhaps most notably in physiologists using a device to measure muscle oxygenation during the hardest efforts. A portable ultrasound machine took readings both prior to and following training runs to determine how the athletes were storing, using, and replenishing carbohydrate in their leg muscles. And the team ensured that each athlete's carbohydrate levels remained sufficient by bicycling beside them as they ran to hand them drinks more often than they would have been available in standard marathon races [7] (p. 78). Movement technologies were present before and during the run. In training, the athletes practiced running directly behind pacers—other runners who took turns leading the way, protecting Desisa, Kipchoge, and Tadese from the elements and, most importantly, eliminating air resistance. "A 2014 analysis argued that the cost of overcoming air resistance, even on a perfectly still day, might amount to 100 s over the course of a two-hour marathon. Studies dating back to the 1970s have suggested that running directly behind another runner can eliminate a tremendous amount of extra effort, but in practice it's difficult to draft that closely behind someone else" [7] (p. 75). The rules for an official world record do not allow pacers to swap in and out, but it would be impossible to find a group of pacers who could run at the prescribed pace the whole way, so Nike abandoned the quest for the world record so that the pacers could take turns and there would always be a group of them leading in a wedge formation. The teams of pacers, dropping in and out every 1.5 miles, followed a Tesla that had lasers projecting green lines of the wedge onto the track for the pacers to follow, taking the most efficient line possible.

Finally, it was an implement technology that many believe had the greatest impact on the event. For this attempt, Nike created a new shoe with a carbon-fiber plate in an extra-cushioned sole. The cushioning both weighs less and is more durable than anything previously tested, but doesn't result in energy loss because that loss is offset by a stiff carbon-fiber plate also in the sole. "External tests conducted at the University of Colorado show that the shoe improves efficiency by about 4 percent on average—a stunning figure that has sparked fierce controversy" [7] (p. 74). The controversy is on account of the perception that the shoe is more responsible for the result than the athletes who wear them. "Technology evolves, but when it evolves so quickly that it effectively picks winners, that's a problem. The top three finishers in the men's Olympic marathon in 2016, it turns out, were wearing disguised prototypes of the new shoe, which Nike has dubbed the Vaporfly. So was the women's winner; so were the men's winners of the 2016 London, Chicago, Berlin, and New York marathons. If we're interested in human limits, what does a sub-two-hour marathon truly tell us if all it takes is a 2:03 runner wearing supershoes?" [7] (pp. 204–205).

Although a version of the shoe is now on the commercial market, its price is roughly double that of other running shoes, effectively limiting it to economically advantaged runners. This adds to the controversy, since the perception is not only that the shoe confers an unfair advantage, but also that it is an advantage not equally available to all.

In the end, even with all of the technological innovation employed in Nike's Breaking2 Project, only one of the three runners came close to the two-hour goal. Eliud Kipchoge covered the marathon distance in 2:00:25. Perhaps if he had accomplished the goal, the reaction would have been kinder, but instead, most viewed the event as mere showmanship on a grand scale, a marketing stunt by Nike.

4. Conceptual Discussion

I want to suggest that the two cases—Boston and Monza—are similar because technology shifted the emphasis in both from sporting competition to quantifiable outcomes. In both, all that seemed to matter in the end was elapsed time. I argue that both races were deeply unsatisfactory for many because of what that focus left out—robust human competition. Looking to the sport philosophy literature, one can find several different ways to characterize this dichotomy. Kretchmar, for example, argues that competition is an essential characteristic of sport; there must be a winner. This requires that a comparison be made between at least two athletes. "Victory is always victory over someone; defeat is forever suffered 'at the hands of,' minimally, a second individual" [8] (p. 27). Certainly, the three runners at Monza were not competing against each other in any reasonable sense. Instead, they were engaged in what Kretchmar calls 'testing.' They were discovering their own limits, 'testing' their skill. But the test of any one is intelligible without reference to either of the other two. We can say the athletes were unsuccessful, but we cannot sensibly say they were defeated [8].

The addition of competition changes a test into a contest; beyond getting from point A to point B in any particular time, the concern changes to getting there *before* one's competitor(s). This is why it seems peculiar to award fifth place to someone simply for crossing the finish line in the fifth fastest net time, even though the athlete had not even visual contact with the athletes who had the fourth or sixth fastest times. We need there to be a race, i.e., at least two athletes engaged in competition against each other (rather than simply against the clock). " ... if two [testing] family members are truly contesting, they are interested in each other's progress in taking the test. Their own strategies, rhythms, their very relationship to the test is, in part, dictated by the other's performance. Contestants watch one another. The contestants cannot be concerned merely with passing the test, for an opponent may pass it in a superior fashion" [8] (p. 29).[2] Recall the competitor cited earlier who claimed it's all about strategy: "You can only race those that you are lined up with. The flow of a race goes up and down based on who wants to press/make a move." The women in the EWS were not truly contesting with the women who started the marathon half an hour later; thus, it is incorrect to assert that any of the women in the first open wave completed the marathon in a superior fashion to the women in the EWS.

Similar to the test/contest distinction, Heather Reid distinguishes between what she calls the holistic Olympic Ethos and the analytic Efficiency Ethos, identifying the former with qualitative knowing and the latter with quantitative. "The Olympic Ethos," Reid says, "connects human beings with each other, as well as with the natural and spiritual worlds. The Efficiency Ethos reduces athletes to quantifiable parts—as analysis that risks leaving their humanity behind" [9] (p. 162). Here, the technological engineering of Nike's Breaking2 Project would obviously be an example of the Efficiency Ethos. On the one hand, it is easy to imagine the teams of pacers moving on and off the track as pistons in a machine, mindlessly pulling Desisa, Kipchoge, and Tadese along behind them, like interchangeable parts rather than unique humans. On the other hand, we see the elite women racing in Boston, connected in competition with each other and with the elements.

Another example of discussion around this sort of distinction is woven through the work of sport philosopher Loland, which refers to the dichotomy variously as the thin and thick theories of competition, the narrow and wide theories of sport, the physiologically inauthentic versus the natural performance, and the logic of quantifiable and qualitative progress [10–13]. In the last, the logic of quantification focuses on record-setting as a sign of progress in sport, while the logic of qualitative progress denies that athletic performances can be compared in such a way as to allow for quantification. "Performances are relative and depend upon interplay between competitors. Every game is different and cannot easily be compared in quantitative terms" [10] (p. 44). The logic of qualitative progress, then, would not characterize the women in the EWS and the women starting thirty minutes later as being in competition with each other since competitors must interact. And the differences in the conditions, both weather and surrounding runners, would make quantitative comparisons impossible. Neither would Loland agree that Monza was a competitive race: "Basic physical qualities, such as endurance, strength, speed and flexibility provide a means only. The primary challenge is on technical and tactical skills that have to be learned through practice and experience in social interaction with others" [10] (p. 45). Thus, we can extend the conclusion also to indicate that Monza was not a real challenge, given that Desisa, Kipchoge, and Taldese exhibited no tactical skill or social interaction.

One might note that I have presumed the superiority of one side of the dichotomy without offering support for that privilege. For that support, I point to Kretchmar and Elcombe's work on sport's potential to enhance human flourishing. As they point out, contesting skills involve more complexity, collaboration, and achievement than tests. It is not simply that more means better; contesting skills are qualitatively superior because they tap into more of what makes us human, rather than cyborg or machine. They "provide enhanced meanings that tell us more about who we are and what we have accomplished" [14] (p. 185). Contests are self-revelatory in a way that tests are not, in part because of their increased requirements. To wit: " Contests introduce a host of additional excellences related to the processes of winning, such as, leading, taking the lead, holding a lead, gambling for a lead, delaying strategically for a reversal late in the contest, intentionally forfeiting a lead, mustering resources that would not be needed just to do well on the test but are necessary to surpass an opponent, intentionally and skillfully deceiving an opponent into thinking that a lead has been lost when it has not, identifying the precise moment when a move will have its greatest impact, and sensing when an opponent is flagging and vulnerable. Clearly, these processes involve a second group of excellences, a group that has been missed or ignored by most commentators" [14] (p. 189). The "excellences" listed here were

---

[2] Sporting activities designed such that participants cannot watch one another, like cycling time trials or downhill skiing events, are most accurately characterized as tests, not contests, and require less complex skills than contests.

entirely absent from the run at Monza, while present but in duplicate (at least) in Boston where the women in the EWS exhibited them and the women in the later start did as well, but not in any relation to each other. We might say there was no contesting at Monza and too much at Boston.

5. Conclusions

The problem with the Boston race is the same as the problem in the Nike Breaking2 Project's Monza attempt—neither was a singular *race*. There was no racing at Monza and there were many races at Boston. One might object that the races were *against the clock*, but that ignores the importance of contesting skills. This accounts for the dissatisfaction many people felt with the outcome of both races. The timing chips at Boston and the scientifically engineered corporate showmanship at Monza shifted the events too far away from what is distinctly human, and for that reason valuable, about sport. Without the interplay of competitors, engaged in display of contesting skills aimed toward victory, human excellence is forfeited to technology.

Funding: This research received no external funding.

Conflicts of Interest: The author declares no conflict of interest.

References

1. Butryn, T. Cyborg Horizons: Sport and the Ethics of Self-Technologization. In *Sport Technology: History, Philosophy and Policy*; Miah, A., Eassom, S.B., Eds.; JAI: Boston, MA, USA, 2002; Volume 21, pp. 111–133.
2. Ryall, E. *Philosophy of Sport: Key Questions*; Bloomsbury: New York, NY, USA, 2016.
3. Tenner, E. *Why Things Bite Back: Technology and the Revenge of Unintended Consequences*; Alfred A. Knopf, Inc.: New York, NY, USA, 1996.
4. Sailors, P. More Than a Pair of Shoes: Running and Technology. *J. Philos. Sport* **2009**, *36*, 207–216. [CrossRef]
5. Reinstein, J. This Woman Placed 5th in the Boston Marathon. If She Were a Man, She'd Have Won $15,000. 2018. Available online: https://www.buzzfeednews.com/article/juliareinstein/boston-marathon-women-prize-money (accessed on 3 May 2018).
6. Reed, K. Personal communication, August 2018.
7. Hutchinson, A. *Endure: Mind, Body, and the Curiously Elastic Limits of Human Performance*; William Morrow: New York, NY, USA, 2018.
8. Kretchmar, R.S. From Test to Contest: An Analysis of Two Kinds of Counterpoint in Sport. *J. Philos. Sport* **1975**, *2*, 23–30. [CrossRef]
9. Reid, H. Why Olympia matters for Modern Sport. *J. Philos. Sport* **2017**, *44*, 159–173. [CrossRef]
10. Loland, S. The logic of progress and the art of moderation in competitive sports. In *Values in Sport: Elitism, Nationalism, Gender Equality and the Scientific Manufacture of Winners*; Tännsjö, T., Tamburrini, C., Eds.; E & FN Spon: New York, NY, USA, 2000; pp. 40–56.
11. Loland, S. Technology in Sport: Three Ideal-Typical Views and Their Implications. *Eur. J. Sport Sci.* **2002**, *2*, 1–11. [CrossRef]
12. Loland, S. The Ethics of Performance-Enhancing Technology in Sport. *J. Philos. Sport* **2009**, *36*, 152–161. [CrossRef]
13. Loland, S. Performance-Enhancing Drugs, Sport, and the Ideal of Natural Athletic Performance. *Am. J. Bioeth.* **2018**, *18*, 8–15. [CrossRef] [PubMed]
14. Kretchmar, R.S.; Elcombe, T. In Defense of Competition and Winning. In *Ethics in Sport*, 2nd ed.; Morgan, W.J., Ed.; Human Kinetics: Champaign, IL, USA, 2007; pp. 181–194.

© 2019 by the author. Licensee MDPI, Basel, Switzerland. This article is an open access article distributed under the terms and conditions of the Creative Commons Attribution (CC BY) license (http://creativecommons.org/licenses/by/4.0/).

Article

Applying Philosophy to Refereeing and Umpiring Technology

Harry Collins

School of Social Sciences, Cardiff University, Cardiff CF10 3WT, UK; CollinsHM@cf.ac.uk

Received: 24 April 2019; Accepted: 8 May 2019; Published: 9 May 2019

Abstract: This paper draws on an earlier book (with Evans and Higgins) entitled *Bad Call: Technology's Attack on Referees and Umpires and How to Fix It* (hereafter *Bad Call*) and its various precursor papers. These show why it is that current match officiating aids are unable to provide the kind of accuracy that is often claimed for them and that sports aficianados have been led to expect from them. Accuracy is improving all the time but the notion of perfect accuracy is a myth because, for example, lines drawn on sports fields and the edges of balls are not perfectly defined. The devices meant to report the exact position of a ball—for instance 'in' or 'out' at tennis—work with the mathematically perfect world of virtual reality, not the actuality of an imperfect physical world. Even if ball-trackers could overcome the sort of inaccuracies related to fast ball speeds and slow camera frame-rates the goal of complete accuracy will always be beyond reach. Here it is suggested that the purpose of technological aids to umpires and referees be looked at in a new way that takes the viewers into account.

Keywords: umpiring and refereeing; technological assistance to match officials; justice and continuity in match officiating; ball trackers; goal-line technology; football; cricket; tennis

1. Introduction

This paper draws on an earlier book (with Evans and Higgins) entitled *Bad Call: Technology's Attack on Referees and Umpires and How to Fix It* (hereafter *Bad Call*) [1] and its various precursor papers [2–4]. These show why it is that current match officiating aids are unable to provide the kind of accuracy that is claimed for them and that sports aficianados have been led to expect from them. Accuracy is improving all the time but the notion of perfect accuracy is a myth. It is a myth in science, where measurement of any kind is always associated with a statement of possible error—and the amount of error is itself uncertain as the so-called 'replication crisis' in medicine and psychology shows. It is clearly a myth in sport because of obvious examples such as that the lines drawn on sports fields and the edges of balls are not perfectly defined. The devices meant to report the exact position of a ball—for instance 'in' or 'out' at tennis—work with the mathematically perfect world of virtual reality, not the actuality of an imperfect physical world. Even if ball-trackers could overcome the sort of inaccuracies related to fast ball speeds and slow camera frame-rates the goal of complete accuracy will always be beyond reach. Here it is suggested that the purpose of technological aids to umpires and referees be looked at in a new way that takes the viewers into account.

2. Justice Not Accuracy. Also Continuity

In *Bad Call*, we argue that match officiating has always been flawed and will always be flawed if the standard is mathematical purity. Traditionally, however, this kind of exactness this was not the aim; the aim was to run the game in a way that kept everyone reasonably satisfied that justice was being done. It was accepted that since the match official nearly always had a better view than anyone else and given the match official's training and experience, no-one could do a better job of providing acceptable judgements. We argue that the match officials' privilege has been eroded with the advent of television replays, especially slow-motion replays; these put the TV viewer in a better position than the match official to make a fair judgement—so long as the official has no access to the replays. Thus the fragility of match officials' real-time judgements, and occasional gross mistakes, have been revealed to a wide audience, causing a sense of injustice in sports fans and spoiling the games. Therefore, we (the authors of the earlier books and articles), recommended the introduction of video-referees and umpires with access to TV replays as aids to the on-field officials.

The crucial thing is that this is not, and should not be seen as, a technological fix for bringing about exact accuracy—inaccuracy will always be there—but a fix for obvious injustices. This philosophical distinction makes a huge difference to the way technological aids are applied to sports-officiating but it is a distinction that does not seem to be widely understood. A second related philosophical principle that goes along with the main principle is that the technologically assisted game should be as like the technologically unassisted game as possible; we should not be playing a completely different game when we move from the lower reaches of amateur sport to the highest level of professional sport, at least, not in terms of the rules. These two principles can be summed up as Justice and Continuity (JAC)

One can see how JAC works with a single example: the skidding ball in tennis. It is (or at least, was) claimed that Hawkeye is more accurate than the human eye in certain circumstances because it takes into account the fact that a hard-driven tennis ball skids when it hits the ground. If the ball is very close to the back edge of the baseline, the human eye (and TV replays will make no difference), sees the ball bounce up from the end-point of the skid and, projecting backwards, humans see the ball as being 'out'. Hawkeye, however, which projects the ball track forward, can show that the ball actually made contact with the baseline before skidding and was therefore 'in'. JAC says that if the human eye and TV always see such a ball as 'out' then there is no felt injustice and the ball simply is 'out' for all practical purposes; it is only the shibboleth of accuracy that would cause us to want to say it was 'in'. If in every game from the Sunday morning romp in the park all the way to non-technically assisted professional games such a skidding ball has always been counted as 'out' with no objection, then the technically assisted game should count it as 'out' too so as to maintain continuity with the rest of the sport.

A more recent event illustrates the same point. (It is proper to point out in reference to this incident that that the author is a Liverpool fan and his analysis of the incident coincides with his loyalties; readers should, therefore, assure themselves that the argument is not a product of bias.) The event in question concerns the 'non-goal' that occurred about 20 minutes into the crucial Premiership game between Manchester City and Liverpool on 3rd January, 2019. The result was a win for City but, other things being equal, it would have been a draw if the disallowed goal had been allowed. It could well be (at the time of the final revision of this paper undertaken with only one match left to play in the season) that this non-goal will mean that 'City' rather than Liverpool win the Premiership this year.

The goal was disallowed after the application of 'goal-line technology'—a technology which was criticised in the book, *Bad Call*, long before this incident, on the grounds that it is expensive and unnecessary, relevant to a vanishingly small number of cases compared to other refereeing errors, and brought in only because TV replays had highlighted goal-line mistakes and so, in all these high-profile cases, TV replays could have corrected them. In this instance the use of goal-line technology has driven a further wedge between the technologically assisted game and the traditional game.

The dispute concerned a clearance by a Manchester City player. Figure 1 shows a TV replay of the clearance and Figure 2 the graphic generated by goal line technology.

Figure 1. TV replay of 'non-goal' scored by Liverpool vs. Manchester City, 3/01/2019.

Figure 2. Goal line technology reconstruction.

It was claimed that goal-line technology showed that the ball had failed to clear the line by 11.2 millimeters subject to a 3.6 millimeter average accuracy. Here we are not questioning the accuracy of the judgment even though we do not know the extent of the scatter of the average error. Also, the presentation of the measurement to one tenth of a millimetre is bizarre given that we are dealing with painted lines on grass and a goal frame that would have to be a fine piece of engineering to preserve a front-to-back plane to within even a centimetre over the course of a game. It is also regrettable that the fact that this must be a virtual reality reconstruction is obscured by the 'realistic' presentation of the grass and the ball; the ball should be presented as a plain disk with fuzzy edges to represent measurement errors while the grass and line should be presented as geometrical blocks without texture, with the line having a fuzzy edge to express its real-world inexactness. Something more in the spirit of Figure 3 would be a more revealing way to present the outcome of the estimate made by goal-line technology. As it is, the way goal-line technology is presented misleads the public.

The main complaint, however, is that the use of goal line technology here offends against JAC. It is hard to imagine that any TV viewer or Video assistant referee would not award a goal after seeing the replay shown in Figure 1. It looks like a goal and in all games that do not use the technology but use TV replays instead, it would be a goal. Given the TV replay, the incident offends against both justice and continuity. In this case, Liverpool fans watching the TV replay will feel they have been robbed by the technology rather than seen an injustice remedied, while Manchester City fans will feel they have been extremely lucky not to be a goal down.

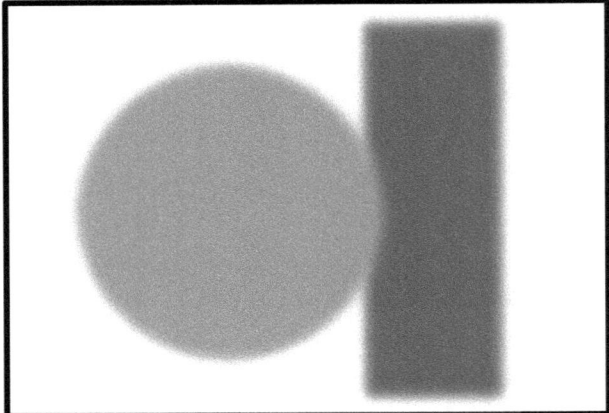

Figure 3. A better way to represent goal line technology.

3. RINOWN

If sports administrators, commentators, and the viewing public could train themselves to understand officiating technology as aiming at justice not accuracy and at maintaining games' traditions as far as possible, the technology could be employed in a very different and very much more efficient way; cricket and some other sports already come close. Under these circumstances on-field match officials would continue to make decisions in real time just as they still do in every game that is not technologically assisted. Then, under circumstances which might vary from sport to sport, the video-assistant would offer a judgement. The on-field official's real-time decision would be taken as right unless the video-assistant could, quickly, show it was unambiguously wrong. This situation is signified by the acronym 'RINOWN', which stands for 'Right If NOt WroNg'. Continuity with the non-technologically assisted game would be preserved because where there was no technological assistance the default position would be that the on-field official was right as is traditionally the case. Given no TV-replays, everything would be just as it has always been through the centuries and a difference with the technologically-assisted game would occur only where the on-field official made the kind of mistake that is obvious to the TV viewer.

What are the circumstances under which the video-assistant's help would be invoked? It could be decided to invoke it only when the players challenged the on-field decision, or when the on-field official decided to ask for help, or when the video-assistant, operating autonomously and monitoring the game continuously, decided to tell the on-field official that they were wrong and have them change their call. Other things being equal, autonomous video-assistants seem best because they have the same view as the TV-watcher and will be alert to exactly the same injustices, caused by same obvious mistakes, as are experienced by the TV watcher; the on-field official will, by definition, miss these, and even the players will not always be aware of injustices that TV viewers may spot.

4. Some Examples

4.1. Cricket

Let us offer some examples of how things could be done differently and better under the principles set out here. We'll start with one that occurred only a couple of weeks before the time of writing. In one of the cricket test matches between Sri Lanka and England in November 2018, a diving catch was taken low to the ground towards the edge of the field. At that distance, no-one near the middle of the field, including the batsman and the umpires, could be absolutely sure that the catch was taken fairly and had not bounced into the fielder's hands; sometimes even fielders are not quite sure. Therefore, the umpires decided to ask the video-assistant to run through some TV replays. Cricket uses its technology properly most of the time and umpires had to give what is called a 'soft signal' before the TV replays were examined. The soft signal represents their unassisted decision—'out' or 'not out'—leaving the video-assistant to decide only if they were obviously wrong, the default being that they were right (RINOWN).

The interesting thing here is the remarks of one of the commentators. He argued that since the umpires were so far from the point at which the catch was taken they could not see whether it bounced or not so they should not be asked to provide a 'soft signal', leaving it entirely to the video-assistant. But here the commentator is being misled by the desire for accuracy rather than justice and continuity. Had there been no TV cameras the umpires, badly sighted though they were, would still have to have made a judgement (incidentally, it would almost certainly have included element based on the trajectory of the ball and the fielder's dive and the demeanor of the fielder—these things, like so many decisions, having nothing to do with exact accuracy). Furthermore, it is quite possible that the TV replays would themselves be indecisive but some decision would still have to be made—preferably as speedily as possible—and, under these circumstances, if it was made by the umpires, no injustice would have been done.

Incidentally, there are two kinds of technologically assisted decisions in cricket (and in some other sports). What we might call Type 1 examples are when the technology is simple, such as TV replay. In this case it is practical for the video-assistant to monitor the game continuously and warn the on-field official when they have made a mistake—'autonomous assistance'. Type 2 is the when the technology is inherently slow, as in the case of ball-tracking and 'ultra-edge' which generates an oscilloscope trace of the sounds made as the ball passes the bat such as would indicate an 'edge' that might lead to a close catch decision—the ball hit the bat and did not just bounce off the pad or miss everything. Type 2 uses of technology invites the 'player-challenge' approach to video-assistance rather than autonomous video-assistance simply because the time taken to generate the images means that play cannot be monitored continuously. It may be that as technology improves, Type 2 will turn into Type 1 and make it possible to have autonomously video-assistance in every case.

In cricket the difference is clear because challenges are used for 'lbw' (this stands for 'leg before wicket' and requires an estimate of whether it was the player's leg rather than the bat that prevented the ball from colliding with the target that the 'bowler' aims for—the three vertical 'stumps') and close catches whereas more distant catches, run-outs (similar to a runner not making his or her ground at baseball), stumpings (where the batter accidentally steps 'out of his ground' and allows the wicket to be broken with the ball), boundary saves and boundary-crossing by the ball 'on the full' (in cricket the 'boundary' is marked by a rope or similar and if the ball rolls across it then four runs are scored but if it flies across it 'on the full'—without hitting the ground—then six runs are scored); these often involve the umpire asking for help which an autonomous video-assistant could provide without asking. At the time of writing there is a debate in cricket about whether the calling of 'no-balls', (when the bowler's foot crosses the legal line), should be passed to an autonomous video-assistant and it seems likely that this will happen.

4.2. Ball Trackers and Tennis

A crucial lesson that has already been mentioned and needs to be widely learned is that technological devices such as ball-trackers, do not show what actually happened but only a statistical estimate of what might have happened, which is subject to unknown errors, often quite large, but which errors are concealed by the exact-looking virtual reality of the reconstruction. This is the argument set out and illustrated in Section 2, above. Thus one may hear cricket commentators complaining that there is something wrong when two lbw challenges, decided on the basis of almost identical ball tracks, result in two different decisions, one 'out' one 'not out', depending on what the umpire had decided in the first place. In cricket this happens because there is, sensibly, a recognised margin of error when it comes to ball-trackers, inside which the umpire's initial decision over-rules the technology. Therefore, the same ball track can lead to different outcomes depending on what the umpire thought in the first place. Certain cricket commentators complain that this is unjust because they do not seem to understand that the same ball-track reconstruction can mask two different actual ball-trajectories. We have to get over the idea in peoples' heads that technological reconstructions present an exactly accurate account of what happened rather than an envelope of possibilities.

Tennis seems to be the sport where ball-tracking is most misused even though the public like the current system and the players have accepted it, some very reluctantly. In tennis the outcome of ball tracking is presented as though it can adjudicate 'in' and 'out' to an indefinitely fine margin with everyone reading the virtual reality reconstructions as reality itself. This, while it might seem like a 'bit of fun', is dangerously misleading in an era where fake news stories promulgated in social media are hard to distinguish from news from trustworthy sources; here tennis is encouraging the public to accept fake news instead of honing their ability to separate the credible from the incredible. Once more, JAC and RINOWN provide an easy solution. It is that the umpire's initial decision should stand unless the ball-tracker shows that there was a clear mistake. In this case 'clearness' is a technical matter which depends on the horizontal component of ball speed and the frame speed of the ball-tracking cameras. When we, working with almost no data, tried to estimate the right kind of error margins in tennis, we thought that nothing within about three millimetres of the edge of the line was secure, and within this margin the umpire's decision should be final. But this 'three millimetres' depends on many factors that, currently, only the ball-tracking companies know and which will be changing all the time as the technology changes. Unfortunately, this material is kept secret under the banner of commercial secrecy. This deliberate misleading of the public sets a bad precedent.

4.3. Rugby

The same considerations apply to rugby. Unlike American football, the rule for scoring a 'try' in rugby is that the ball has to be carried over the line and placed on the ground with momentary downward pressure. An opposition team can stop the ball touching the ground even though it is over the line; this is referred to as the ball being 'held up'. Sometimes there are a huge pile of bodies over or around the edge of the line with the ball invisibly buried somewhere toward the base of it. In the technologically assisted game the referee nowadays calls for the video-assistant to try to untangle the decision. Under JAC the referee would have to make a decision, as they have to when there is no technological assistance, and the video assistant's job would be to say whether that decision was obviously and visibly wrong and if not, the decision would stand. This would remove the grounds for argument about the true outcome and the sense of injustice, while markedly speeding up the decision-making process.

4.4. Football

What is known as VAR, or the 'video assistant referee', is currently being brought into football (known in the USA as soccer) at an ever-increasing rate. We like to think that this is partly a result of our arguments and analysis of three seasons of English Premier League football in our book, *Bad Call*, but it is hard to find any acknowledgement of this work. In Chapter 7 of our book we put forward a scheme for introducing TV replays into football while minimising delays in the game. The central principle is, once more, RINOWN—the referee makes the decisions just as now and that decision is the default unless it is obviously wrong to the TV viewer; this, of course, also satisfies JAC. Unfortunately, VAR seems to be being introduced into football in a variety of different ways and its future promises to be attended by a lot of confusion.

5. Goal-Line Technology

As an example, consider, once more, goal-line technology. This is a technological device that tells a referee via a wristwatch-type indicator whether the ball has fully crossed the goal-line in case of a disputed goal. As explained in Section 2, exactly what is meant by 'fully crossed the goal line' is difficult to say given that goals and goal lines are not exact but no comprehensive estimates of possible error, which would include the scatter rather than being an average, are provided. To repeat, the clamour over goal-line technology was caused by well-publicised mistakes in important televised matches, notably an England World Cup semi-final against Germany, but in all these cases the mistake was obvious on the TV replay and this makes it difficult to see why any more advanced technology was called for unless the pressure emerged from the idea that technology could provide exactness. In our analysis we showed that over three seasons of English Premiership football the number of disputed goals that might be affected by goal-line technology was about 11 whereas the number of potential goal-related mistakes arising from flawed penalty, offside and red card decisions was well over 300. Of these 11, the number which would not have been obvious to an appropriately located TV replay camera would have been a very small subset.

It is obvious that the large majority of these 'well-over 300' mistakes could not possibly have been settled by an exactly accurate technology since such mistake often depend on judgement of intention, in the case of penalties and red-cards, and 'interference' with play' in the case of offside and there is no foreseeable technology that can measure these things. It is obvious then, that starting with the notion of accuracy as the foundation of the introduction of VAR in football is going to lead to confusion. Starting with the notion of justice, continuity, and RINOWN, will resolve it.

Our recommendation is the same as for other sports. On-field referees make decisions and video-assistants monitor the game in the same way as TV viewers monitor it—with the same or better access to replays. Video assistants call play back when, and only when, an obvious mistake has been made—that is, a mistake that is obvious to anyone with the benefit of TV replays including viewers at home and video assistant referees. Given that the mistake must be obvious, this kind of judgment is quick and aligns with the TV viewer at home, thus eliminating injustice. We suggest various ways of halting and restarting the game under different circumstances in Table 7.2 (p124) of *Bad Call* but this is something that can only be refined with experience. The crucial arguments here are about resolving confusion about what decision-aid technology in sport is for, and the arguments are necessarily philosophical, at least in part.

Funding: This research recieved no external funding.

Conflicts of Interest: The author declares no conflict of interest.

References

1. Collins, H.M.; Evans, R.; Higgins, C. *Bad Call: Technology's Attack on Referees and Umpires and how to Fix It*; MIT Press: Cambridge, MA, USA, 2016.
2. Collins, H. The philosophy of umpiring and introduction of decision-aid technology. *J. Philosophy Sport* **2010**, *37*, 135–146. [CrossRef]
3. Collins, H.; Evans, R. Sport-decision aids and the "CSI-effect": Why cricket uses Hawk-Eye well and tennis uses it badly. *Public Underst. Sci.* **2012**, *21*, 904–921. [CrossRef] [PubMed]
4. Collins, H.; Evans, R. You Cannot Be Serious! Public Understanding of Technology with special reference to 'Hawk-Eye'. *Public Underst. Sci.* **2008**, *17*, 283–308. [CrossRef]

© 2019 by the author. Licensee MDPI, Basel, Switzerland. This article is an open access article distributed under the terms and conditions of the Creative Commons Attribution (CC BY) license (http://creativecommons.org/licenses/by/4.0/).

Article

Why You Don't Have to Choose between Accuracy and Human Officiating (But You Might Want to Anyway)

S. Seth Bordner

Department of Philosophy, University of Alabama, Tuscaloosa, AL 35487-0218, USA; seth.bordner@ua.edu; Tel.: +1-205-348-5942

Received: 13 May 2019; Accepted: 5 June 2019; Published: 14 June 2019

Abstract: Debates about the role of technology in sports officiating assume that technology would, *ceteris paribus*, improve accuracy over unassisted human officiating. While this is largely true, it also presents a false dilemma: that we can have accurately officiated sports or human officials, but not both. What this alleged dilemma ignores is that the criteria by which we measure accuracy are also up for revision. We *could* have sports that are so defined as to be easily (or at least *more* accurately) judged by human officials. A case from the recent history of science provides an instructive example. I argue that *if* we insist on human officials, we can still aim for maximal accuracy, though there will be tradeoffs. With compelling reasons to want accuracy in officiating, however, these tradeoffs effectively serve as a *reductio* against the use of human officials unaided by technology.

Keywords: accuracy; officiating; justice; the human element; technology; Hawk-Eye; aesthetics of sports

1. Introduction

In the debate about whether to use technology in sports officiating—and if so, how much—it is widely agreed that adding technology would improve accuracy relative to unaided human officiating, but at the loss of some sort(s) of value. Collins, Evans, and Higgins [1] worry about the degradation of the officials' authority. Ryall [2] considers the loss of entertainment value that would follow the reduction in controversial missed calls. Johnson and Taylor [3] value the lessons in humanity and humility provided by having to suffer bad calls.

I disagree that such values, either separately or together, count strongly enough against the value of accuracy that we should forego more accurate (technologically-assisted) officiating—where and when it's available—in favor of (less accurate) human officiating. But setting this matter aside, the current debate is premised on a false dilemma. Human officiating *need not* be *less* accurate than technology; thus, the choice between maximal accuracy and human officiating is not an exclusive one. The way through the horns of the dilemma lies in appreciating that accuracy is *relative to criteria* that we are free to specify. We may thus freely specify them in ways that unaided human beings can reliably judge.

In what follows, I argue that sports—much like science—rely on classification under concepts, the criteria for which *we choose* based on our values and interests. Accuracy, in turn, requires correctly applying the criteria. This task is made more or less difficult for human beings to accomplish depending on how fine- or coarse-grained the criteria are. So, in effect, we choose which facts will matter, as well as how to track them. If we insist on tracking them with unaided human officials, then we should choose facts that such people *can accurately track*. I also suggest some possible changes that might be made to existing sports if we take seriously the idea of tracking those facts that human beings can reliably judge. Whether these suggestions are welcome or repugnant, they can serve either as guides for how to change our sports or as an indictment of the desire for human officiating at the expense of accuracy.

2. A Lesson from Astronomy

When Clyde Tombaugh discovered Pluto in 1930 it was, by the definition of 'planet' in use at the time, the ninth known planet: it was a massive, spherical, non-luminous body that orbited a star, our Sun, like the other known planets, albeit on an unusually inclined orbit. Even being smaller than our moon, Pluto was a significant body orbiting our Sun, and so for 75 years, it remained the ninth of nine planets; the smallest of what astronomers considered the most basic components of our solar system.

All of that changed in 2005 when Caltech astronomer Mike Brown discovered Eris. Initial measurements indicated Eris was both bigger and more massive than Pluto—surely, the tenth planet![1] What followed was not celebration, however, but crisis. On the one hand, the case for counting Eris as a planet was clear. Pluto was a planet, and Eris was at least as big as Pluto; ergo, Eris was a planet. But at the same time, Eris' discovery undermined the case for counting Pluto as a planet in the first place. Until then, Pluto was unique—small, yes, but notably bigger than any of the thousands of other bodies in the Kuiper belt beyond Uranus. But Eris showed that Pluto was not all that special after all, in either size or in location.

Eris' discovery threw the astronomical community into dispute over one of its most basic concepts: what is a 'planet'? The dispute was ultimately settled in 2006 by the International Astronomical Union's adoption of a new definition of 'planet'. To the old definition was added the criteria that a planet must have sufficient mass to have "cleared the neighborhood" of its orbit: roughly, that any other object in its orbit will orbit *it*. Since Pluto, as was long known, shared its orbit with many other objects of comparable size to its own satellite Charon, it failed to meet this new criteria and was defined out of existence as a planet. Pluto was no longer a planet; Eris would never be one. And instead of being credited with the discovery of the tenth planet, Brown is known instead as the man who killed Pluto.

Pluto's undoing was probably inevitable, but it was prompted by advances in technology. Brown's discovery of Eris (and dozens of other nearly-Pluto-sized bodies) was made possible by improvements in telescopic design, image capturing, and data analysis. These improvements in studying the stars ultimately showed that how scientists classified the objects orbiting our Sun was, for astronomical purposes, *wrong*. But the error here is instructive. By the time Pluto's planetary status came into question, its size, shape, mass, and orbit were long known. The question was not, *do Pluto's physical parameters meet the criteria for planetary status*, but rather was, *what should the criteria be*? Crucially, what the criteria *should* be is not an empirical question but a normative one—one that bears on the interests and aims of scientists rather than measurable features of the world.

Revising the definition of 'planet' was fraught and controversial. In doing so, astronomers had to navigate competing interests of scientific utility, conceptual naturalness, and cultural familiarity. One of the biggest objections to any official revision was that it would do violence to the colloquial use of the term. Schoolchildren since the 1930s learned the names of *nine* planets and some worried the familiarity with astronomy that this promoted would be undermined by a revision. But how a scientific concept is employed by non-scientists does not necessarily track the sorts of natural properties that scientists want to study and which constitute the reason for considering objects as belonging to the same kind in the first place. So, there is the opposing concern that technical concepts that also have use in ordinary language need to remain tethered to their scientific origins or risk further confusing a public that already struggles to understand its theories.[2]

---

[1] At the time, Eris was estimated to be both larger and more massive than Pluto. The subsequent flyby of Pluto by NASA's New Horizons probe showed that Pluto (2370 km) is *very slightly* (1.8%) larger than Eris (2326 km) in diameter. Eris is still estimated to be 27% more massive than Pluto, however [4]. Brown's memoir [5] of the discovery of Eris and the resulting demotion of Pluto from planetary status is fascinating and delightful.

[2] In the case of Pluto, the interests that ultimately won were those of keeping the criteria for planets closely aligned with the idea that planets were the most important and most fundamental objects in a solar system other than a star. This meant, in effect, that a body's impact on its neighborhood becomes more significant a criteria than its being round and/or orbiting the Sun. Defining 'planet' in such a way conveys more valuable information about the nature of the solar system than other ways might. As Brown writes, "Most people ... will know what a planet is and how many planets there are and what their

Classification under concepts is a fundamental scientific practice and problem. Since Galileo first looked through his telescope to discover the moons of Jupiter, however, sometimes advances in our knowledge and technological capabilities put pressure on those concepts and the roles they play in scientific practice. The wealth of information provided by newer, better technology poses problems as well as opportunities for scientists and their conceptual scheme. Accommodating this information into theories is how science (eventually) progresses.

In Pluto's demise, there are lessons to be learned for sports theorists as well. Sports, as well as science, depend on classification under concepts. Often these concepts are put under pressure by new information discovered through advances in technology. Like in the case of Pluto and Eris, sometimes sports face difficulties concerning what the criteria *should* be. This is particularly the case in sports officiating where advances in technology have shown us the sometimes-wide gap between how sports define the criteria and how officials apply them. The job of sporting officials is not unlike that of scientists, as it were, observing, measuring, recording, certifying, and curating the "data" produced by the athletes.[3] And it is in this respect that innovations and improvements in technology raise both problems for sports as they are officiated, and opportunities for how officiating can be improved.

Thus far, the debate about what role technology should play in sports officiating has largely centered around one question: should sporting officials be given use of—or even replaced by—technology to improve officiating accuracy, or not?[4] More technology, or not? Previously, I have argued for more, maybe much more, as long as it improves accuracy [6]. The counterpoint has been, not so much that more technology would *not* be more accurate, but that accuracy itself is overrated [1,7], or that the costs of introducing technology may outweigh the benefits [10], or even that the inaccuracy of human officials *improves* sports in a way [3].[5]

There has been much less discussion about what accuracy in officiating means. Largely, it has been assumed an official's call is accurate to the extent that it *correctly applies the criteria*—accuracy means "getting it right."[6] This takes for granted that there is a right way to get it: that there are objective facts about the players or pieces of the game that can be correctly or incorrectly judged by officials. And indeed, there are often such facts and officials often do judge them incorrectly. A baseball pitch that passes through no part of the strike zone and is not swung at by the batter has not met the criteria to be called a strike. It *ought not* to be called a strike. An umpire who calls it a strike anyway would be wrong to do so; they would be applying the criteria incorrectly. But even in the relatively well-defined case of balls and strikes, the criteria can be problematic in at least two ways. First, some degree of vagueness is likely ineliminable in defining any criteria. Often, it will be unclear *whether* the criteria apply in a case or not; in baseball, for example, the criteria for balls and strikes are not exhaustive—some pitches are technically neither balls nor strikes.[7] Second, it can be practically impossible for officials to apply the criteria to the events as they happen. Primarily, this will be due to the simple difficulties of seeing all of what one is supposed to judge or seeing it clearly enough. The human being as a measuring device is rather limited under the best of conditions, and conditions are not always best. Moreover, humans have cognitive biases in addition to their perceptual limitations that further complicate the already-difficult task facing officials [11].

Technology can at best help address the second problem by seeing what the human eye cannot see or seeing it free from biases. This is not an insignificant benefit, but as is well known, it comes at some

---

names are. Their entire mental picture of what the solar system is, of how our local bit of the universe is put together, will be carried in the understanding of that simple word. The definition of the word *planet*, then, had better carry with it the most profound description of the solar system possible in a single word. If you think of the solar system as a place consisting of eight planets . . . , you have a profound description of the local universe around us." [5] (p. 235).

[3] Of course, the analogy is not perfect. Scientists and sports officials might have very different aims and motivations, and sports are by no means controlled experiments. I thank two anonymous referees for stressing this point.
[4] See, for example, Bordner [6], Collins [7], Collins, Evans, and Higgins [1], Griffioen [8], and Royce [9].
[5] On this last point—the alleged positive value of inaccurate officiating—see n. 14 below.
[6] This is certainly an assumption I made in [6].
[7] See [6] n. 10.

costs. Largely unexplored, however, is the role that poorly defined criteria play in making officiating too difficult for human beings to do well. It is partly *because* of how the strike zone is defined—"that area over home plate the upper limit of which is a horizontal line at the midpoint between the top of the shoulders and the top of the uniform pants, and the lower level is a line at the hollow below the kneecap, [...] determined from the batter's stance as the batter is prepared to swing at a pitched ball"—that calling balls and strikes is as challenging as it is. Tracking a baseball with the naked eye is not by itself too much for the human perceptual system to handle; catchers almost always catch the ball, after all. What is not so easy is telling whether any part of a spinning, speeding ball passes through any part of a vaguely defined, invisible, three-dimensional region of space. Human eyes are not built to see invisible lines. Cameras *can be* and have been; it is in virtue of them that we now know just how wide the gap is between where the strike zone is supposed to be and where umpires think it is.

The problem can be even worse for officials tasked with judgments of a player's intention, such as whether a foul was flagrant or whether a player's conduct was unsporting. In such cases it is not so much that we lack the perceptual abilities to determine the facts, it is that *what counts as the relevant fact* is poorly or vaguely defined. It is not clear what the criteria even are, so questions of whether an official's call is accurate are unanswerable.

Everyone agrees that we can do better; in particular, (almost) everyone agrees that using technology would improve accuracy. But, recall, the debate has largely taken for granted that "accuracy" has been thought of in terms *accuracy with respect to the current criteria*. It is in this context that the desire for more accurate officiating pushes in favor of advanced technology and against human officials.

Acknowledging the roles that definitional vagueness and ambiguity play in making the job of officiating more difficult, however, presents us with a unique opportunity: it allows us to consider how our sports, like our sciences, might be improved by *clarifying or refining the criteria* we use to measure and judge them. If we take seriously the costs of officiating technology—both the financial costs as well as the potential negative effects on entertainment value—it is worth exploring ways in which we might still aid the goal of maximal accuracy in officiating by *refining our criteria* to make them simpler and/or easier for human officials to adjudicate. In much the same way that the astronomical community made studying astronomy easier—by redefining 'planet' with clearer, more easily measurable criteria—sports might likewise improve accuracy and make the jobs of officials easier by redefining the phenomena they are tasked with judging.

3. The Challenge of Sports Officiating

Sporting officials have both epistemic and judicial duties. As Royce aptly states, "[r]eferees have to decide rather than discover what to do, and not merely what happened. But we expect them to *decide* what to do partly on the basis of *discovering* what happened, and to interpret and apply rules in relation to what happened when arriving at their decision" [9] (p. 62). The principal difficulty facing officials is not *deciding what to do*, as such, though certainly applying the rules can be challenging even when it is clearly known what happened.[8] Rather, officials often don't know *what happened*—either because they did not or could not see the relevant facts—and so cannot *decide what to do* appropriately within the rules.

But what exactly counts as *what happened*? Not every fact is relevant to the athlete or the official. No player or official is concerned to know or measure the average number of kernels in boxes of popcorn sold during the game, for instance. Even many facts that affect or partially constitute the relevant events are not relevant *per se*. The exit velocity of a batted ball is in part determinative of whether it leaves the yard for a homerun. But the speed itself is irrelevant—what matters to players and officials alike is only where the ball ends up. The simple reason for this is that the rules of baseball

---

[8] For an introduction to the difficulties facing officials even under the best conditions, see the work of J.S. Russell, e.g., [12,13].

nowhere make reference to exit velocity. In short, the rules specify both which sorts of facts are relevant to the game *and* what officials are supposed to decide *given what happens* in the set of relevant facts.

Not only do the rules specify which facts matter, they often specify *what counts as a fact*. Whether a batted ball leaves the field of play is an empirically discoverable fact, but it is not a natural fact.[9] That is, the concepts of a "batted ball" or the 'field of play' are not to be found in any natural scientific theory; they are artificial inventions of the rules of the game. Our best physical theories recognize hard bits like protons and electrons, but not hardball; they acknowledge electromagnetic fields, but not ball fields. Sporting facts are social facts, as Borge argues, in that "the attitude we take towards the phenomenon ... is partly constitutive of the phenomena" [14] (p. 356).

So, in deciding what the rules of the game should be, we also decide what the relevant sorts of facts will be that we want officials to pay attention to, as well as what officials should do if certain facts obtain or certain conditions are met. That is, we decide *what the criteria will be*. Our decisions are, in a sense, arbitrary and unnecessary [15]. There is no moral or metaphysical requirement that we have foot races with hurdles, for example.[10] To justify having hurdles in a race, we need only insist that *we want to see a race like that*. We are not *wrong* to want such races, nor are we *wrong* to prefer races without hurdles. Choosing what games to play is exercising our autonomy.

That said, we might have reasons to prefer some rules and some criteria over others. Once decisions are made about what the relevant sorts of facts are, there will be better and worse ways of organizing, playing, *and officiating* games. That is, once it is decided that the first person to reach the line is the winner, it will be true that running will be a better tactic than walking, *ceteris paribus*. Likewise, once it is decided that the official's job is to determine which person reaches the line first, it will be true that marking the line clearly and visibly with chalk or paint (and conducting the race in the daylight) will be a better choice than, say, using invisible ink or a single thread of spider silk (or running the race in total darkness). That is, once we decide what the relevant facts are, we have decided that those facts matter to the game. If we then adopt unreliable or inconsistent methods for tracking those facts (when more reliable or consistent methods are available), we make *bad choices* given our prior decision that those facts matter.[11]

The point here is that, since we not only define the game but also the criteria by which it will be measured and judged, we are free to set those criteria wherever—and define them however—we like. So, the central problem for officiating in sports—deciding *what to do* in on the basis of *what happened*—can be recast in this light: *what sorts of happenings* should we keep track of, and how should we track them? What *should* the relevant criteria be? As with the question of what the criteria for 'planet' should be, this is not primarily an empirical question; answering it requires consulting our values.

In considering potential rules or rule changes in sports, we might *discover* what our values are through reflective equilibrium. But we might also *insist* on values and let these dictate how we craft the rules. One significant value is justice or fairness.[12] Another is accuracy. Together, these push strongly in favor of using the most accurate means of officiating without regard to concerns about the impact on gameplay or spectator enjoyment.[13] We might also value elegance, the "flow" of the game, a sense of drama, or more to the present concern, *the role of human officials*. We need not have an argument for insisting on human officials, any more than we need an argument for why the 110-m

---

[9] As Borge [14] argues, sporting facts are *social facts*. Whether natural facts are *also* social facts is outside the scope of this paper. In any case, even if they are, there is still a distinction between, say, the scientific-even-if-social fact of the location of a ball and the sporting-social fact that the ball was in (or out) of bounds.
[10] This is not to say that there are *no* moral requirements for games-makers. I would insist that there are—for example, the moral requirement not to make a game of hunting human beings—, though this is beyond the scope of this paper.
[11] This applies *ceteris paribus*. More reliable and/or consistent methods may be "available" in theory but not in practice. The sense of "available" will vary depending on context. This does not affect the underlying point.
[12] I here leave aside questions about the relationship between justice and fairness.
[13] See, for instance, [3,6].

high hurdles should have hurdles. Indeed, I think no such argument is possible.[14] We need only insist that *we want it that way*. As things stand, valuing human officiating cuts against the interest in "getting it right", in large part because getting it right given the current criteria is often too difficult for unaided human officials to accomplish on their own and requires technological intervention.[15] Thus, the central question of the debate: more officiating technology or not?

This question, I contend, presents a false dilemma between accuracy, on the one hand, and a human-officiated game. Human officials *could be* as accurate as we liked if only we *decided* that the relevant facts were ones that human beings are well-suited to measure. However, we have not; instead, our sports have largely been defined in quasi-scientific terms, as if the playing field were a Cartesian plane and the players and equipment idealized solid bodies with discreet outer envelopes. Thus, sports have become scientized experiments studying the movement of bodies in bounded but infinitely divisible spaces across infinitely divisible times where the margins between success and failure might resolve down to the millimeter or the thousandth of a second. These are the decisions that have been made about *what count as the relevant facts* in sports. *Given this*, the choice to use human beings as measuring devices is a bad one—human beings are not well-suited to resolve the position of bodies in motion down to the millimeter or the thousandth of a second—and the choice to continue doing so only gets worse as technology gets better.

But the sports we play and the facts we decide are relevant are not forced on us. We do not have to insist on *both* using criteria that cannot be judged accurately by human officials *and* using human officials. If we want to insist on human officials, then, it is worth considering how sports might be designed or modified not just for humans to play, but also for humans to judge *excellently*.

4. What Sports Designed for Human Officials Might Look Like

In general, the criteria used in sports are too fine-grained for humans to judge nearly as accurately as technology can. Baseball umpires are, by the most optimistic estimates, only 90% accurate in calling balls and strikes.[16] While this might sound impressive, we only know this because of the already-99%-accurate Pitchf/x system Major League Baseball uses in every ballpark to evaluate its umpires. Moreover, the 9% difference in accuracy between human umpires and Pitchf/x is enormous: for context, MLB umpires missed more than 34,000 ball-strike calls in 2018 alone [17]. And as determinations of sporting facts go, ball-strike calls are relatively simple: the umpire, from a static position, need only track one object moving directly toward him/her with the plate and the batter's stance to help indicate the strike zone. Things are much more complicated and difficult in other sports such as (American rules) football, basketball, or soccer/football, where officials themselves are in motion along with 10–22 players and a ball, and where the sorts of determinations that need to be made concern spaces and times measured in fractions of inches or seconds. In general, we should expect human officials to perform relatively poorly in judging these events.

---

[14] Johnson and Taylor [3] argue that the fallibility of human officials contributes positively to sports in that "there is something important about recognizing and accepting our vulnerability as part of who we are as human beings" (p. 154). Following Simon [16], they contend the degree of luck that fallible human officiating adds to sports "is important because it promotes an appreciation of arbitrariness in life and accordingly fosters humility of character" (p. 155). But this is not an *argument* that fallible officiating *is valuable*, it is an announcement that *they value it*. (I place *no* such value on it, yet I fail to see how I am making a *mistake* by not doing so, any more than I would be making a mistake by preferring to watch baseball played with a designated hitter than without.) But, *even if* one values the promotion of character that playing a game in which luck significantly infects officiating, this does not yield their conclusion that *human* officiating should be preferred and technology resisted. As they note, error is ineliminable in even the most advanced technologies, and error rates could easily be increased to more "accurately" model human officiating if so desired. If the possibility of error and the presence of luck is what constitutes the "human element" of officiating, then technology can be effectively "human".

[15] For example, Johnson and Taylor [3] (p. 156) write, "by their nature game aesthetics require compromising accuracy and justice as it is".

[16] Williams [17] found that in 2018, MLB umpires incorrectly called 9.21% of pitches—the best rate since the MLB started tracking pitches with Pitchf/x.

If we define the relevant facts more coarsely, however, we can reasonably expect that human beings will be correspondingly more accurate at determining them. For example, rather than making relevant *precisely* where a ball leaves the field of play, or *precisely* where it was positioned when a player was downed, we could make relevant only whether the ball (or player) crossed a certain clearly marked threshold.

Consider: gridiron football is often called "a game of inches", but the field is measured in yards, lines are drawn at intervals of whole yards, and statistics are recorded only in whole yards. Teams have four downs to advance the ball ten yards. If they succeed, they earn another four downs. Yet despite this, the ball can be "spotted" (placed) at any point on the field, meaning that if the ball carrier is tackled between yard lines, the ball will be placed there to begin the next play; territory can be gained or lost in any fraction of a yard (or foot, or inch). There are no markings *between* the yard lines, though, and moreover only the lines marking five-yard intervals are marked all the way across the field. When the ball carrier is tackled outside of the hash marks, the ball is subsequently moved (by being tossed from the official to pick it up to an official standing at the nearest hash mark) and placed at the same yardage (which can be anywhere between two yard lines). And when there is a close call as to whether the ball has been advanced 10 yards, since there is often no yard line to go by, a comically low-tech ritual occurs. The chain crew—a pair of officials bearing poles with a 10-yard long chain between them—marches out from the visiting team sideline to the hash line where the ball is spotted, which can be more than halfway across the field. One pole is supposed to mark the previous spot of the ball and the other the line to gain a first down. A marker is attached to the chain denoting the point at which the chain crosses a five-yard line, so as to calibrate its placement upon moving it across the field. All of this takes time, and every step of the process is an opportunity for introducing error; the initial spot of the ball could be off, the poles could be misplaced, the chain could kink or stretch, etc. Each movement of the poles and chain is based solely on an individual's *estimate* of where the ball (or the pole) was relative to the sideline. But, recall, these are estimates of where things are supposed to stand *precisely*.

The farcical nature of this has not gone unnoticed and regularly prompts calls for advanced technology to more accurately track the exact position of the ball [18]. But the technology isn't ready yet, nor is it necessarily needed. Nearly all such measurements could be eliminated by redefining 'the spot' as *the last yard line the ball carrier contacts* in the direction of travel from the previous spot.[17] That is, in a game measured only in whole yards, we could stipulate that ground can be gained only occur in whole yards, whether forward or backward.[18] As a result, the precise location of the ball would seldom be of concern; it would only matter whether the ball carrier makes contact with the next yard line. If he comes up short, clearly landing somewhere between yard lines (which will be true in the vast majority of cases), there will be no question as to where the ball should be spotted (namely, the last yard line contacted). It is very easy for a human official to be mistaken by an inch or two about a ball's location; it is much harder to be mistaken by three feet.

There are other changes we might effect to make officiating easier for humans. Many of these will involve physically altering the playing space to make boundaries more salient. Here I have in mind what Collins, Evans, and Higgins [1] call "level 1" devices for "capturing" events, such as the bails in cricket, the bar in high jump, or the cup in golf. The falling of the bails *constitutes* the breaking of the wicket; the falling of the ball into the cup *constitutes* completing the hole. It is normally a simple matter for a human official to judge whether the bails have fallen or the ball is in the cup; indeed, it is hard to even imagine a scenario where human perception alone would be insufficient to decide whether the bails or a high-jump bar have fallen *and* where some more advanced technology would do better. In such a case, unaided perception would be *no worse than* more advanced technology.

---

[17] A similar rule already applies for the goal line. There, it is sufficient that any part of the ball "breaks the plane" of the goal line before being downed. It does not matter where exactly in the end zone the ball ends up; so long as it ends up somewhere past the plane of the goal line and short of the back of the end zone, it is a touchdown.

[18] The idea is to make the yard a quantum. Thus, I affectionately refer to this as "quantum football".

We could introduce similar methods for capturing events in other sports. For instance, in professional tennis, line calls are still made by humans but challenges are settled by consulting the Hawk-Eye track estimating system. The speed of the game makes it quite difficult for the human eye to tell whether the ball bounces in (which means on the line) or out; if any part of the ball touches any part of the line, the ball is in. But such calls would be much easier to make with the eye alone if tennis were more like squash. In squash, lines are *out* and the bottom half-meter of the front wall is covered by "the tin", the upper edge of which is beveled. The beveled edge of the tin is also the line above which shots must hit the front wall. Thus, when shots hit on the bottom line (out), they hit the bevel and ricochet at an unmistakably different angle than compared to a flat wall; the carom and the sound of the ball striking the tin clearly indicate the shot was out. Tennis *could be* modified analogously, by changing the criteria to make lines out of bounds and physically modifying the lines to cause the ball to rebound differently. The resulting sport would hardly ever require a system as sophisticated as Hawk-Eye to settle in/out questions. Whether such a sport is one we want to play or watch is another question.

5. Conclusions

Many will react to these proposals or others in the same vein with incredulity or revulsion. So be it. (Indeed, I think tennis modified as suggested would be ridiculous, though I am quite partial to the idea of quantum football.) These are not proposals to make sports *better tout court*. Rather, I offer these as potential examples of what sports would have to look like *if* we view *both* accuracy *and* human officiating as desiderata for sports. It is a false dilemma that we necessarily need to choose one or the other, but this is not to say there aren't tradeoffs. To have both would require making changes to how our sports are defined and played, to make the relevant facts coarse enough to be reliably judged by unaided human perception. Those who do find such changes repugnant should consider these proposals as the sort of absurdity to which a commitment to both desiderata reduces. For my part, insofar as I find the principal value in sports being the display of excellence by *the players*, I would prefer even more fine-grained criteria to allow for even finer margins of measurement and comparison. At the same time, I think the arguments in favor of maximal accuracy in officiating are compelling and conclusive. As a result, I place no value whatsoever in human officiating *as such*: if it is the best we can do given our resources, so be it; if we can do better, *let us do so*.

Others may prefer the aesthetics of sports officiated by all and only humans. As I have said, it is not wrong to want it so in and of itself. Indeed, if given the choice between an impersonal technological system and an *equally accurate* human official, I have no objection against those who would prefer the human. I wonder, though, what choice the proponents of human officiating would make between an often-inaccurate technology and a *nearly perfect human* official. I have a suspicion that the supposed good-making features of error-prone officiating would disappear if it were fallible robots in contrast to nearly-infallible humans.

In any case, this is not a choice we are likely to ever face. Our sports are not likely to be revised radically so as to bring the criteria for judging them to well within the limits of human perception. For those that admire the undeniable skills of human officials and who appreciate the excellence that they too often display, I would urge them to consider incorporating the fact-determining tasks of human officials into a sport of its own. In so doing, the inherent perceptual limitations that human officials face would become a feature, not a bug, of the contest, and the resistance to allowing them the use of technology would be more well-motivated on the grounds that doing so would make the game too easy. After all, choosing what games to play is exercising our autonomy.

Funding: This research received no external funding.

Acknowledgments: I am grateful to Adam Arico, Andrew Grace, Stuart Rachels, and Chase Wrenn for helpful conversations and feedback.

Conflicts of Interest: The author declares no conflict of interest.

References

1. Collins, H.; Evans, R.; Higgins, C. *Bad Call: Technology's Attack on Referees and Umpires and How to Fix It*; Bijker, W.E., Carlson, W.B., Pinch, T., Eds.; Inside Technology; MIT Press: Cambridge, MA, USA, 2016.
2. Ryall, E. Are there any good arguments against goal-line technology? *Sports Ethics Philos.* **2012**, *6*, 439–450. [CrossRef]
3. Johnson, C.; Jason, T. Rejecting Technology: A Normative Defense of Fallible Officiating. *Sport Ethics Philos.* **2016**, *10*, 148–160. [CrossRef]
4. Redd, N.T. Eris: The Dwarf Planet That is Pluto's Twin. 2019. Available online: https://www.space.com/28379-eris-dwarf-planet.html (accessed on 25 April 2019).
5. Brown, M. *How I Killed Pluto (and Why It Had It Coming)*; Speigel & Grau: New York, NY, USA, 2012.
6. Bordner, S.S. Call 'Em as they are: What's Wrong with Blown Calls and What to do about them. *J. Philos. Sport* **2015**, *42*, 101–120. [CrossRef]
7. Collins, H. The Philosophy of Umpiring and the Introduction of Decision-Aid Technology. *J. Philos. Sport* **2010**, *37*, 135–146. [CrossRef]
8. Griffioen, A.L. Why Jim Joyce Wasn't Wrong: Baseball and the Euthyphro Dilemma. *J. Philos. Sport* **2015**, *42*, 327–348. [CrossRef]
9. Royce, R. Refereeing and Technology - Reflections on Collins' Proposals. *J. Philos. Sport* **2012**, *39*, 53–64. [CrossRef]
10. Ryall, E. *Philosophy of Sport: Key Questions*; Bloomsbury Sport: London, UK, 2016.
11. DeLong, J.E. Neuropsychology Behind the Plate. *Sport Ethics Philos.* **2017**, *11*, 385–395. [CrossRef]
12. Russell, J.S. The concept of a call in baseball. *J. Philos. Sport* **1997**, *24*, 21–37. [CrossRef]
13. Russell, J.S. Are Rules All an Umpire Has to Work With? *J. Philos. Sport* **1999**, *26*, 27–49. [CrossRef]
14. Borge, S. Sport Records Are Social Facts. *Sport Ethics Philos.* **2015**, *9*, 351–362. [CrossRef]
15. Suits, B. *The Grasshopper: Games, Life and Utopia*; Broadview Press: Peterborough, UK, 2005.
16. Simon, R. Deserving to be lucky: Reflections on the role of luck and desert in sports. *J. Philos. Sport* **2007**, *34*, 13–25. [CrossRef]
17. Williams, M.T. MLB Umpires Missed 34,294 Ball-Strike Calls in 2018. Bring on Robo-Umps? Boston University, 2019. Available online: https://www.bu.edu/today/2019/mlb-umpires-strike-zone-accuracy/ (accessed on 30 April 2019).
18. Victor, D. Why Doesn't the N.F.L. Use Tracking Technology for First-Down Calls? 2019. Available online: https://www.nytimes.com/2017/12/18/sports/nfl-first-down-measurement.html (accessed on 29 April 2019).

© 2019 by the author. Licensee MDPI, Basel, Switzerland. This article is an open access article distributed under the terms and conditions of the Creative Commons Attribution (CC BY) license (http://creativecommons.org/licenses/by/4.0/).

Article

Something's Got to Give: Reconsidering the Justification for a Gender Divide in Sport

Andria Bianchi [1,2]

[1] Department of Bioethics, University Health Network, Toronto, ON M5G 2A2, Canada; andria.bianchi@uhn.ca; Tel.: +1-416-333-6677
[2] Department of Philosophy, University of Waterloo, Waterloo, ON N2L 3G1, Canada

Received: 19 April 2019; Accepted: 12 May 2019; Published: 15 May 2019

Abstract: The question of whether transgender athletes should be permitted to compete in accordance with their gender identity is an evolving debate. Most competitive sports have male and female categories. One of the primary challenges with this categorization system, however, is that some transgender athletes (and especially transgender women) may be prevented from competing in accordance with their gender identity. The reason for this restriction is because of the idea that transgender women have an unfair advantage over their cisgender counterparts; this is seen as a problem since sports are typically guided a principle called 'the skill thesis', which suggests that sports are supposed to determine who is most skillful by maintaining a fair starting point. In this paper, I argue that if the skill thesis ought to be maintained and there continues to exist no conclusive evidence in support of unfair advantages possessed by trans women, then we may want to re-consider the gender binary in sport. Rather than having male/female categories, it may make more sense to categorize athletes based other sport-specific factors (e.g., height, weight, etc.). This may help to maintain the skill thesis while at the same time removing potentially unfair and discriminatory barriers against transgender athletes.

Keywords: transgender; trans women; sport; testosterone; gender; gender binary

1. Introduction

Mainstream discussions centred on trans-inclusivity have become ubiquitous. This increase has influenced some common social practices to change, such as having gender neutral washroom facilities and developing gender neutral dance studios (where traditional male/female roles are non-existent) [1,2]. The sports world, however, continues to grapple with challenges and controversies involving transgender people. The male/female gender binary continues to exist in most sporting events, and the idea that transgender women may possess unfair advantages is a widespread belief.

In 2017, I responded to the claim that transgender women possess unfair advantages when competing in female categories because of high testosterone levels [3]. The argument against trans women competing in female categories is motivated by the idea that a person's success in sports should be based solely on skill and not on unequal advantages or starting points between competitors; this is referred to as the skill thesis. In response, I suggested that genetic advantages already exist in sports, making it such that a fair and equal starting point is impossible to achieve. I ultimately suggested, however, that if maintaining the skill thesis *and* mitigating unfair advantages is important, then both transgender and cisgender athletes should be subjected to a handicap system.

There continues to be significant ethical debate regarding how to manage transgender women in sport; minimal headway has been made since 2017. In response to the ongoing debate, this article expands on my previous argument by considering the importance and suitability of the male/female gender binary. While recognizing that the skill thesis may not be seen as entirely foundational for everyone, I suggest that *if we want to maintain the skill thesis* as a guiding principle in sport (since it is currently, indeed, a guiding principle), then we need to reconsider whether it makes sense to categorize athletes based on their sex assignment at all. Perhaps it may be more sensible to categorize athletes based on other potentially relevant factors, such as height, weight, testosterone levels (if it is found that testosterone levels are, in fact, relevant), etc. In the first section of this paper, I offer a brief description of what it means to be transgender. I subsequently give an overview of some of the primary cases and controversies involving transgender women competing in female categories. The third section of this paper describes my previous proposal to implement a handicap system for both transgender and cisgender athletes. Finally, I expand on this proposal and ultimately suggest that it may be time to reconsider the gender binary in sports; this proposal also serves as a different, yet relevant expansion of Torbjörn Tännsjö's argument and Melanie Newbould's proposal to eliminate sex specific categories [4,5]. Reconsidering the gender binary may be a worthwhile pursuit in order to: (1) maintain the skill thesis and (2) establish an inclusive and equally competitive environment for all athletes. An alternative approach may be to simply abandon the skill thesis and allow transgender women to compete in female categories. Because the skill thesis is so pervasive, however, this paper considers strategies that maintain it as a guiding principle.

2. What Does it Mean to be Transgender?

The term 'transgender' or 'trans' is used to describe people "with diverse gender identities and gender expressions that do not conform to stereotypical ideas about what it means to be a girl/woman or boy/man in society [6]." A transgender person identifies with a gender that differs from their sex, where a person's sex is usually assigned at birth and based on factors such as hormones and reproductive systems. It is typically assumed that a person who is transgender is either a trans man (i.e., a person whose sex assignment is female and gender identity is male) or a trans woman. However, the term can more broadly refer to a person who "identif[ies] themselves as having no gender, a mix of both genders, or a gender that changes over time [7]." The term 'cisgender' or 'cis' describes people whose gender identity accords with their sex assignment (e.g., a person with a female sex assignment who identifies as a woman).

According to the National Center for Transgender Equality in the United States, a person of any age may realize they are transgender [8]. Some people know that they are trans from a young age. Others may spend much of their life feeling as though they do not fit in and/or do not accord with expectations and assumptions regarding their gender but are unable to name the reason. However, "[a]s transgender people become more visible in the media and in community life ... more transgender people are able to name and understand their own experiences and may feel safer and more comfortable sharing it with others [8]." This may be, at least in part, the reason that an increasing number of people have been openly identifying as trans over the last few years [9–11].

Although more people are identifying as transgender, normative assumptions regarding the male/female gender binary continue to exist (e.g., ideas about what a person's sexual anatomy should be, appropriate pronoun usages, etc.). Consequently, people whose gender identities extend beyond and/or differ from normative conceptions are often judged, marginalized, and shunned from the normalcy that cisgender people are granted in society (more specifically, cisgender people whose gender expression[1] accords with normative expectations) [12]. There are many examples of some of the challenges that transgender people encounter on a regular basis. One of these examples is that of employment, where occurrences such as the "refusal to hire, privacy violations, harassment, and even physical and sexual violence on the job" are prevalent amongst the trans population [13]. A high risk of suicidality is another consequence that sometimes stems from the discrimination and stigma that trans people face [14]; the TransPulse Survey (a survey that considered the health needs

---

[1] The term 'gender expression' is the way that a person expresses their gender identity.

of transgender people in the province of Ontario, Canada) found that 77% of survey respondents seriously contemplated and 45% attempted suicide [15]. Moreover, a 2017 poll found that "[r]oughly one in six LGBTQ[2] people say they have avoided medical care (18%) and calling the police (15%), even when in need, due to concern that they would be discriminated against because of their LGBTQ identity [16,17]."

As a result of these challenges and possible consequences, there are a growing number of support services available for transgender citizens and new human rights policies that aim to protect them from discrimination and marginalization [18,19]. Additionally, there are "an increasing number of countries liberalising their regulations on [sex] assignment (and reassignment) of legal sex [20]." In response to this liberalisation movement and in order to promote inclusion and equality, some common social practices have changed. More specifically, social practices that used to be based on the male/female gender binary have expanded their scope to accommodate those whose gender identity extends beyond the binary. A good example of this change is washroom accessibility, where the idea is that transgender people should have the right to access a washroom that accords with their identified gender [1,2]. While this is still a growing phenomenon in North America, it is becoming more common in the United Kingdom to not have gendered washrooms at all.[3] Additionally, and while there is still much work to be done, some healthcare organizations are starting to explicitly inform potential patients that they are an inclusive and welcoming space for the LGBTQ community [21,22].

3. Involving Trans Persons in Sport: A Brief Overview of Cases and Controversies

Although some organizations and social practices now support and accommodate transgender people, one industry that continues to grapple with transgender participation is that of the sports industry. Most sporting events categorize athletes based on the male/female gender binary (e.g., male cycling and female cycling, male swimming and female swimming). This poses a challenge for transgender athletes who want to compete in accordance with their gender identity and how they live the rest of their life. The reason that transgender people are often not automatically allowed to compete in the category that aligns with their gender identity is because of a widespread idea that they may possess an unfair advantage in comparison to their cisgender counterparts. This argument is specifically used to criticize and/or to prevent *transgender women* from competing in female categories, where the idea is that trans women may have an unfair competitive advantage in comparison to cisgender women athletes. The advantage is supposedly based on the effects that may result from a cisgender male's androgen levels (i.e., testosterone), where increased testosterone is thought to contribute to increased strength and speed. As noted in their evaluation of gender segregation in athletics, Foddy and Savulescu say that "[i]t is entirely because of this difference [in having higher levels of androgens] that we consider it unfair to expect women to compete with men in athletic sports." [23] (p. 1184). So, if a trans woman has the biological characteristics of a cisgender male, then the idea is that they will possess athletic advantages that a cisgender woman is unable to naturally attain, thereby making their participation unfair.

The argument that trans women may possess an unfair advantage is seen as problematic by the sports industry because sports are typically guided by a principle called the 'skill thesis' which I have discussed before [3]. The skill thesis is the idea that athletes ought to be rewarded based on skill; the most skillful athlete should be the person who wins [3] (p. 233), [24] (p. 13). The skill thesis is not based on motor skills in particular, but rather the skill(s) that may result from a person having physiological strength, speed, and power, which may be influenced by testosterone levels.[4] In order for the skill thesis to be realized, athletes need to start from an equal playing field; this requires

---

[2] LGBTQ is the acronym that is used to describe the lesbian, gay, bi-sexual, transgender, and queer community.
[3] Thanks to Dr. Emily Ryall for informing me of this more common practice in the United Kingdom.
[4] Thanks to Dr. Emily Ryall for highlighting this distinction for my consideration.

that advantageous external influences (e.g., equipment) and internal influences (e.g., steroid use) are mitigated and monitored. It is widely thought that trans women possess excessively high levels of testosterone in a way that upsets the skill thesis.

While the focus of this paper is on transgender women, it is also the case that some intersex people have encountered similar criticisms to trans women because of the idea that they also possess high testosterone levels and have an unfair advantage. The term 'intersex' is used to classify people who are "born with reproductive systems, chromosomes and/or hormones that are not easily characterized as male or female. This might include a woman with XY chromosomes or a man with ovaries instead of testes [25]." It is important to highlight that transgender women and intersex persons are importantly distinct; "transgender persons are typically born with male/female anatomy but feel as though they are in the wrong body [26] (p. 99)", whereas intersex persons do not necessarily feel as though they are in the wrong body, even though their "phenotype or genotype is atypical with respect to sex markers [26] (p. 99)." The only commonality that may exist amongst transgender and intersex athletes (that is relevant for this paper) is that they are both criticized for having an unfair advantage due to high testosterone levels. Because of this same criticism, I consider examples involving both transgender and intersex athletes below. Ultimately, however, the crux of this paper is focused on transgender women athletes who arguably encounter greater criticisms because of their cisgender male anatomy and changed gender identity.

There have been a number of cases discussed in the media that consider whether transgender women and/or intersex athletes should be allowed to compete in female categories—I will discuss a sample these of cases below.

One of the first controversial cases involving a transgender woman athlete occurred in 1976, involving a professional tennis player named Renee Richards. Richards was scheduled to compete in the female category in tennis, and she was asked to take a sex test. Upon refusing to take the test, Richards was banned from competing [27] (p. 235). She subsequently brought her case to the US Supreme Court who agreed that the sex test requirement was 'grossly unfair, discriminatory and inequitable' [3] (p. 232), [27] (p. 235). Although Richards was permitted to compete in female categories after this ruling, 25 women withdrew from a future tournament because of the belief that Richards retained unfair benefits and muscular advantages of a cisgender male [3] (p. 232), [27] (p. 236).

An additional case which I have described previously [3], is that of mixed martial artist (MMA) Fallon Fox, who was also criticized for having an unfair advantage over her competitors because of her testosterone levels. Fox is a transgender woman and was criticized for competing in the female division because of her differing sex assignment. In 2011 (shortly after Fox's controversial case), the International Association of Athletics Federation (IAAF) developed new regulations for determining athletes' eligibility to compete in female categories. The new regulations required athletes to have testosterone levels of less than 10nmol/L at least twelve months before competing [28].

A more recent case involving a transgender woman is that of Laurel Hubbard. Hubbard is a weightlifter and a transgender woman from New Zealand who competed in the female weightlifting category. In 2017, Hubbard won an international weightlifting title in the over-90-kilogram division. Although Hubbard had "a year's worth of blood tests showing . . . no more testosterone running through her veins than any of the other female weightlifters competing in the Australian International" [29], the idea that she had an unfair advantage due to her testosterone levels remained present.

Another case where a female athlete was criticized for her testosterone levels is that of intersex athlete Dutee Chand. Chand is a sprinter from India who was criticized for having high testosterone levels after winning gold in the 200-m sprint and the 400-m relay race at the 2014 Asian Junior Athletics Championships. In order to determine her gender, Chand was subjected to a blood test, in addition to "a chromosome analysis, an M.R.I. and a gynecological exam that she found mortifying [30]." She was banned from competing in female categories and advised to take hormone-suppressing drugs or have surgery in order to mitigate her testosterone levels. In response, Chand appealed to the Court of Arbitration for Sport (CAS) in 2015 "questioning why she should be forced to have surgery if her condition was natural and she was not ill [31]." Among a number of arguments, Chand claimed that "there was no scientific support for the performance-enhancing effect of high levels of endogenous testosterone [20]."

As a result of Chand's appeal, the CAS questioned whether and/or to what extent an athletic advantage may be possessed by athletes who have naturally high levels of testosterone. In light of this question, the CAS suspended the IAAF's hyperandrogenism regulation and gave them two years to offer more scientific evidence demonstrating the link between "enhanced testosterone levels and improved athletic performance [31]." If no scientific evidence is produced, then the hyperandrogenism regulation would be void. In support of their decision, the CAS said that "[a]lthough athletics events are divided into discrete male and female categories, sex in humans is not simply binary [31]." Moreover, they argued that "[s]ince there are separate categories of male and female competition, it is necessary for the I.A.A.F. to formulate a basis for the division of athletes into male and female categories for the benefit of the broad class of female athletes. The basis chosen should be necessary, reasonable and proportionate to the legitimate objective being pursued [31]." Finally, the CAS found Chand to have established that:

> "[I]t is prima facie discriminatory to require female athletes to undergo testing for levels of endogenous testosterone when male athletes do not. In addition, it is not in dispute that the Hyperandrogenism Regulations place restrictions on the eligibility of certain female athletes to compete on the basis of a natural physical characteristic (namely the amount of testosterone that their bodies produce naturally) and are therefore prima facie discriminatory on that basis too [32]."

In alignment with the CAS, the International Olympic Committee (IOC) stopped regulating women's natural testosterone levels until the IAAF case concluded. The IAAF did not produce sufficient evidence about potential advantages assumed by hyperandrogenous women as a result of increased testosterone levels by the 2017 deadline.

In 2018, however, the IAAF published new criteria for athletes competing in female categories [32]. The new criteria apply to five track events and require all female athletes with 'differences of sexual development' (DSDs) to reduce their testosterone levels to below 5 nmol/L. The change of acceptable testosterone level was based on research conducted by Dr. Bermon of the IAAF Medical and Science Department, who said that there is a "performance advantage in female athletes with DSD over the track distances covered by this rule [32]." Although this is the present standard, the research produced by Dr. Bermon was recently contested by Pielke et al., who suggest that the scientific integrity of the research is flawed [33]. So, it appears that we may be back to a place of uncertainty in terms of knowing whether and/or how much testosterone may lead to significant advantages.

The final and most recent case that I will discuss here is that of Caster Semenya. Semenya, who is believed to be intersex, was the 800-metre track and field winner at the 2009 world championships, 2012 Olympics, and 2016 Olympics. After her victory in 2009, she was criticized for being "too masculine", barred from the competition, and subjected to sex tests. According to available reports, Semenya has a condition called hyperandrogenism, which is when a person's body produces a large amount of testosterone [34]. Consequently, Semenya was seen as having an unfair advantage in comparison to other athletes in the female category.

As mentioned above, the IAAF published new criteria for athletes competing in female categories in response to Chand's case. The criteria were supposed to come into effect in November 2018, but Semenya challenged the rules to the CAS [34]. In response, the CAS granted a panel of three judges the responsibility of performing an evaluation and reaching a verdict about Semenya's appeal. After months of deliberation, the verdict was finally announced, requiring Semenya and others with high testosterone levels to lower them [35]. While some agree with the CAS verdict, many athletes, fans, and organizations have spoken out against the ruling. For instance, Canada's sport and science minister, Kirsty Duncan, reportedly said "I do not think a sport organization should be deciding who is a woman or what makes a woman. I don't think any sport organization should be telling an athlete to alter their body chemistry. We ask that our athletes do not take drugs. Now an athlete is being told her alter her natural body chemistry [35]." While this ruling was initially motivated by and challenged by intersex athletes, the outcome of requiring athletes to have certain testosterone levels will plausibly influence transgender women as well.

4. Trans Women in Sport: Discussing a Previous Argument

In a 2017 article, I discussed the skill thesis and the topic of transgender women competing in female categories [3]. The purpose of the article was to respond to the question of whether trans women should be allowed to compete in female categories. I will briefly describe my previous argument here and then propose a novel expansion of it in the section below (Section 4).

I commenced my 2017 article "Transgender Women in Sport" by suggesting that while the idea that transgender women possess high testosterone levels is a frequently used justification to preclude them from competing in female categories, the science behind this argument is vague.[5] In fact, it may be the case that "'the presence of high testosterone does not guarantee an increased level of performance. Rather, the way that one's body responds to testosterone is relevant (Schultz 2011) [3] (p. 233).'" I subsequently argue that *if* this is correct (i.e., the idea that high testosterone does not guarantee an increased performance level in and of itself)[6] then it seems that the *real argument* against trans women competing in female categories is "based on the assumption that they have a higher level of *effective* testosterone in comparison to their cisgender competitors [3] (p. 233)." I use the term effective testosterone to refer to "the testosterone that can be effectively used by one's body in order to benefit or enhance one's performance [3] (p. 234)." And if it is the case that trans women have unfairly high levels of effective testosterone, then they may be unfairly advantaged from the perspective of the skill thesis.

After considering the possibility that trans women may have high effective testosterone levels such that skill thesis is undermined, I argue that the skill thesis is, in fact, already undermined because of the natural genetic lottery. The genetic lottery makes it such that some people are going to be advantaged in ways that others are not, making it impossible to commence a sporting event from a place of even proximate equality amongst athletes; a male/female gender binary in sports does not allow the skill thesis to properly exist [3,23]. I draw on a couple of examples to illustrate this point, such as the case of Michael Phelps, whose genetic attributes provide him with many advantages that his competitors probably lack (e.g., size 14 feet, the fact that he is double jointed, his large 'wingspan') [3,23,36]. So, if genetic advantages already exist in sport even though the skill thesis exists, then there may be a reason to question the legitimacy of the argument against trans women competing in female categories.[7]

After highlighting that genetically advantageous attributes already exist in sport, I argue that we can proceed in either one of two ways when it comes to considering if transgender women should be permitted to compete in female categories: (1) we can accept that the skill thesis is unrealistic and allow trans women to compete in female categories even if they have an increased level of effective testosterone or (2) we can argue that the skill thesis ought to be maintained and that all potentially unfair genetic advantages need to be mitigated in male and female categories for both cisgender and transgender athletes. While I recognize that skill thesis/striving for equality amongst athletes may be problematic (as also mentioned by Gleaves and Lehrbach [37] (pp. 314, 315)), I ultimately decide to explore the second option (i.e., mitigating potentially unfair advantages) given the prevalence of

---

[5] Furthermore, it appears that the science is still vague if Dr. Bermon's narrow research produced flawed results.
[6] The idea that trans women have a high level of effective testosterone is still unproven.
[7] In my former article, I discuss that there may be a distinction to be made between different kinds of genetic features. When considering transgender women in sport, it may be relevant to consider whether cisgender women would be capable of achieving the same kinds of advantages that trans women possess. If no, then it may be the case that only trans women who undergo certain hormonal interventions should be permitted to compete in female categories. While recognizing that this may be a possibility, I focus the article on all trans women given the broad range of persons who may identify as a woman irrespective of interventions [3].

the skill thesis. I specifically focus on mitigating effective testosterone levels since that is the primary attribute that seems to preclude trans women from competing in accordance with their gender identity.

In concluding the 2017 paper, I argue that one way to maintain the skill thesis and to mitigate effective testosterone levels is to implement a handicap system that focuses on effective testosterone levels.[8] Handicap systems are already used in some sports (e.g., golf) to "assist players to play on somewhat equal terms so that the results accurately reflect players' skill [3] (p. 238)." With this goal in mind, I argue that a handicap system may be the most helpful way to allow transgender women to compete in female categories by recognizing and accounting for the way that effective testosterone levels may undermine the skill thesis. Ultimately, I propose that the effective testosterone levels of transgender and cisgender athletes ought to be calculated and compared to one another in order to determine if anyone is unfairly advantaged. If an athlete has an excessive amount of effective testosterone then I argue that the corresponding advantage would need to be considered when determining their ranking (e.g., whether they deserve to be granted first place or, in fact, whether their effective testosterone level provided them with an unfair advantage such that a first place finish does not accord with the skill thesis). By using a handicap system, I argue that the appropriate winner can be determined while at the same time allowing trans women to fairly compete in female categories.

5. Next Steps: A Potential Re-Consideration of the Gender Divide in Sport

The question of whether transgender women athletes should be permitted to compete in female categories has not been resolved. In fact, the CAS is currently exploring the issue in order to determine an ethically defensible and scientifically valid solution [38]. Perhaps this provides some justification to revisit my proposed handicap system mentioned above. The other option previously put forward (which may also be worth reconsidering) is to abandon the skill thesis and allow transgender athletes to compete in accordance with their gender identity; this option may be justified by the fact that genetic advantages already exist in sport. However, it also seems plausible that a third option may be worth considering, and this option may serve as a natural extension to my previous proposal.

As mentioned above, my previous article concluded that a handicap system ought to be implemented in order to maintain the skill thesis and allow trans women to participate in female categories. This conclusion begs the question, however, as to whether a gender divide is necessary to maintain at all, or whether a larger change may be warranted. More specifically, it seems that my previous proposal leads to the suggestion that instead of trying to maintain the skill thesis by mitigating unfair advantages within sex specific categories, it may make more sense to simply abolish the categories themselves.

There are a couple of theorists who have already considered the relevance of maintaining sex specific categories in sport. In 2011, Foddy and Savalescu considered whether segregating sports based on gender performance is defensible, where they focus on intersex athletes and Semenya's case [23]. The authors highlight that gender is not binary and they briefly consider the possibility and challenges of using testosterone levels to categorize athletes (similar to my previous proposal) [23] (p. 1187). Ultimately, they conclude that there is no justification for excluding intersex athletes from current categories because of genetic variants [23] (p. 1188).

Another theorist who has considered sex specific categories in sport is Torbjörn Tännsjö [4]. Tännsjö argues that sex specific categories ought to be abolished. Rather than being primarily motivated by the skill thesis, however, Tännsjö's argument is based on the idea that sexual discrimination is morally objectionable. More specifically, he argues that if sexual discrimination (namely, the idea that women are treated differently and as less capable than men) is morally objectionable in most contexts, then it should also be deemed problematic in the sports industry [4] (p. 347). In order to truly promote

---

[8] My argument in this paper is based on the assumption that effective testosterone levels are, in fact, relevant to determining whether a transgender woman is unfairly advantaged.

gender equality and to achieve the primary purpose of sporting events (namely, to determine the best athlete), Tännsjö says that a gender binary system should not exist. All athletes should compete against one another and the best athlete should have the opportunity to win, regardless of whether this is a cisgender or transgender male or female.[9]

There exist two potential challenges in response to Tännsjö's argument. First, one may respond by arguing that sex specific categories in sport are not an unjust form of sexual discrimination in and of themselves and only *unjust* discriminatory categories are problematic. For instance, if evidence *does* exist which suggests that male and female athletes ought to be categorized separately in order to maintain fairness and/or if female athletes *want* to be categorized separately, then perhaps sex specific categories may be justifiable. Tännsjö's argument does not lend any possibility to these potential responses because his view is based on the assumption that the gender binary in sports is a form of unjust sexual discrimination.

The second argument that could be used to oppose Tännsjö's proposal has to do with ensuring that cisgender women are provided with the opportunity to compete in competitive sports in general; proponents of this argument would support the maintenance of sex specific categories (based on sex assignments). Originally, competitive sporting events, such as the Olympics, only permitted male athletes to compete. It was not until the 1900 Paris Summer Games that sex specific events were established and women were allowed to participate [39]. The fact that female categories in sport were established after male categories, in addition to the challenges that many cisgender women continue to experience when it comes to being treated as equal members of society, has led some scholars to maintain a protective lens in support of specific female categories for cisgender women athletes. The argument goes as follows: Allowing transgender women (i.e., people with a male sex assignment) to compete against cisgender women in sport may result in more transgender women being successful because of their male physiology (e.g., increased testosterone, height, weight, foot size, arm length, etc.), consequently resulting in less representation from cisgender women athletes. This consequence would be detrimental to the progress that women have made in in the sports industry. Thus, the argument ultimately suggests that sex specific categories ought to be maintained, and that transgender women should not be permitted to compete in female categories in order to (1) maintain the skill thesis and (2) ensure equal representation in sport for cisgender women athletes.

In response to this argument regarding cisgender representation, it may be worth noting that there is still no conclusive evidence to support the claim that transgender women are higher performers than their cisgender counterparts, and evidence is important when it comes to developing rules [40] (p. 14). As discussed in their systematic review about sport and transgender people, Jones et al. say that there is "no direct or consistent research suggesting transgender female individuals (or male individuals) have an athletic advantage at any stage of their transition (e.g., cross-sex hormones, gender-confirming-surgery) [41]." Melanie Newbould makes a similar claim, saying that "the hypothesis that women with testes have an advantage has not been subjected to close scientific scrutiny [5]." Furthermore, Newbould says that even if high testosterone levels provide athletes with some helpful benefits, "athletic ability depends on a much wider range of factors such as natural talent for the sport, genetic composition, personal interest and motivation, appropriate training, nutrition and so on [5] (p. 257)." One may respond to Jones et al. and Newbould, however, by saying that the majority of world sport records are held by cisgender men, thereby suggesting that that there appears to be some advantageous differences that are a consequence of cisgender male physiology [42]. Relatedly, one may argue that transgender women who have *not* undergone any physiological transition measures may possess certain advantages in comparison to those who have pursued hormonal interventions. Although there may be differences amongst some cisgender men and women making it such that some transgender women may possess certain advantages, the lack of conclusive evidence makes it such

---

[9] Note: Tännsjö does not focus on transgender men and women but rather cisgender women in general.

that it may be premature to preclude an entire group of people (i.e., transgender individuals) from competing in accordance with their gender identity at this point in time.

Since there currently exists no strong conclusive evidence in support of the unfair advantages possessed by transgender women (who either have or have not undergone a transition-related surgery), it may be unfair to prevent them from competing in female categories. However, *even if* evidence eventually shows that some transgender women have an unfair advantage, then this still does not necessarily mean that preventing them from competing in female categories is the best option to pursue *if* we want to maintain the skill thesis. As mentioned above, the skill thesis is a prevalent guiding principle in sport, where the goal is to ensure that the most skillful athlete can win in the absence of unfair advantages [3,40] (p. 10). The skill thesis does *not* suggest that that sex specific categories should be the focus of enabling athletes to start from an equal playing field. So, instead of categorizing and separating athletes based on sex, perhaps athletes should instead be categorized based on something else. This is precisely the idea that Newbould considers when contemplating options for transgender athletes who have and have not undergone surgical interventions. Newbould proposes that it may make sense to categorize people based on their testosterone level rather than sex assignment (e.g., high testosterone and low testosterone groupings) [5] (p. 258). This is similar to my 2017 proposal regarding effective testosterone and the handicap system.

There are multiple problems with Newbould's suggestion and my previous proposal. One of these problems is that effective testosterone levels cannot be measured at the present time. And if it is the case that how one's body *uses* testosterone (i.e., effective testosterone) is the primary indicator of potentially unfair advantages, then the inability to measure it is problematic. Also, and most importantly, it is still unclear whether testosterone is, in fact, the primary factor that poses possible advantages for transgender women. Because of this uncertainty, it seems moot to focus on testosterone levels when it comes to considering advantages within sex specific sports categories and/or as the primary factor for new categories.

Instead of pursuing my previous proposal or Newbould's suggestion, perhaps considering factors other than solely testosterone would be more apt when it comes to contemplating what fair categories in sport might look like. So, rather than categorizing people based on their sex assignment, a new system might categorize athletes based on potentially more relevant factors, where the factors could be sport-dependent (e.g., high jump might primarily take into account athletes' heights and testosterone levels, swimming might primarily take into account athletes' foot sizes, heights, arm spans, etc.). According to this proposal, the development of and any changes that are made to categorization criteria would be based on characteristics that are most relevant to specific sports as determined by pertinent stakeholders (e.g., sports organizations, athletes, etc.), thereby allowing sports organizations to separate athletes with certain types of genetic advantages into categories of their own, if possible. If this kind of categorization system were to occur, then it might be the case that some sports would end up separating persons based on their sex assignment, but their sex assignment alone would not determine the categories. So, if some athletes just so happen to compete against others who have the same sex assignment, then this would be dependent on factors that extend beyond their sex.

The proposal to eliminate sex specific categories in favour of categorizing athletes based on other potentially more relevant criteria seeks to maintain the skill thesis, making it a natural extension to my previous proposal (i.e., the handicap system) [3]. It also seeks to eliminate potentially discriminatory and/or unjustified/arbitrary classifications based on sex assignment alone. The difference between this new idea of categorizing people based on factors other than sex and the handicap system is that my former proposal still maintained sex specific categories and tried to mitigate unfair advantages within the gender binary system; the new proposal does not. Furthermore, my motivation for reconsidering the defensibility of male/female categories in sport is different from Tännsjö's. My primary motive is based on maintaining the skill thesis given its prevalence in the sports world, and the skill thesis cannot be achieved with sex specific categories irrespective of whether evidence develops that deems transgender women to have an unfair advantage. As a consequence of reconsidering the gender divide, a more inclusive athletic environment for transgender athletes will be established. At the present time, transgender women athletes are frequently shunned from competitive sport environments at least in part because sex specific categories exist and the idea that they have an unfair advantage is widespread. One way to address this problem is to reconsider the gender divide and eliminate sex specific categories in favour of a different categorization system. The option to abolish the gender divide would also influence athletic events to be more welcoming and accepting of non-binary athletes since one's sex assignment and gender identity would be irrelevant to the categories.

One potential problem with this new proposal is that if cisgender male athletes just so happen to have physiological advantages that enable them to compete at a different (i.e., higher) performance level than cisgender women, then cisgender women may be excluded from competitive sports. This is a significant concern from an equality standpoint, especially since women often encounter disadvantages in society and this performance variance could potentially and negatively influence their status in other domains [43]. In one respect, however, if every competitive sport has multiple categories based on relevant factors then there will plausibly be a smaller likelihood that cisgender women will be completely excluded. For instance, if all competitive swimming events have categories for people with wingspan X (i.e., a large span) and wingspan Y (i.e. a shorter span), in addition to other factors, then cisgender women may be more likely to be included if it just so happens that most cisgender male competitors have wingspan X + other relevant factors and most cisgender women have wingspan X. If this turns out to not be the case, however, then perhaps sports organizations would want to develop categories for certain sports that will take into account cisgender women athletes for representation and inclusivity purposes. At the same time, it would be important to ensure that any categories developed are not seen as 'lesser than' the others, which may be hard to achieve. Ultimately, the existence of this potential problem does not in and of itself justify the maintenance of our current sport categories, but it does encourage us to ensure that we thoughtfully approach any new recommendations.

6. Conclusions

Most sporting events are currently based on the male/female gender binary. This sex specific categorization is unhelpful, however, when it comes to managing transgender women athletes who are criticized for having an unfair advantage over their cisgender counterparts. One of the primary reasons that transgender women are criticized is because of the idea that they may have high testosterone levels, resulting in increased levels of performance. Cases such as Renee Richard's, Caster Semenya's, Fallon Fox's, Laurel Hubbard's, and Dutee Chand's have brought this issue to the forefront of the sports world. Although the topic of including transgender women in sport is being debated, there currently exists no conclusive evidence to support the argument that some trans women may possess unfair advantages and/or that these advantages are somehow different than other advantages that may already exist in sport.

Current efforts to manage the debate are primarily based on the maintenance of sex specific categories in sport, which is guided by the skill thesis. In a previous article, however, I showed that the skill thesis cannot be achieved because of the natural genetic lottery, which offers potentially unfair advantages to certain athletes. If the skill thesis continues to be a guiding principle in sport, then it may make sense to not only mitigate potentially unfair advantages in sex specific categories (which is what I previously suggested) but also to abolish the gender divide. Rather than separating athletes based on their sex assignment to try to achieve the skill thesis, perhaps alternative factors ought to be considered. Newbould proposes that factors such as testosterone levels ought to be the basis from which athletes are categorized. Similarly, I suggest that factors such as testosterone or other relevant factors (depending on the sport) ought to be taken into account. Reconsidering the legitimacy of the current gender divide in sport may allow the skill thesis to be better attained and lead to a more inclusive environment for all athletes, regardless of their gender identity and sex assignment.

Funding: This research received no external funding.

Acknowledgments: I would like to thank Dr. Christopher Grafos for his thoughtful feedback on earlier versions of this manuscript. Also, many thanks to Dr. Emily Ryall for her recommendations and support on the development of this paper.

Conflicts of Interest: The author declares no conflict of interest.

References

1. Goodyear, S. Transgender Bathroom Debate Has Students Wondering What the Big Deal Is. *CBC News*, 24 May 2016. Available online: https://www.cbc.ca/news/canada/transgender-school-policies-bathrooms-student-voices-1.3589717 (accessed on 19 April 2019).
2. U.S. Department of Labor-Occupational Safety and Health Administration. A Guide to Restroom Access for Transgender Workers. 2015. Available online: https://www.dol.gov/asp/policy-development/TransgenderBathroomAccessBestPractices.pdf (accessed on 19 April 2019).
3. Bianchi, A. Transgender Woen in Sport. *J. Philos. Sport* **2017**, *44*, 229–242. [CrossRef]
4. Tännsjö, T. Against Sexual Discrimination in Sports. In *Values in Sport: Elitism, Nationalism, Gender Equality and the Scientific Manufacturing of Winners*, 1st ed.; Tamburrini, C., Tännsjö, T., Eds.; Taylor & Francis: London, UK, 2000; pp. 101–115.
5. Newbould, M.J. What do we do about women athletes with testes? *J. Med. Ethics* **2016**, *42*, 256–259. [CrossRef] [PubMed]
6. Trans/Transgender. The 519 Glossary of Terms. Available online: http://www.the519.org/education-training/glossary (accessed on 19 April 2019).
7. Ryall, E. *Philosophy of Sport: Key Questions*; Bloomsbury: London, UK, 2016.
8. National Center for Transgender Equality. How Does Someone Know That They Are Transgender? 2016. Available online: https://transequality.org/issues/resources/frequently-asked-questions-about-transgender-people (accessed on 19 April 2019).
9. Increase in Transgender Kids. *Castanet.net*. 2012. Available online: http://www.castanet.net/news/World/71255/Increase-in-transgender-kids (accessed on 19 April 2019).
10. Associated Press. Sex Change Treatment for Kids on the Rise. *CBS News*. 20 February 2012. Available online: http://www.cbsnews.com/news/sex-change-treatment-for-kids-on-the-rise/ (accessed on 19 April 2019).
11. Weiler, N. Transgender Kids: 'Exploding' Number of Children, Parents Seek Clinical Help. *Mercury News*, 5 June 2015. Available online: http://www.mercurynews.com/2015/06/05/transgender-kids-exploding-number-of-children-parents-seek-clinical-help/ (accessed on 19 April 2019).
12. Gender Expression. Available online: http://www.the519.org/education-training/glossary (accessed on 28 January 2019).
13. National Center for Transgender Equality. Housing & Homelessness. Available online: https://transequality.org/issues/housing-homelessness (accessed on 19 April 2019).
14. National Center for Transgender Equality. Health & HIV. Available online: https://transequality.org/issues/health-hiv (accessed on 19 April 2019).
15. Bauer, G.; Boyce, M.; Coleman, T.; Kaay, M.; Scanlon, K.; Travers, R. *Who Are Trans People in Ontario?* Report No:1(1); Trans PULSE E-Bulletin: Toronto, ON, Canada, 2010; Available online: http://transpulseproject.ca/research/who-are-trans-people-in-ontario/ (accessed on 19 April 2019).
16. NPR; The Robert Wood Johnson Foundation; Harvard T.H. Chan School of Public Health. *Discrimination in America: Experiences and Views of LGBTQ Americans*. Available online: https://www.npr.org/documents/2017/nov/npr-discrimination-lgbtq-final.pdf (accessed on 19 April 2019).
17. Powell, A. The Problems with LGBTQ Health Care. *The Harvard Gazette*. 26 March 2018. Available online: https://news.harvard.edu/gazette/story/2018/03/health-care-providers-need-better-understanding-of-lgbtq-patients-harvard-forum-says/ (accessed on 19 April 2019).
18. United Nations. *Ban Calls for Efforts to Secure Equal Rights for LGBT Community*; United Nations: New York, NY, USA, 2016. Available online: https://www.un.org/sustainabledevelopment/blog/2016/09/ban-calls-for-efforts-to-secure-equal-rights-for-lgbt-community/ (accessed on 18 April 2019).
19. Ontario Human Rights Commission. Gender Identity and Gender Expression (Brochure). Available online: http://www.ohrc.on.ca/en/gender-identity-and-gender-expression-brochure. (accessed on 19 April 2019).

20. Ljungqvist, A. Sex segregation and sport. *Br. J. Sports Med.* **2018**, *52*, 1481–1482. [CrossRef] [PubMed]
21. Rainbow Health Ontario. Service Provider Directory. Available online: https://www.rainbowhealthontario.ca/service-directory/ (accessed on 19 April 2019).
22. Roussy, K. Hospital Staff in Toronto Learn the Dos and Don'ts of LGBTQ Lingo. *CBC News*, 1 July 2016. Available online: https://www.cbc.ca/news/health/transgender-hospital-toronto-lgbtq-canada-1.3655169 (accessed on 19 April 2019).
23. Foddy, B.; Savulescu, J. Time to re-evaluate gender segregation in athletics? *Br. J. Sports Med.* **2011**, *45*, 1184–1188. [CrossRef] [PubMed]
24. Simon, R. Deserving to Be Lucky: Reflections on the Role of Luck and Desert in Sports. *J. Philos. Sport* **2007**, *34*, 13–25. [CrossRef]
25. Intersex. The 519 Glossary of Terms. Available online: http://www.the519.org/education-training/glossary (accessed on 19 April 2019).
26. Dea, S. *Beyond the Binary: Thinking About Sex and Gender*; Broadview Press: Peterborough, ON, Canada, 2016.
27. Schultz, J. Caster Semenya and the "Question of Too": Sex Testing in Elite Women's Sport and the Issue of Advantage. *Quest* **2011**, *63*, 228–243. [CrossRef]
28. Karkazis, K.; Carpenter, M. Impossible Choices: The Inherent Harms of Regulating Women's Testosterone in Sport. *Bioethical Inq.* **2018**, *15*, 579–587. [CrossRef] [PubMed]
29. Payne, M. Transgender Woman Wins International Weightlifting Title amid Controversy Over Fairness. *Washington Post*, 22 March 2017. Available online: https://www.washingtonpost.com/news/early-lead/wp/2017/03/22/transgender-woman-wins-international-weightlifting-title-amid-controversy-over-fairness/?noredirect=on (accessed on 19 April 2019).
30. Padawer, R. The Humiliating Practice of Sex-Testing Female Athletes. *New York Times*, 28 June 2016. Available online: https://www.nytimes.com/2016/07/03/magazine/the-humiliating-practice-of-sex-testing-female-athletes.html (accessed on 19 April 2019).
31. Branch, J. Dutee Chand, Female Sprinter with High Testosterone Level, Wins Right to Compete. *New York Times*, 27 July 2015. Available online: https://www.nytimes.com/2015/07/28/sports/international/dutee-chand-female-sprinter-with-high-male-hormone-level-wins-right-to-compete.html (accessed on 19 April 2019).
32. IAAF Introduces New Eligibility Regulations for Female Classification. Available online: https://www.iaaf.org/news/press-release/eligibility-regulations-for-female-classifica (accessed on 19 April 2019).
33. Pielke, R., Jr.; Tucker, R.; Boye, E. Scientific integrity and the IAAF testosterone regulations. *Int. Sports Law J.* **2019**, 1–9. [CrossRef]
34. Campigotto, J. The Caster Semenya Case Could Shape the Future of Women's Sports. *CBC News*. 30 April 2019. Available online: https://www.cbc.ca/sports/olympics/trackandfield/caster-semenya-explainer-1.5116897 (accessed on 8 May 2019).
35. Dunbar, G. Caster Semenya Loses Appeal Against IAAF Testosterone Rules. *CBC News*, 1 May 2019. Available online: https://www.cbc.ca/sports/olympics/trackandfield/caster-semenya-appeal-1.5117936 (accessed on 8 May 2019).
36. Hadhazy, A. What Makes Michael Phelps So Good? *Scientific American*, 18 August 2008. Available online: http://www.scientificamerican.com/article/what-makesmichael-phelps-so-good/ (accessed on 19 April 2019).
37. Gleaves, J.; Lehrbach, T. Beyond fairness: The ethics of inclusion for transgender and intersex athletes. *J. Philos. Sport* **2016**, *43*, 311–326. [CrossRef]
38. Koshie, N. Indian Express. 6 April 2019. Available online: https://indianexpress.com/article/sports/sport-others/cass-verdict-on-caster-semenya-testosterone-case-5661681/ (accessed on 19 April 2019).
39. Reeser, J.C. Gender identity and sport: Is the playing field level? *Rev. Br. J. Sports Med.* **2005**, *39*, 695–699. [CrossRef] [PubMed]
40. Coggon, J.; Hammond, N.; Holm, S. Transsexuals in Sport—Fairness and Freedom, Regulation and Law. *Sportsethics Philos.* **2008**, *2*, 4–17. [CrossRef]
41. Jones, B.A.; Arcelus, J.; Bouman, W.P.; Haycraft, E. Sport and Transgender People: A Systematic Review of the Literature Relating to Sport Participation and Competitive Sport Policies. *Sports Med.* **2017**, *47*, 701–716. [CrossRef] [PubMed]

42. IAAF. Olympic Games Records. Available online: https://www.iaaf.org/records/by-category/olympic-games-records (accessed on 19 April 2019).
43. English, J. Sex Equality in Sports. *Philos. Public Aff.* **1978**, *7*, 269–277.

 © 2019 by the author. Licensee MDPI, Basel, Switzerland. This article is an open access article distributed under the terms and conditions of the Creative Commons Attribution (CC BY) license (http://creativecommons.org/licenses/by/4.0/).

Article

Testosterone: 'the Best Discriminating Factor'

Jonathan Cooper

Law School, Oxstalls Campus, University of Gloucestershire, Gloucester GL2 9HW, UK; jcooper8@glos.ac.uk

Received: 6 June 2019; Accepted: 8 July 2019; Published: 11 July 2019

Abstract: In 2011 the IAAF introduced the Hyperandrogenism Regulations in an attempt to deal with a difficult problem; that of ensuring 'fair' competition in female athletics as a result of athletes with differences in sexual development competing against women without such conditions. In 2015, following a challenge to those regulations by Indian athlete, Dutee Chand, The Court of Arbitration for Sport (CAS) considered the merit of the regulations and determined that there was insufficient scientific evidence to justify their imposition. The regulations were suspended by the CAS, until more convincing evidence could be provided (CAS 2014/A/3759 *Chand v AFI and IAAF*). The IAAF duly commissioned further research (Bermon and Garnier, 2017) and introduced amended regulations (the Eligibility Regulations for Female Classification (the DSD Regulations)). Although not universal, the IAAF has faced significant criticism from several angles about its approach to the problem. In particular, there has been criticism of the value of the scientific research on which the regulations are based (Franklin et al., 2018; Karkazis et al., 2012; Koh et al., 2018; Sőnksen et al., 2018; Tucker, 2017, Pielke, Tucker & Boye 2019) and also from those in the ethical and human rights fields seeking to ensure that the rights of individual athletes are protected (Adair, 2011; Buzuvis, 2016; Koh et al., 2018). In light of such criticism, this paper considers the IAAF's approach in dealing with the perceived problem and considers its conduct against an objective framework of 'good sporting governance' (Geeraert, 2013; Henry and Lee 2004). It is this paper's contention that the IAAF's approach to rule creation in this area demonstrates less than ideal governance practice and, in doing so, notes the role of historical, cultural and institutional barriers as well as an over-reliance on insufficiently conclusive scientific evidence to provide a seemingly objective solution to a fundamentally more complex problem.

Keywords: governance; ethics; testosterone; discrimination; integrity; science; fair-play; sport; athletics

1. Introduction

1.1. Background and Aims

That compelling sport requires a level playing field is a well-used metaphor and one that is often taken to be the cornerstone of competitive sport. In short, the metaphor expresses the idea that competitors are required to follow the same rules and are given the same opportunity to compete. Of course, sport does not require complete equality between competitors. As a meritocracy, compelling sport actually requires inequality; it requires that individuals or teams can be ranked by reference to how they make use of their natural biological advantages (both physiological and psychological) or to find advantages through strategy or, in some cases, even through technology and financial power. Sport, therefore, requires merely an approximation of equality between competitors; enough equality to make it interesting but not so much that it makes it impossible to determine winners and losers. However, it is important to emphasise that the notion of a level playing field represents only part of a wider notion of sporting 'fair play' (Loland, 2002 [1]), an important point that will be returned to.

As quasi-monopolies (Geeraert, 2015 [2]) International Sporting Federations (ISFs) have the power and authority to create and maintain 'the rules of the game' and, therefore, to determine how level the playing field is and which advantages are fair and which are unfair. Inevitably, in determining what is fair and what is not, ethical issues should be central.

Justifying the limits of fair advantage in sport is easier when the advantage in question is clearly separable from the qualities that are being ranked. For example, it is easier to justify regulating against the wearing of swimsuits that provide a performance advantage because swimming as a sport does not seek to rank competitors by how good their equipment is. However, when the advantage in question is genetic and directly influences the qualities that are being ranked, such as a competitor's ability to generate speed, power and demonstrate endurance in athletics, the decision to regulate and limit specific advantages and not others, raises difficult ethical questions about fairness, discrimination and the role of sport in society. When, in 2011, the International Association of Athletics (IAAF) introduced the Hyperandrogenism Regulations, thereby limiting eligibility to compete in female events by reference to naturally occurring (endogenous) levels of testosterone, the IAAF seemingly became the first international sporting federation to *exclude* athletes from competing on the basis of a natural genetic trait due to the 'unfair' competitive advantage it was perceived to provide (Professors Sonksen and Holt in *Chand v AFI & IAAF* [3]).

To emphasise the underlying issues surrounding fairness and discrimination, the situations of Caster Semenya and Usain Bolt are worth considering. Both athletes have dominated their respective athletic events for a substantial period of recent history. Whilst dedication and training was, of course, part of Usain Bolt's success, it would be hard to maintain that his recent domination of sprinting was not due, in part, to natural genetic advantages he enjoyed over his competitors. It has been suggested that Bolt, like many other top sprinters, has the 'sprinting gene', meaning he may have particularly fast-twitch muscle reflexes and longer muscle fibers than most. Unlike a lot of sprinters, however, he is 6ft 5 inches tall (Thomas, 2016 [4]). These genetic advantages almost certainly contributed to what makes him especially adept at sprinting. Yet there appears to have been no consideration of whether he had an unfair advantage from one, or indeed, a combination of these genetic factors or the size of advantage that such genetic factors might play. Instead, his success is simply ascribed to 'talent', with the incumbent suggestion of a 'positive' and fair advantage.

In contrast, the perceived increased lean body mass (and the additional strength and power that is said to come from it) that Caster Semenya has over other female middle distance runners has been the subject of significant IAAF attention in order to quantify the performance advantage and regulate the genetic advantage said to be behind it.

Outside of athletics, there are plenty of other examples of natural genetic advantage leading to domination of sport which have not raised the concerns of relevant ISFs or lead to regulation. Two of the most obvious being Eero Mäntyranta's domination of cross country skiing in the 1960's (genetic mutation that increased his red blood cell concentration) and Michael Phelps, the most decorated Olympian in history, who dominated several swimming events intermittently from 2000-2016 (arm length, hand and relative torso size). They, like Usain Bolt, just won the genetic lottery.

The comparison made is not to suggest it is inherently wrong to treat what are, after all, different natural advantages in a different way, it is merely to observe from a reductionist standpoint, that when the aim of a sport is to rank individuals using criteria that that are strongly influenced by natural genetic advantages, it is hard to see a rationale and ethical justification for focusing solely on one natural advantage and ignoring others. In Bolt's case, it might prove difficult to pinpoint and attribute specific performance advantages to specific genetic factors, but it does not follow that this should be ignored, especially if you have already identified genetic traits resulting in increased speed and power as fair game for regulation; it smacks of discrimination.

The difference in approach is, of course, possible to justify, but the tenor of this paper is that the justification for focusing *only* on testosterone needs to be 'good' and, to do so, it should be grounded on principles of good sporting governance, having considered fully all relevant ethical, legal and scientific factors as well as the stated purposes of the IAAF. The aim of this paper, therefore, is to scrutinize, by reference to good governance principles by which the IAAF strives to adhere, the approach of the IAAF to the introduction and implementation of regulations limiting the eligibility of female athletes based on a perceived unfair advantage resulting from naturally high levels of testosterone (the Testosterone Regulations).

Before turning to principles of good governance, it is necessary to briefly consider the background to the IAAF's introduction of the Hyperandrogenism Regulations and their successor, the DSD Regulations.

1.2. Classification by Sex and Regulation of Eligibility to Compete in Female Category

For virtually as long as women have been allowed to compete in Athletics (and indeed other sports), there have been rules to segregate competition into male and female categories, a distinction that has historically been made by reference to biological sex. The rational for segregation was, no doubt, initially based on observations, assumptions and generalizations about the athletic ability of men and women, the perceived 'weakness' of the feminine form and cultural stereotypes about the role of women (Adair, 2011; McDonagh and Pappano, 2008 [5,6]). Over time there has been scientific flesh added to the assumption of 'male athletic advantage'; the often quoted statistic is that an average male has a 10–12% athletic advantage over an average female (IAAF DSD Regulations, 2019, IAAF Explanatory Notes [7,8]). According to medical experts relied on by the IAAF, the advantage is due to the significantly increased Lean Body Mass (LBM) of average males when compared to average females as well as other athletic advantages that are likely to stem from testosterone, such as larger bones, numbers of red blood cells and 'possible' psychological advantages through increased aggression (Professors Ritzen and Hirschberg in *Chand*; Auchus, 2018; Handelsman et al., 2018 [3,9,10]). There also seems to have been increasing recognition of ethical arguments surrounding equality of opportunity for women. As a result, there seems to be little dispute about the justification of classification by sex in most sports, particularly where natural biological advantages play a significant role and where there is a perceived risk of injury to female athletes if competition was not segregated (Adair, 2011; McDonagh and Pappano, 2008 [5,6]). In the context of athletics, where success depends heavily on maximization of natural biological advantages linked to strength, power and endurance, the rationale is largely undisputed (Krech, 2017; McDonagh and Pappano, 2008 [6,11]) and seems to underpin the ongoing use of classification by sex, despite the risk of injury not being a concern.

Prompted, primarily, by fears of men posing as women to gain an unfair advantage, screening of athletes to ensure only biologically female athletes compete against each other has been embedded in the governance of athletics for over 50 years (Krech, 2017; Xavier and McGill, 2012 [11,12]). Various methods of seeking to determine the biological sex of athletes have come and gone over the years, including 'nude parades', chromosomal testing of saliva and briefly, full medical examinations (Ha et al., 2014; Krech, 2017 [11,13]). The decision of the IAAF to abandon screening based on chromosomal tests reflected the dawning scientific realization that biological sex is not binary; that there are several different indicators of biological sex in addition to chromosomal sex and that in some individuals not all of them necessarily point in the same direction towards traditional conceptions of male and female.

Prior to the 2009 World Athletic Championships, there was a growing concern that athletes with 'differences in sexual development' (DSDs) might have an unfair advantage by competing in the female classification. Between the jettisoning of chromosomal testing and Caster Semenya's victory in the 800m at the 2009 World Championship, the IAAF's policy for dealing with athletes with suspected DSDs is probably best described as 'ad-hoc', with testing to determine the biological sex of individuals taking place following the recommendation of a medical director of a relevant athletics meeting, which could be on the basis of observations or 'tip offs' (Ha et al., 2014 [13]). It was, no doubt, the mess of the Semenya investigation and catalogue of potential ethical and human rights violations that finally prompted the IAAF to seek a different approach.

Accordingly, in 2011, the IAAF introduced the Hyperandrogenism Regulations. Ostensibly, the regulations recognized competition is built around the division of athletes by their legal status as male or female (now Rule 141.3, IAAF Competition Rules 2018–2019 [14]). However, the Hyperandrogenism Regulations made an athlete ineligible for the female category if she had endogenous testosterone levels above 10 nmol/L, a figure that was reached by virtue of the fact it would not exclude women with polycystic ovary syndrome (PCOS), which also accounts for elevated levels of testosterone (at an average level of 4.5 nmol/L) (Professor Ritzen in *Chand* [3]).

The change of tack came in the fact that the Hyperandrogenism Regulations sought to avoid external classification of athletes by biological sex, a point stressed by professors Ritzen and Hirschberg in giving evidence for the IAAF in *Chand* [3]. Instead, the purpose of the Hyperandrogenism Regulations was, apparently, 'to address the position of female athletes who, due to a special condition, have functional levels of testosterone that are usually only seen in males' (*Chand* [3]). At least on the face of it, by focusing on testosterone levels, the regulations focused instead on the underlying reasons for the 'male performance advantage' and in so doing, presented an objectively measurable variable as a determiner of eligibility (Handelsman et al., 2018 [10]), rather than eligibility being based on the assignment of biological sex as determined by a third party. However, as several commentators have observed, the actual effect, inevitably, was still to assign athletes as male or female (Krech, 2017 [11]). The fact that this assignment is 'only' supposed to be for the purpose of athletics is unlikely, it is suggested, to reduce the magnitude of the effect of being told your understanding of your own sexual and gender identity is wrong in the context of an activity that is central to your life.

In 2015 the Indian athlete Dutee Chand challenged the validity of the Hyperandrogenism Regulations at the CAS on the grounds of discrimination as to sex and/or gender and in relation to individual physiological traits. In *Chand* the CAS accepted the IAAF's stated justification for the rule, and in doing so, tacitly acknowledged that creating a 'level playing field' in female athletics could be legitimately achieved by the exclusion of female athletes based on levels of testosterone, even though this approach was discriminatory. The problem was that the CAS was not satisfied that there was sufficient evidence that female athletes with levels of testosterone above the IAAF's cut-off point (10 nmol/L) did, in fact, have a competitive advantage 'of the same order' as male athletes (*Chand*; Pielke et al., 2019 [3,15]). Accordingly, the CAS suspended the Hyperandrogenism Regulations but provided an opportunity for the IAAF to furnish further evidence.

The IAAF duly commissioned further research (Bermon et al., 2018; Bermon and Garnier, 2017 [16,17]) the results of which were clearly insufficient, even on the IAAF's own interpretation, to convince the CAS that the performance advantage was of the same magnitude as male athletes or significant across all athletic events. Accordingly, the Hyperandrogenism Regulations were dropped and a variation was introduced that was drafted to focus on certain events where the evidence of performance advantage was deemed by the IAAF to be significant. The 'restricted' events are the 400 m, 800 m, 1500 m, and the mile (DSD Regulations 2018 [7]). Furthermore, the serum levels of testosterone at which an athlete becomes ineligible was reduced to 5 nmol/L and the regulations only apply to athletes with XY chromosomes. The IAAF's stated reason for the focus on particular events is due to the over-representation of DSD athletes in those events and their relative success in those events (IAAF, Explanatory Notes, 2019 [8]). In terms of the reduction in serum level, the justification was that 'absent a DSD or a tumor no female would have serum levels of testosterone of 5 nmol/L' (IAAF Explanatory Notes, 2019 [8]).

Before the regulations were introduced, Caster Semenya challenged the validity of the DSD regulations at the CAS, which left the imposition of the regulations in suspense until the outcome of the CAS decision. The CAS eventually upheld the validity of the regulations, albeit with some reservations concerning the practical application of the regulations and the paucity of evidence relating to some of the events (*Semenya v IAAF*, Court of Arbitration for Sport, 2019 [18]). Despite those reservations, the DSD Regulations came into force on 8 May 2019. The full decision of the CAS has not been published, and detailed scrutiny of this decision is, therefore, not possible at present. At the time of writing, it should be noted that the Swiss Federal Court has suspended the application of the regulations in respect of Caster Semenya (but not other athletes) whilst her appeal of the CAS decision is ongoing.

2. Methodology

2.1. A Question of Good Governance

Unfortunately, despite being recognized as a key ingredient for good governance, full transparency in the decision making of International Sporting Federations (ISFs) is not the norm (Geeraert, 2015 [2]) and the IAAF is no exception. The IAAF's constitution, for example, gives the power of adopting and amending rules and regulations to the IAAF Council (IAAF Constitution, Article 47.2 (d) [19]) but there is no requirement to publish the minutes or a summary of them and the IAAF does not appear to do so on its website. Accordingly, stakeholders are left to scrutinize that which the IAAF is prepared to provide. In that regard, the IAAF has set out the key aspects of its rationale for introducing the Testosterone Regulations both in the regulations themselves and in explanatory notes which accompany them. However, the rationale provides little more than a self-justifying summary of the decision and, it is hoped, only reveals the tip of the iceberg in terms of the ethical, legal and scientific considerations that were taken into account when deciding to adopt the policy. Some further detail was revealed following publication of the judgment of the CAS in *Chand* and in the executive summary of *Semenya*. However, this is far from full transparency, and without this stakeholders must either take it on trust or look to legal accountability to ensure that the IAAF Council has considered and given appropriate weight to all of the relevant factors, and did not take into account, or give inappropriate weight to, irrelevant or less relevant factors.

Given this lack of transparency, this article attempts to clarify some of the important considerations that *ought* to have been taken into account and uses inference to consider the weight that they seem to have been given. However, it attempts to do so not by applying the author's own moral framework, but by reference to generally accepted notions of good governance in sport, which provides a practical normative framework about how ISFs ought to behave (Ryall et al., 2019 [20]). These are notions which have been tacitly and overtly approved by the IAAF as a member of Association of Summer Olympic International Federations (ASOIF), and in the IAAF's own stated aims and purposes.

To emphasise the importance of such scrutiny, it is important to recognise the limitations of legal accountability demonstrated by the recent decision in *Semenya*.

2.2. Limits of Legal Accountability

As in *Chand*, the CAS determined that the DSD Regulations were discriminatory on the basis of sex and/or gender and towards individuals with certain physiological traits. However, as it was accepted that the IAAF was pursuing a legitimate aim, the key question was whether the regulations were necessary and proportionate to achieve that aim (CAS, 2019 [18]). By a majority, the CAS panel determined that they were.

The decision (or at least the executive summary of it), highlights that legal accountability of ISFs is limited both by the terms of reference to the CAS (i.e., what the CAS is asked to determine) and the reality that sport has a large degree of autonomy in which to shape its own legal norms (Ryall et al., 2019 [20]; Gardiner, 2012 [21]).

With regard to terms of reference, the executive summary makes it clear (just as in *Chand*) that CAS was not asked to consider the validity of segregation between male and female athletics in the context of its stated purposes as it was accepted (without argument) to be a 'legitimate aim' of the IAAF. For reasons explained more fully below, this means that when it comes to scrutinising the approach of the IAAF, the fundamental basis of rules for policing the male/female divide and its relevance to the Testosterone Regulations avoids examination.

Second, that its decisions are constrained by its 'judicial function'. In other words, the framework of legal reasoning dictates that the CAS is not free to substitute what it would have done for the decision of the IAAF or what it thinks is 'fair' or appropriate (Ryall et al., 2019 [20]). In doing so the CAS is both explaining the limits of its powers and function and providing an example of the limit of legal accountability for the decisions of ISFs in general and the IAAF in particular.

Further consideration of the limits of legal accountability are beyond the scope of this paper; but the recognition that there *are* limits in legal accountability of the decisions of ISFs is important in highlighting the need for other forms of scrutiny and accountability. The key point being that, even though the decision of the IAAF has been legally 'vindicated' (albeit with some reservation), this does not mean that it is necessarily a 'good' decision from a wider governance perspective (a point which, it is suggested, the executive summary alludes to in noting the reservations). Accordingly, outside the narrow legal sphere, there is room (and a need) for wider scrutiny of the decision making process of the IAAF. ISFs enjoy monopolistic type powers (Geeraert, 2015 [2]) over a large number of participants in sport and over a social activity that is undoubtedly seen as a 'public good'. As such, ISFs have obligations not only to the majority of athletes, but also to protect minorities within the sports community and, more widely, to the societies they operate within. As such they should also have to meet demanding procedural and performance requirements or they risk losing legitimacy (Tallberg and Zürn, 2019 [22]).

2.3. Principles of Good Sporting Governance

Over recent years there have been an increasing number of studies on what 'good governance' means in a sporting context and there are now well-established sets of good governance principles in sport utilised in both literature and policy (Chappelet and Mrkonjic, 2013; Mrkonjic, 2016 [23,24]). Despite variations, they generally reflect a core of well accepted aspirational principles about the processes and policies of ISFs that revolve around accountability, transparency, democracy, treating stakeholders fairly and equally and ensuring there are control mechanisms on those wielding power (Ryall et al., 2019 [20]).

Given this paper's concern is scrutinising governance decisions of the IAAF, it seems appropriate to take the principles of good governance as espoused by ASOIF (of which the IAAF is a member) as the starting point from which to evaluate its decision making and general approach to the introduction of the Testosterone Regulations.

The ASOIF Governance Task Force Report (ASOIF, 2016 [25]) recommends five key principles that should be included by their member federations in their statutes and should be embraced in all of their activities, decisions, processes and regulations. The principles being integrity, transparency, democracy, sports development & solidarity, and control mechanisms.

To carry out the analysis, this paper will consider the principles of good governance in turn, the extent to which they are reflected in the IAAF's constitution and, importantly, the extent to which they appear to have been translated into the individual decision making of the IAAF concerning the Testosterone Regulations. However, also included in the analysis of good governance is a principle related to 'effectiveness', which allows consideration of the quality of individual decisions in terms of furtherance of the IAAF's *own* constitutional purposes. Although there will be an inevitable overlap in the analysis of the IAAF's adherence to ASOIF's principles and its own stated purposes, evaluation against its own internally set purposes provides an additional level of scrutiny about the appropriateness and legitimacy of the decision making. Whilst not adhering to generally accepted external standards of governance practice clearly raises legitimacy and governance concerns, failing to fulfill the purposes that an organization states it is in existence to achieve raises an even more fundamental concern.

It should be noted that as considerations about transparency have been discussed above, they will only be touched on again in context the other principles of good governance.

3. Discussion

3.1. Integrity & Solidarity

The relevant ASOIF guidelines on implementing integrity primarily rest on the ethical principles set out in the IOC Code of ethics (ASOIF, 2016 [25]). Article 1 of the IOC code sets out fundamental principles and states that ISFs should have respect for the Olympic spirit, requiring mutual understanding with a spirit of friendship, solidarity and fair play (International Olympic Committee, 2016, Code of Ethics, Article 1.1. [26]).

The Sports Governance Observer explains solidarity as recognizing responsibility towards internal and external stakeholders (Geeraert, 2015 [2]) and, it is suggested, encapsulates the need to support all internal stakeholders (including athletes), to promote inclusivity as well as recognition of a wider obligation towards society. As such it makes sense to consider the principle of solidarity together with integrity as they raise similar concerns in the context of the Testosterone Regulations.

Article 1 states that ISFs should have respect for international conventions protecting human rights which ensure, in particular, respect for human dignity and the rejection of discrimination of any kind on whatever ground (Art. 1.4). It is worth emphasizing that the wording is unequivocal and there is no qualification to the objective of rejecting discrimination; there is nothing to suggest that discrimination is acceptable in some circumstances or in relation to some characteristics.

The IAAF's has, to some extent, embedded these principles in its constitution, the current version of which recognizes that one of its purposes is to 'preserve the right of every individual to participate in Athletics, without unlawful discrimination of any kind undertaken in the spirit of friendship, solidarity and fair play' (IAAF Constitution, 2019) Art 4.1 (j) [19]).

As such, there is a slight mismatch between the more complete statement of IOC Code of ethics and the IAAF's recognition of its constitutional obligations to ensure integrity.

In identifying potential human rights concerns raised by the Testosterone Regulations the Universal Declaration of Human Rights (UDHR) provides an obvious and extremely useful framework against which to identify such concerns (Larson, 2011 [27]). Of particular relevance are Articles 1, 7, 12, 22 and 29 of the UDHR [28].

Article 1 makes an explicit acknowledgement that 'all human beings are born free and equal in dignity and rights and should act towards one another in a spirit of brotherhood'. Article 22 recognizes that everyone is entitled to realize their economic, social and cultural rights *indispensable for their dignity and the free development of their personality* (emphasis added).

Article 12 expressly protects an individual's rights to privacy and from suffering attacks on their reputation.

Article 7 and 22 both recognize that individuals should not be discriminated against. Article 22 makes specific reference to the need to ensure that individuals have their rights and freedoms protected without distinction of any kind, such as race, colour, sex ... birth or other status.

Article 23 protects the right to work and free choice of employment

Article 29 recognizes the possibility of limitations on these freedoms, but only lawful limitations 'solely for the purpose of securing due recognition and respect for the rights and freedoms of others and of meeting the just requirements or morality, public order and the general welfare in a democratic society'.

This is far from the only relevant international convention relating to the protection of Human Rights. The UNESCO International Charter of Physical Education, Physical Activity and Sport recognizes as a fundamental principle that access to sport should be without discrimination and that sport should be inclusive and promote equal opportunities for all. The International Covenant on Civil and Political Rights and the European Convention on Human Rights also protect against non-discrimination. Beyond embedding these commitments in their constitutions, Schwab makes the point that ISFs need to translate the general commitments into actions and decisions taken by conducting due diligence in assessing and mitigating against human rights risks; and dealing with human rights issues transparently (Schwab, 2017 [29]).

Thus, if the IAAF is to adhere to ASOIF principles of integrity and solidarity, it has an obligation to ensure protection of every individual's rights to dignity, privacy, non-discrimination and the development of their personality not only in the creation and implementation of regulations and policies, but also in their application and implementation on a day to day basis. According to the

UDHR, failure to adhere to this obligation is only be permissible if it is to secure the rights and freedoms of others.

The historic treatment of Caster Semenya (and other athletes with DSDs) resulting from the introduction and implementation of policies and regulations designed to police female eligibility raised serious concerns about human rights violations. Using Semenya's case as an example, specific potential violations by the IAAF might have included: restricting the free development of her personality by the assignment of biological sex (against her own perceptions), which would also likely interfere with her dignity; being forced to undergo invasive assessment to verify biological sex (dignity, privacy), having no control over information about your own medical conditions (dignity, privacy), being forced to divulge information about extremely personal medical issues that go to a sense of identity (dignity, privacy), being prevented from competing without taking medication (expression of personality, dignity, freedom to work); having the whole issue played out in public (privacy); being required to undertake the process of sex verification when others are not (discrimination); having your reputation muddied by being labelled a cheat (reputation). Add to this the potential psychological damage resulting from such violations and the fact that the verification only applies to selected women (and no men) and you have a lengthy list of human rights concerns.

Of course, the IAAF sought to address some of these concerns through the use of testosterone levels to determine eligibility for competing in female events rather than testing for biological sex per se. However, as already discussed, it is difficult to distinguish the effect. From the perspective of an athlete with a DSD, the distinction between being told you are not biologically female and being told you are not 'athletically' female is one that is likely to get lost in explanation.

The Testosterone Regulations have explicitly recognized the need to protect the dignity and privacy of relevant athletes (DSD Regulations, Art 3.4 [7]) and the process of investigation has been made clearer, including an attempt to define the basis on which an investigation would begin (DSD Regulations, Art 3.3 [7]). However, this does not change the fact that the substance of the regulations mean that there will always be significant interference with the athlete's right to express her personality, her dignity, her right to privacy, her right to not be discriminated against and her right to realize her economic potential. For example, an athlete is still required to report sensitive, private medical information to the IAAF and, although 'reasonable grounds' are required, an investigation can still be undertaken on the instigation of the IAAF, provided it has a 'reliable source' (leaving plenty of scope for subjective selection of athletes and influence from those with their own motives).

The IAAF constitution recognizes that discrimination might be 'lawful'. As illustrated in *Semenya*, lawfulness of discrimination is considered a question of 'proportionality' and is limited to considering whether the regulations are necessary and proportionate to the legitimate aim to be achieved. In *Semenya*, the CAS, starting from an assumption about the legitimacy of the aim, found that it was proportionate. Whilst the legal principle recognizes that there is a 'margin of appreciation' for rule creators to determine both what is a legitimate aim and what is necessary to achieve that aim, that freedom is not absolute (Rivers, 2006 [30]) and the appropriate exercise of that freedom was not considered in *Semenya*. Outside the narrower question of lawfulness of the discrimination, there is also a wider 'good governance' question posed by the UDHR, which acknowledges that an individual's rights and freedoms should *only* be infringed in the interests of protecting the rights and freedoms of others. In other words, the fundamental question is whether the Testosterone Regulations strike an appropriate balance between protecting the rights of athletes to whom the regulations will be applied and protecting the rights and freedoms of others. The difficulty of the balancing exercise for the IAAF, which was not considered in *Semenya*, is that it is not immediately obvious which UDHR rights and freedoms are being infringed by DSD athletes being allowed to compete. Presumably the IAAF would consider that the right of others (i.e., 'normal' females) to compete on a 'level playing field' trumped the various infringements of the rights of athletes with DSDs and is necessary to ensure 'fair play' (Krech, 2017 [11]). However, referring to the IAAF's own scientific evidence and considering what 'normal females' would be losing by competing against athletes with DSDs, it is far from clear that it would be much more than a reduced opportunity of winning. As a pure human rights question, it seems difficult to justify that a reduced opportunity of winning should outweigh the potential serious infringements of the rights and freedoms of individual DSD athletes, a task made even harder when you consider more fully the whole notion of fair play in sport.

3.1.1. The Meaning of Fair Play

Whilst it is not the purpose of this article to re-enter the debate about the concept of 'fair-play', it is important to make some observations about key aspects of it. First and foremost, fair play incorporates the requirement to play by the rules, at least in terms of the spirit or ethos of them, if not always the 'letter' of them (Butcher and Scheider, 2003 [31]). Secondly, and importantly in the context of the Testosterone Regulations, it would also seem to import an idea of equality of opportunity. This is, of course, at the heart of the IAAF's reasoning for pursuing both the retention of the male/female classification and the imposition of the Testosterone Regulations. However, it is important to recognize that equal opportunity does not *require* segregation of events into male and female classifications and that doing so is an ongoing choice by the IAAF and a means to achieve the wider aim of fair play. That choice of means may be justified when considered against other possible means of achieving the aim and against the other aims and purposes of the IAAF (such as development of the sport), but it is an ongoing value judgement that needs to be recognized as such and re-evaluated from time to time.

Third, fair play encapsulate abstract, non-sport specific values that are seen by society, generally, as positive; the types of values that have historically been used to justify playing and watching sport as a social or public good, such as understanding and empathy for others (Butcher and Scheider, 2003 [31]) and an appreciation that winning is not everything. Embracing such values is important in demonstrating solidarity by promoting values and practices that contribute towards a better society (Geeraert, 2015 [2]). Although these values are not always present in sport there are enough examples of conduct which is rightly lauded for demonstrating 'fair play' and which have the power to showcase and encourage positive social values (the memory of Paulo Di Canio playing for West Ham and catching the ball when the opposition goalkeeper collapsed to the turf instead of heading the ball into an empty net sticks in the author's mind).

Accordingly, when ISFs are considering how to promote and achieve 'fair play', it should be appreciated that the concept itself encapsulates more than ensuring approximate equality of opportunity and playing by the rules and, as such, there is an inherent difficulty in using 'fair play' to justify infringements of human rights and human dignity before you even consider wider purposes such as ensuring solidarity and integrity.

3.1.2. Medical Care and Solidarity

It should be appreciated that, as a matter of solidarity, the IAAF have stressed that the Testosterone Regulations will help athletes receive medical care for conditions of which they were unaware (*Chand*, DSD Regulations, 2018 [3,7]). However, it is submitted that this justification does not really support the need for testosterone based regulations that exclude athletes from competition. Medical diagnosis and support could clearly be provided without the need to determine eligibility based on testosterone levels.

3.2. *Democracy*

The ASOIF's governance task force report focusses on democracy in terms of the process of electing members to executive bodies and in ensuring representation of key stakeholders in the governing body. However, it is suggested that democracy goes further than this and should include wider participation by both internal stakeholders (such as athletes and national federations, clubs etc.) and external stakeholders (the public, governments, NGOs and those interest in human rights) in the creation and development of specific policies (Geeraert, 2015 [2]).

Given the lack of full transparency concerning the rationale and processes for the adoption of the Testosterone Regulations, it is difficult to comment fully on the extent to which the voices of all stakeholders were considered. Karkazis et al. have shed some light on the evolution of the Hyperandrogenism Regulations highlighting that a range of stakeholders were consulted (including human rights experts, female athletes and a representative of the intersex community), but also pointing out obvious limitations (in terms of the composition of the IAAF's working group, the selection of stakeholders asked to input in to the decision making process and the clarity of the goal to be achieved) (Karkazis et al., 2017 [32]). What input athletes with DSDs had into the continuing process up to the introduction of the DSD Regulations is not entirely clear.

Of course, the input of voices from stakeholders is important, but as they are not the decision makers, we can only speculate as to the impact and the weight that different stakeholder's views were given. However, it might be noted that there was, apparently, only one representative of the intersex community (a non-athlete) (Karkazis et al., 2017 [32]), which, given the potentially disproportionate effect on athletes with a DSD, might be considered somewhat of an underrepresentation. As alluded to above (as a matter of solidarity), ISFs should be alert to the need to protect minorities as well as listening to the interests of majorities, a point underlined by Madeleine Pape, a former competitor of Semenya who moved from being a supporter of testosterone based regulations as an athlete to a critic of them once the 'bigger picture' became clearer to her (Pape, 2019 [33]).

3.3. Sports Development

The development of individual sports and sports in general, in terms of participation, attention and securing resources are reflected in the ASOIFs principles and in the IAAF's constitution (IAAF Constitution, 2019, Art 4.1 (b) and (l)).

In the context of the Testosterone Regulations, the potential development effect on participation of females in elite athletics if they were required to compete against men has always formed an important part of the rationale for segregation by sex (IAAF Explanatory Notes 2019; *Chand*; *Semenya* [3,8,18]). However, it is difficult to see how that rationale supports the Testosterone Regulations themselves, *unless* it is backed up by evidence that athletes with DSDs enjoy such an advantage that normal female athletes could not and would not compete at all or, at least, that there would be a significant reduction in participation. Whilst it may be plausible to accept (without any empirical evidence) that few, if any, females would be seen in the majority of elite athletic events if they had to compete against men it does not follow that we should accept, without evidence, that there is or would be an significant effect on participation in elite female athletics if athletes with DSDs were allowed to compete without restriction. Without such evidence, the justification is no more than a hunch, raising an important question about the role of factual evidence in the IAAF's decision making. This concern is particularly warranted given that the IAAF's evidence about performance advantage of females with high levels of testosterone does not seem to suggest, from what we have seen at present, that athletes with high levels of testosterone benefit from close to the 10–12% 'male' performance advantage.

Whilst the 'development' of athletics might have been a relevant factor justifying the segregation of male and female athletes historically, it should not be confused with a relevant justification for the Testosterone Regulations, which it is suggested can, at present, only be justified by reference to the notion of fair play. In using the 'sports development' or 'protection of female athletes' argument as a justification for the Testosterone Regulations, the IAAF is conflating two different issues.

3.4. Control Mechanisms

The ASOIF principles on control mechanisms focus heavily on financial irregularity and the danger of corruption, rather than wider ethical considerations. This is also reflected in the IAAF code of conduct and remit of its ethics panel, which seems to focus on corruption, rather than having a wider ethical due diligence remit (IAAF Integrity Code of Conduct, 2019 [34]). Although ethical issues may be picked up in the decision making process as a matter of 'democratic' input (discussed above), perhaps the input of a formal ethics committee into a wider range of decisions might be a step forward in ensuring ethical due diligence in governance decisions.

3.5. Good Governance and Effectiveness

Some sets of good governance principles also incorporate notions of performance or effectiveness (Henry and Lee, 2004; Parent, Naraine & Hoye, 2018 [35,36]) and therefore extend the ambit of good governance to include an assessment of whether the *implementation* of processes and individual decisions achieve (or at least advance) the ISFs stated aims and purpose. There has been some implicit criticism of the inclusion of performance as a measure of good governance in that it confuses governance and management (Chappelet and Mrkonjic, 2013 [23]). However, it is submitted that this is an artificial distinction. Consideration of the 'quality' of individual decisions made by ISFs by reference to internal stated purposes is important in considering issues of legitimacy and accountability and therefore plays a central role in any assessment of good governance (Tallberg and Zürn, 2019 [22]). As such this paper will also consider how well the IAAFs approach to adopting the Testosterone Regulations accords with its own constitutional purposes before commenting further on any additional observations about complying with a wider sense of good governance.

3.6. Testosterone Based Regulations; an Appropriate Policy to Further the IAAF's Stated Purposes?

In the DSD Regulations and the explanatory notes that accompany them (IAAF, 2019 [7,8]) the primary reasons for adopting the policy were (1) to ensure 'fair competition in female athletics' and (2) to protect 'the protected class' of female athletes. These reasons were also highlighted by the CAS in *Semenya* as the legitimate objective that the IAAF was pursuing (CAS, 2019 [18]).

However, it should be appreciated that the IAAF constitution contains no specific purposes which relate to ensuring fair competition in *only* female athletics or to ensuring a male/female categorisation is retained in order to protect female athletes. The relevant provision would seem to be Article 4.1(j) which illustrates that the purpose that the IAAF should be seeking to achieve is to (1) 'to preserve the right of every individual to participate in Athletics without unlawful discrimination of any kind', and (2) to ensure that athletics is 'undertaken in a spirit of friendship, solidarity and fair play' (IAAF Constitution, 2019 [19]). This is important as it clarifies that both the decision to retain separate male/female categories and to pursue the Testosterone Regulations are merely *possible* means towards achieving the IAAF's wider purposes. Whether they are an appropriate means requires a value judgement based on a proper consideration of all of the IAAF's stated purposes (including adherence with external principles of good governance) and the impact of the means on achieving its stated purposes. That judgement requires full consideration of other possible means of achieving those purposes, and particularly, any means that might cause less conflict with other purposes such as non-discrimination, integrity, solidarity and which also underpin (the wider notion of) fair play.

Other possible means of achieving those purposes might have been: classifying by legal gender; classifying by lean body mass; classifying by testosterone levels alone; introducing a handicap system within sub-categories or a handicap system that applies to all athletes regardless of sex or gender. From the decisions in *Chand* and *Semenya*, we can observe that the IAAF rejected classification by legal gender on the basis of potential for unfair advantage. However, due to a lack of transparency about the decision making process, it is impossible to know what other possibilities have received serious consideration as a potentially 'better' means of advancing the IAAF's purposes as a whole and the reasons for their rejection. Inevitably, this raises questions about the quality of decision making and whether 'external' motivations are driving the policy. This is particularly so given the evident conflicts of purpose and principles of good governance that the current policy creates with regard to integrity, solidarity, non-discrimination and fair play.

Furthermore, as already pointed out, the protection of the female athletes cannot form the basis of a justification for the testosterone regulations unless there is reliable evidence that the unrestricted participation of athletes with DSDs would result in reduced participation and interest in athletics. It is possible that such evidence exists, but it does not seem to have been referred to in any rationale that the IAAF has put forward. As such the only plausible justification has to rest on the notion of fair play.

3.7. The Problem with Integrity, Solidarity and Fair Play

As already alluded to, it is difficult to see how the possible reduction in the likelihood of 'normal' female athletes winning could ever be appropriately balanced against the consequential interferences of human rights associated with the application of the Testosterone Regulations. This is so even if you accept the argument that the medical intervention required to reduce testosterone to eligible levels will amount to no more than taking oral contraceptives (something that seems to have been accepted by the CAS in *Semenya*). This balancing exercise becomes even harder still when you consider the evidence that the IAAF has relied on seems to demonstrate, at best, a relatively small performance advantage (0.3–3.1%) for women in the highest tertile of testosterone levels over those in lowest tertile of testosterone levels, and then only in the handful of events to which the regulations apply (Bermon et al., 2018; Bermon and Garnier, 2017). It is suggested that, in order to 'warrant' the discrimination and other human rights interferences, it would be necessary to demonstrate the advantage that females with DSDs enjoy is so large that 'normal females' cannot compete at all. Only then will 'normal' female athletes be losing something that could be recognisable as a human right or freedom.

At the very least, forced medication (even if it is 'only' oral contraceptives) with, presumably, unknown effects on individual athletes, seems an odd way of balancing human rights issues. If the effect of testosterone is to provide a quantifiable performance advantage; wouldn't a less invasive solution be to compensate by reference to time? The IAAF has referred to evidence that female athletes who took medication to suppress testosterone levels from 21–25 nmol/L to 2 nmol/L had a reduced performance of 5.7% (IAAF Explanatory Notes, 2019 [5]). If that evidence is scientifically reliable, then why not require a percentage time handicap?

A particular concern is that historical, cultural and institutional barriers are unduly influencing the approach that is now being taken. When little was known about either the underlying reasons for the 'male advantage', or the complexities of biological sex, categorisation by biological sex may well have been appropriate (or at least practical) as a proxy for ensuring both fair play and the protection of female athletes, but that does not necessarily make it so now. If, as the IAAF suggests, testosterone levels are the primary reason for the 'male advantage' and seemingly, provide a measurable and quantifiable advantage (key to the reasoning of the IAAF and the decisions in the CAS (Pielke et al., 2019 [15]) then we have gone beyond crude observations about men being faster than women and the consequence would seem to be that segregation by sex is no longer needed as a proxy means of ensuring fair play or 'protecting' female athletes. Segregation by sex is, therefore, more clearly shown for what it is, a policy *choice* of the IAAF. If that choice creates significant conflicts with the IAAF's stated purposes then other options that better reflect its purposes (and good governance principles), should be considered. Perhaps the prospect of men and women competing against each other is too radical, but why that is a problem and the basis of the decision ought to be properly justified in a transparent and democratic way.

Furthermore, to reflect its stated purposes, the IAAF's wider policy should be about protecting against 'unfair' advantages regardless of sex or gender. The concern should not be about protecting only female athletes, it should be about protecting *all* athletes from those that might have an unfair advantage. It is that purpose which should inform a search for scientific evidence to determine the size of the advantage enjoyed and, only then, regulation to address any significant unfairness. If the scientific evidence supports the conclusion that testosterone (or indeed any other genetic factor) provides a sufficiently large advantage and possibly affects women and men significantly differently, then subsequent regulation may be necessary and might need to reflect that. However, from the historical background to the Testosterone Regulations and from the scientific evidence on which the IAAF purports to rely, that does not appear to be the approach that has been taken. For example, in the Bermon and Garnier studies (Bermon et al., 2018; Bermon and Garnier, 2017 [16,17]) on which heavy reliance is placed, the data in relation to male performance differences based on testosterone levels is far less than the female data (the female data is taken from both the Daegu and Moscow IAAF world championships, but the Daegu world championships is not used in relation to male athletes) and there is a fairly blunt conclusion that there is no significant performance difference between the males with low testosterone levels and those with high levels. Since the whole basis of the Testosterone Regulations is that increased testosterone *does* provide a performance advantage, it seems strange that the IAAF have not sought to explain or investigate this further, especially given that other academic evidence relied on by the IAAF suggests increases in testosterone in healthy adult males increases muscle strength and size in a linear fashion (Auchus, 2018 [9]). When you also take into account that the revised figures produced by the amended Bermon & Garnier 2018 study suggest that there is no statistically significant performance advantage for females in the higher tertile of testosterone in three of the four events that are now regulated (Pielke et al., 2019 [15]), this seems to suggest a blinkered agenda. Quite why the cut-off point for eligibility is 5 nmol/L to ensure that women with PCOS are not caught is not fully explained (despite noting the higher level of testosterone and the disproportionate numbers in elite athletics) and again is suggestive of an agenda beyond simply levelling out unfair performance advantages.

Finally, if the Testosterone Regulations are to be ultimately justified by the level playing field argument it is difficult to see why one natural biological advantage is unfair without having evidence of the advantage that other natural biological advantages actually play. The answer seems to be to refer to the fact that 'the male advantage' is the single most significant biological factor in determining athletic performance and testosterone is the primary cause of that advantage. However, if ensuring fairness is the aim, the only question should be whether the performance enhancing effects of testosterone provide a significant advantage beyond other genetic advantages. It is totally irrelevant whether testosterone is the primary reason for the 'male advantage'; the only question should be what performance advantage it provides and whether it is out of sync with other genetic advantages. So if, as the IAAF evidence suggests, a female with high testosterone levels has a 5.7% performance advantage (IAAF Explanatory Notes, 2019 [8]), surely the question should be how that compares against other genetic advantages, such as having the 'sprinting' gene for example.

4. Conclusions

The above discussion suggests that, in pursuing the adoption and implementation of the Testosterone Regulations, the IAAF has not necessarily advanced their own stated purposes or adhered to the principles of good governance to which it aspires. There are particular concerns about upholding and promoting principles of integrity, solidarity and fair play stemming from human rights interferences that necessarily result from implementation of the regulations. There are also concerns in terms of transparency and democracy in the decision making.

However, there is also an additional concern raised about how the IAAF has made use of scientific evidence as a basis for justifying the Testosterone Regulations. Most obviously, there are compelling arguments that the central plank of the IAAF's evidence (Bermon et al., 2018; Bermon and Garnier, 2017 [16,17]) may be scientifically flawed, both in terms of what it is capable of showing (only correlation not cause) and in terms of the data resulting in a lack of scientific integrity (Karkazis et al., 2017; Franklin et al., 2018; Pielke et al., 2019 [15,32,37]). In particular, the Pielke study highlighted real concerns about the independence of the Bermon and Garnier studies, the ability of other scientists to re-create and verify the results and, from an evaluation of the revised data in the 2018 Bermon et al. study, the statistical significance of almost all of the observed performance advantages (it was suggested that there was only one event where the performance advantage of female athletes with higher testosterone levels was statistically significant (Pielke et al., 2019 [15]). The concern about independent verification and external scientists not having access to the same data to reproduce results clearly reinforces concerns about transparency.

Even taken at face value, the Bermon and Garnier studies suggest that there was zero advantage in several events, and even a disadvantage in events such as the 100m (where the power advantage of increased lean muscle mass associated with higher testosterone levels might be expected to provide a benefit) (Bermon et al., 2018; Bermon and Garnier, 2017 [16,17]). In other events, where a performance advantage was observed for female athletes (hammer and pole vault) no restrictions have been introduced, and there does not appear to be an explanation for this in the DSD Regulations or the explanatory notes to them (IAAF, 2019, IAAF Explanatory Notes, 2019 [7,8]). There is an inference from the 2017 Bermon and Garnier study that there are outliers within the highest tertile of female athletes that would have a much greater performance advantage (Bermon and Garnier, 2017 [17]). However, no direct evidence is provided of the performance advantage actually enjoyed by these outliers and as such there is a concern that it is the inference, more than the empirical evidence, which is influencing the policy.

These observations on the use of scientific evidence tend to suggest that the IAAF has sought the scientific evidence to justify the evolving policy, rather than approaching the scientific evidence with an open mind and deciding the policy based on that evidence. It was suggested earlier in this paper that for the IAAF to limit specific genetic advantages it needed a good justification for doing so. However, taking into account principles of good governance reflected in the IAAFs stated purposes and the criticsms of the scientific evidence, it is difficult to agree that the policy is currently justified.

Funding: This research received no external funding.

Conflicts of Interest: The author declares no conflict of interest.

References

1. Loland, S. *Fair Play in Sport: A Moral Norm System*; Routledge: London, UK, 2002.
2. Geeraert, A. *Sports Governance Observer*; The Legitimacy Crisis in International Sports Governance; Play the Game c/o Danish Institute for Sports Studies: Aarhus, Denmark, 2015.
3. CAS 2014/A/3759. *Chand v AFI and IAAF*; CAS: Boston, MA, USA, 2015.
4. Thomas, C. *Built for Speed: What Makes Usain Bolt So Fast?* The Telegraph: Nashua, NH, USA, 2016; Available online: https://www.telegraph.co.uk/usain-bolt-worlds-fastest-man/0/built-for-speed-what-makes-usain-bolt-so-fast/ (accessed on 2 June 2019).
5. Adair, J.L. In a League of Their Own: The Case for Intersex Athletes. *Sports Law J.* **2011**, *18*, 121.
6. McDonagh, E.; Pappano, L. *Playing with the Boys: Why Separate is Not Equal*; Oxford University Press: Oxford, UK, 2018.
7. IAAF. *Eligibility Regulations for Female Classification (Athletes with Differences in Sexual Development) 2018*; IAAF: Monaco, 2019.
8. IAAF. *Explanatory Notes: Eligibility Regulations for Female Classification (Athletes with Differences in Sexual Development) 2018*; IAAF: Monoco, 2019.
9. Auchus, R.J. Endocrinology and Women's Sports: The Diagnosis Matters. *Law Contemp. Probl.* **2018**, *80*, 127.
10. Handelsman, D.J.; Hirschberg, A.L.; Bermon, S. Circulating Testosterone as the Hormonal Basis of Sex Differences in Athletic Performance. *Endocr. Rev.* **2018**, *39*, 803–829. [CrossRef] [PubMed]
11. Krech, M. To be a Woman in the World of Sport: Global Regulation of the Gender Binary in Elite Athletics. *Berkeley J. Int. L.* **2017**, *35*, 262–290.
12. Xavier, N.A.; McGill, J.B. Hyperandrogenism and Intersex Controversies in Women's Olympics. *J. Clin. Endocrinol. Metab.* **2012**, *97*, 3902–3907. [CrossRef] [PubMed]
13. Ha, N.Q.; Dworkin, S.L.; Martínez-Patiño, M.J.; Rogol, A.D.; Rosario, V.; Sánchez, F.J.; Wrynn, A.; Vilain, E. Hurdling Over Sex? Sport, Science, and Equity. *Arch. Sex. Behav.* **2014**, *43*, 1035–1042. [CrossRef] [PubMed]
14. IAAF. *Competition Rules 2018*; IAAF: Monaco, 2018.
15. Pielke, R.; Tucker, R.; Boye, E. Scientific integrity and the IAAF testosterone regulations. *Int. Sports Law J.* **2019**, 1–9. [CrossRef]
16. Bermon, S.; Hirschberg, A.L.; Kowalski, J.; Eklund, E. Serum androgen levels are positively correlated with athletic performance and competition results in elite female athletes. *Br. J. Sports Med.* **2018**, *52*, 1531–1532. [CrossRef] [PubMed]
17. Bermon, S.; Garnier, P.-Y. Serum androgen levels and their relation to performance in track and field: Mass spectrometry results from 2127 observations in male and female elite athletes. *Br. J. Sports Med.* **2017**, *51*, 1309–1314. [CrossRef] [PubMed]

18. CAS. *Semenya v IAAF Executive Summary*; CAS: Boston, MA, USA, 2019.
19. IAAF. *Constitution*; IAAF: Monaco, 2019.
20. Ryall, E.; Cooper, J.; Ellis, L. Dispute resolution, legal reasoning and good governance: Learning lessons from appeals on selection in sport. *Eur. Sport Manag. Q.* **2019**, 1–17. [CrossRef]
21. Gardiner, S. Legal Regulation of Governing Bodies. In *Sports Law*; Routledge: New York, NY, USA, 2012.
22. Tallberg, J.; Zürn, M. The legitimacy and legitimation of international organizations: Introduction and framework. *Rev. Int. Organ.* **2019**. [CrossRef]
23. Chappelet, J.-L.; Mrkonjic, M. *Basic Indicators for Better Governance in International Sport (BIBGIS): An Assessment tool for International Sport Governing Bodies*; IDHEAP: Chavannes-près-Renens, Switzerland, 2013.
24. Mrkonjic, M. *Enlarged Partial Agreement on Sport: A Review of Good Governance Principles and Indicators in Sport*; Council of Europe: Strasbourg, France, 2016.
25. ASOIF. The Association of Summer Olympic International Federations: Governance Task Force. Available online: https://www.asoif.com/governance-task-force (accessed on 11 April 2019).
26. International Olympic Committee. *IOC Code of Ethics*; International Olympic Committee: Lausanne, Switzerland, 2016.
27. Larson, S. Intersexuality and Gender Verification Tests: The Need to Assure Human Rights and Privacy. *Pace Int. Rev.* **2011**, *23*, 215–247.
28. United Nations. Universal Declaration of Human Rights. Available online: https://www.un.org/en/universal-declaration-human-rights/index.html (accessed on 12 March 2019).
29. Schwab, B. "When We Know Better, We Do Better." Embedding the Human Rights of Players as a Prerequisite to the Legitimacy of Lex Sportiva and Sport's Justice System. *Md. J. Int. L* **2017**, *32*, 4.
30. Rivers, J. Proportionality and Variable Intensity of Review. *Camb. Law J.* **2006**, *65*, 174–207. [CrossRef]
31. Butcher, R.A. Fair Play as Respect for the Game. In *Sports Ethics*; Blackwell: Columbus, OH, USA, 2003.
32. Karkazis, K.; Jordan-Young, R.; Davis, G.; Camporesi, S. Out of Bounds? A Critique on the New Policies on Hyperandrogenism in Elite Female Athletics. In *The Ethics of Sport*; Oxford University Press: Oxford, UK, 2017; pp. 119–143.
33. Pape, M. I Was Sore about Losing to Cater Semenya. But This Decision against Her Is Wrong. 2019. Available online: https://www.theguardian.com/commentisfree/2019/may/01/losing-caster-semenya-decision-wrong-women-testosterone-iaaf (accessed on 3 May 2019).
34. IAAF. Integrity Code of Conduct. 2019. Available online: https://www.iaaf.org/about-iaaf/documents/rules-regulations (accessed on 12 May 2019).
35. Henry, I.; Lee, P. Governance and Ethics in Sport. In *The Business of Sport Management*; Pearson: London, UK, 2004.
36. Parent, M.; Naraine, M.; Hoye, R. A New Era for Governance Structures and Processes in Canadian National Sport Organizations. *J. Sport Manag.* **2018**, *32*, 555–566. [CrossRef]
37. Franklin, S.; Ospina Betancurt, J.; Camporesi, S. What statistical data of observational performance can tell us and what they cannot: The case of Dutee Chand v. AFI & IAAF. *Br. J. Sports Med.* **2018**, *52*, 420–421. [CrossRef] [PubMed]

© 2019 by the author. Licensee MDPI, Basel, Switzerland. This article is an open access article distributed under the terms and conditions of the Creative Commons Attribution (CC BY) license (http://creativecommons.org/licenses/by/4.0/).

Article

Sports Tournaments and Social Choice Theory

Rory Smead

College of Social Sciences and Humanities, Northeastern University, Boston, MA 02115, USA; r.smead@northeastern.edu

Received: 28 April 2019; Accepted: 24 May 2019; Published: 30 May 2019

Abstract: Sports tournaments provide a procedure for producing a champion and ranking the contestants based on game results. As such, tournaments mirror aggregation methods in social choice theory, where diverse individual preferences are put together to form an overall social preference. This connection allows us a novel way of conceptualizing sports tournaments, their results, and significance. I argue that there are genuine intransitive dominance relationships in sports, that social choice theory provides a framework for understanding rankings in such situations and that these considerations provide a new reason to endorse championship pluralism.

Keywords: sports tournaments; team rankings; intransitive dominance; win-loops; social choice theory; Condorcet's paradox; championship pluralism

1. Introduction

The New York Giants won the Superbowl in 2008, but most fans do not consider them the best NFL team that year. In fact, it is relatively clear that the team the Giants defeated, the New England Patriots, were better even though the Giants outplayed them on the day of the big game. So it goes. Most fans would agree that the best team does not always win the game. Poor refereeing, bad luck, an uncharacteristic mistake, or just a great day from a scrappy underdog can cost the better team victory. Upsets happen [1], and since tournaments are just collections of games, it follows that the best team is not always declared a champion.

Of course, it is more complicated than that. While the Giants were not the best team that year, they arguably had the best overall performance in the NFL playoffs. Afterall, they won the Superbowl! Also, if we knew what team was best, why do we need the playoffs? Why do we need the tournament at all? Performance in a tournament is often taken to be a sign of quality, as evidence about the true nature of the team or athlete. If the label "winner" was not supposed to indicate quality, we could simply flip coins or roll dice to decide the results. When we, as spectators or participants, buy into a sports tournament we do not think about it as a fancy slot-machine. We think about it as a decision procedure. It is a method for choosing a champion. There are reasons to think that the victorious team and the better team do not always coincide [2], but it is generally supposed that there is a correlation between the two. And success in games (and tournaments) is at least taken as an indication of team quality, even if not always a perfect one.

But what does a tournament really tell us about the contestants? If the aim is to identify the "best" team, then what kind of tournament structure should we have? And, how does a tournament's structure, apart from the quality of the contestants, impact the results? These questions have close parallels in social choice theory, which explores how individual preferences or judgements should be aggregated to produce a single preference or judgement for a social group [3]. The analogous question in sports is how specific performances and game results should be compiled to produce a champion. Here, I will explore some central results in social choice theory and their implications for how we ought to interpret and understand sports tournaments.

After drawing parallels between tournaments and social choice (Sections 2 and 3), I argue that there are genuine intransitive dominance relationships in sports, as there are in social choice theory (Section 4). I then argue that key impossibility results from social choice theory do not apply to sports tournaments as readily as they do democratic choices (Section 5). I conclude with a discussion on how this impacts our understanding of tournaments and suggest that we should embrace championship pluralism.

2. Condorcet's Paradox: World Cup Edition

The 1994 FIFA World Cup Group E consisted of four teams: Mexico, Republic of Ireland, Italy, and Norway. They played a round-robin, each playing against every other team. As has become standard in association football, a win earns a team 3 points, a draw 1 point. The teams are then ranked by total number of points, the top 2 teams advancing to the next round, with the third-place team possibly advancing depending on how it compared with other third-place teams.

After all the games were played, every team had one win, one draw, and one loss, for a total of 4 points each. Table 1 shows the complete standings.

Table 1. FIFA 1994 World Cup Group E Final Standings [4].

TEAM	Games	Win	Draw	Loss	GS	GA	GD	PTS
Mexico	3	1	1	1	3	3	0	4
Rep of Ireland	3	1	1	1	2	2	0	4
Italy	3	1	1	1	2	2	0	4
Norway	3	1	1	1	1	1	0	4

Who should win this group? According to FIFA rules in 1994, Mexico won the group on the strength of goals scored (GS) and Republic of Ireland defeated Italy in their match and so was ranked above them on the head-to-head tiebreaker. So, one might argue that Mexico should have won, as those were the rules established. The tournament rules are simply an agreed upon convention for picking a champion, and the team that ought to win is simply the team that actually wins (assuming they followed the rules).

But there are other ways to understand the question of who ought to win this group. Perhaps we want our tournament to identify the objectively "best" team, or at least the one that had the "best" set of performances according to some true standard of the sport. In which case, there may be questions about whether some tournament rules or structures are better at identifying quality. Such considerations assume that there is something about the teams beyond the mere results that tournament rankings should track. Setting aside concerns about cheating or foul-play, debates over whether the "right team won" would seem to imply such a view.

Assume, for now, that there is some objective "ranking" among teams that tournaments are supposed to help us discern. Mexico won the group by total goals scored, which may arguably track offensive performance. But why favor offense rather than defense? If defensive performances were treated as more "important" than offensive performances in the tiebreaking rules, Norway would have switched places with Mexico and won the group. The argument may be that we want to incentivize scoring because it makes the games more exciting, but is excitement an indicator of team quality?

Taking a closer look at the specific results of the group games makes this even more interesting. Here are all 6 matches:

1. Republic of Ireland defeats Italy 1-0
2. Norway defeats Mexico 1-0
3. Italy defeats Norway 1-0
4. Mexico defeats Republic of Ireland 2-1
5. Italy and Mexico draw 1-1
6. Republic of Ireland and Norway draw 0-0

It is natural to think that a victorious team ought to be ranked higher than the defeated team. But if so, the first four matches generate an intransitive cycle: Republic of Ireland > Italy > Norway > Mexico > Republic of Ireland. I will call such a set of results a "win-loop". Such loops mirror the Condorcet Paradox in social choice theory [5].

Condorcet's paradox occurs when there are three or more candidates (e.g., A, B and C) in an election and where a majority of voters prefer A to B, B to C and C to A. This can occur if one-third of the population prefers A to B to C, one-third prefers B to C to A and the remaining third prefers C to A to B. Then, a total of two-thirds prefer A to B, two-thirds also prefer B to C, and two-thirds prefer C to A. There is no majority winner and an intransitive cycle occurs if we vote on pairwise comparisons.

To avoid the paradox in the context of the World Cup group one of the first four results must be effectively ignored or weighted less than others. In this case the Norway defeat of Mexico is not counted as significantly as others. Norway defeated Mexico, tied them on points, and yet it was Mexico that won the group and Norway that was eliminated. It would be easy to make the case that the most surprising result, however was Ireland defeating Italy. Italy was the top seeded team in that group and Ireland was the only team of the 4 that did not finish at the top of their groups during the qualifying phase. If we ignore game #1 instead and respect the other results, the ranking becomes Italy > Norway > Mexico > Ireland. However, then Ireland is in the situation where they defeated the winner, tied them on points, and yet are eliminated. What the paradox shows us is that some team was necessarily going to be aggrieved.

3. Condorcet's Jury Theorem and Series of Games

One might think that the problem is just an artifact of not enough games. Condorcet paradoxes are typically more likely to occur when there is a relatively small number of voters [6]. Perhaps the same is true with a small number of games played between sports teams. The thought is that if each team had played each other 10 times, we would better avoid this kind of problem. This is the rationale behind having teams play a series of games against one another. Any individual game may be subject to a chance outcome, but the victor in a best-of-five or a best-of-seven series (e.g., the playoffs in American Baseball, Hockey, or Basketball) is less likely to be determined by accidental outcomes.

This relates to another result from social choice theory: Condorcet's Jury Theorem (Condorcet 1785, Boland 1989). The theorem states that if you have several independent people making a judgement of some fact, provided each is (even slightly) more likely to make the correct determination than the incorrect one, the more people you have the more likely the aggregate is to be correct. The parallel in sports is that the more games are played, the more accurate the overall results will be.

However, this requires that the results be independent of one another and that the different games played between the teams be roughly equivalent, which is not generally true in sports. Some "bias" in game outcomes can be counter-acted and balanced between different games, such as having both teams play at their home field, as is done in two-legged contests in European soccer. In the best-of-seven series in many American sports, one team (usually the one with the better record) gets 4 games at home, the other 3. Regardless, the core idea is that the more results we have between teams, the more confident we can be in declaring one team better.

To illustrate this, suppose team A has a 60% chance to beat team B on any given day. For simplicity, let us ignore any homefield advantage or other exogenous factors. Here are the chances that A will win a "best-of" series: best-of-1 (60%), best-of-3 (64.8%), best-of-5 (68.3%), and best-of-7 (71%). This trend continues. The more games played, the more likely it is that the better team will be the winner of the series.

If this is correct, the tournaments that have more games will be more likely to truly select the best team as a champion. Single-elimination tournaments are prone to flukes and upsets, which is why the NCAA collegiate basketball tournament is so hard to predict every year. On the other hand, in best-of-7 tournaments, such as the NBA playoffs, it seems that the better teams are almost always the

4. Win Loops and Intransitive Dominance

The jury theorem reasoning works well when there are two teams involved, but it can break down when there are three or more teams. If team A defeats team B and team B defeats team C, this does not mean that A will defeat B, or even that it is probable that A will defeat B. Transitivity may fail accidentally or systematically.

Let A > B represent that team A is in fact more likely than not to beat team B (although team B may happen to win on any given day). Accidental failures of transitivity occur when we have A > B, B > C and A > C, but it just so happens that A defeats B (as expected), B defeats C (as expected), and C defeats A (in an upset). With respect to accidental failures of transitivity, the task of a ranking system is (arguably) to identify which results were accidents and remove them from consideration. By playing multiple games those "accidental" results become less likely and we can be more confident that the final rankings represent the true rankings. However, when win-loops are non-accidental, this no longer works.

It may be that the "true" relationship between the three teams is intransitive. Just as there is no best-move in rock-paper-scissors, teams or competitors can find themselves in situations where transitivity fails systematically. Seth Bordner argues that such genuine win-loops probably occur and that if they do occur "it poses immense problems for ranking conventions" [7] (p. 223). To explore this possibility here, consider the 2017 National League East Division in Major League Baseball. There are 5 teams and each played every other 19 times during the season. Table 2 shows the win-loss splits among those teams.

Table 2. National League East head-to-head records for 2017 [8].

TEAM	vs. ATL	vs. MIA	vs. NYM	vs. PHI	vs. WSH
ATL	N/A	11-8	7-12	6-13	9-10
MIA	8-11	N/A	12-7	8-11	6-13
NYM	12-7	7-12	N/A	12-7	6-13
PHI	13-6	8-11	7-12	N/A	8-11
WSH	10-9	13-6	13-6	11-8	N/A

The official final standings, based on total win-loss records were WSH (97-65), MIA (77-85), ATL (72-90), NYM (70-92) and PHI (66-96) [8]. However, looking at the team vs. team splits a more interesting relationship emerges. WSH is still clearly the top team, having a winning record against all other teams. However, the remaining four teams are more difficult to place in an ordering due to an intransitive relationship: MIA > NYM > PHI > ATL > MIA.

Is this win-loop representative of some genuine intransitive relationship between teams, or is it merely the result of some fluke in results? First, consider the latter possibility. Which ordering is the "fluke"? The only single result that could be removed to break the loop is the MIA > NYM. So, maybe that result is an accident and should be disregarded. But it is not so simple. That result is also consistent with the overall rankings and only has about an 0.18 probability of occurring by chance alone (assuming each team is expected to win half of their games). Moreover, these kinds of win-loops occur regularly in Major League Baseball. In the 2018 season for example, every team in the National League was involved in at least one such loop.

Could such an intransitivity represent the true relationship between the teams? The following simple model shows that such intransitive relationships are genuine possibilities and should not always be understood as mere statistical flukes. Suppose we have three tennis players, A, B, and C who each have distinct skills in serving, returning, and volleying. Suppose further that we can precisely quantify these skills on a 1 (poor) to 4 (excellent) scale and that each player has the skill levels in Table 3.

Table 3. Skills of three tennis players in a simple model.

Player	Serving	Returning	Volleying
Player A	4	2	1
Player B	1	4	2
Player C	3	1	3

Consider an idealized representation of a tennis match, where player i is playing against player j and the net expected points earned are calculated as follows.

- The fraction of serves that result in a volley (*v*) depends on the difference in serving and returning skills such that smaller differences mean volleys are more likely:

$$v = 0.8 - |S_i - R_j| * 0.1 - |S_j - R_i| * 0.1. \tag{1}$$

- Player i's net expected points earned on volleys is proportional to the difference in volleying skill and the percentage of volleys that occur:

$$v * (V_i - V_j)/4. \tag{2}$$

- Player i's net expected points earned on serves is:

$$(1 - v) * (S_i - R_j)/4. \tag{3}$$

- Player i's net expected points earned on returns is:

$$(1 - v) * (R_i - S_j)/4. \tag{4}$$

S_i is i's serving skill, R_i is i's returning skill, and V_i is i's volleying skill. Note that the "4" is simply a normalizing term representing the maximum possible difference in skill levels as it relates to expected points earned. Likewise, the other specific numbers chosen are not essential for the point, nor are they based on any precise data from tennis, they are merely chosen for ease of illustration and to capture the qualitative descriptions.

In this model, we can calculate the expected points for any given serve of a tennis match between any two players. Table 4 shows the expected outcome of each matchup.

Table 4. Expected points and results from each matchup in a simple tennis model. Net points are the average expected points earned for the first player listed in the matchup.

Matchup	Net Points for P1 on Serves	Net Points for P1 on Returns	Net Points for P1 from volleys	Total	Expected Result
A vs. B	0	0.075	−0.175	−0.1	B defeats A
A vs. C	0.45	−0.15	−0.2	0.1	A defeats C
B vs. C	0	0.075	−0.175	−0.1	C defeats B

Note that these expected points reflect the true skill levels of the players in the different aspects of the game and how they compare. There simply is not a transitive ordering of the players with respect to their quality. It will not help to play more games. Because the intransitivity is real and not an artifact of luck, the more games we play, the more probable it is that we see an intransitive cycle.

Given the frequency of win-loops occurring in sports and the fact that relatively simple models can be constructed that generate plausible intransitive relationships, it is reasonable to believe that there are genuine intransitive loops in sports. Note that intransitive dominance occurs in other domains as well. In ecology, for example, there is an ecological version of rock-paper-scissors among males of the side-blotched lizard *Uta stansburiana* [9]. These lizards have three distinct mating strategies: a harem-building strategy, a mate-guarding strategy, and a cuckolding strategy. Harem-building does well amongst mate-guarders, cuckolding does well against harem-building, and mate-guarding does well against cuckolding. Which strategy is best (from a biological perspective) depends on the rest of the population. There simply is no true biological ranking of the behaviors. Another example is seen in games of chance with Nontransitive dice [10]. These are sets of dice which form intransitive win-probability cycles when played against one another. Every die can be beaten by some other die in these games.

If dominance is not a transitive relationship in sports, then perhaps there simply is not a best team or athlete [7]. This may be an acceptable conclusion for those that think we ought to participate in or watch sports simply for the love of the game. However, such a conclusion will be unsatisfying for the rest of us who like to think that sports tournaments and the crowning of a champion carry a special significance. Social choice theory shows us a way forward despite these difficulties.

5. Arrow's Theorem

Social choice theory has long had to deal with the intransitive relations that occur in Condorcet's paradox. It is easy to imagine cases where candidate A easily beats candidate B in an election, B easily beats candidate C, and C easily beats candidate A. Nevertheless, we cannot simply say "there is no true best candidate" and call it a day. Even if we think that's true, we still need to pick a winner. Many probably feel the same way about sports—the whole point is to have a winner, so we need to have a way of determining one.

This turns out to be much more difficult than simply settling on a conventional method for aggregating preferences. Arrow's Impossibility Theorem is a result that shows what kind of constraints social choice functions face [11,12]. It states that no social choice function can satisfy five desirable conditions: (i) have an unrestricted domain of individual preferences; (ii) have a positive association of social and individual values; (iii) be independent of irrelevant of alternatives; (iv) be non-imposed; and (v) be non-dictatorial.

Arrows theorem has corollaries in judgement aggregation [13,14], as well as in contexts such as scientific theory choice [15]. It also can be interpreted in the context of sport, where a particular set of game results is analogous to a voter's preferences and the social choice function, which aggregates preferences, is the tournament. The five conditions then become: (i) able to accommodate any possible set of game results and produce a complete ranking; (ii) winning games does not hurt a team's ranking in the tournament; (iii) the relative ranking of two teams should not depend on some other team; (iv) the ranking should not be determined by factors outside the results of the games and performances; and (v) we should not privilege one set of games over all others. Perhaps these are all desirable conditions for sports tournaments. However, each of them is violated in some contexts (see the Table 5), and considering the examples reveals that these are not usually taken as serious requirements for sports tournaments.

Table 5. Arrow's conditions and sports tournaments.

Condition	Example of Violation
(i) All possible game results are allowed, and the final ranking is complete.	Many tournaments do not allow for ties in match results, disallowing logically possible team comparisons. Additionally, not all tournaments require that the inputs (the individual games) be transitive or complete, they can be partial and intransitive. Likewise, the final ranking need not be complete (e.g., elimination tournaments often settle 1st, 2nd, 3rd, and 4th place, but do not settle lower rankings).
(ii) Winning never hurts a team's ranking.	Winning can hurt a team's chances of overall tournament success if the win causes a pairing in the next round that is significantly more difficult. The 2018 world cup featured such a game between Belgium and England. The winner (Belgium) faced a significantly more difficult slate of games in the elimination round as a result of defeating England.
(iii) The relative ranking of teams depends only on games between those teams.	Most round-robin style tournaments will violate this criteria as the overall ranking depends on how a team performs against the field rather than any specific team. For example, Arsenal defeated eventual Premier League champions Leicester City in both of their matches in 2015/16 but finished in second place.
(iv) Rankings are not imposed by anything other than game results.	The NCAA college football rankings dictate the entrants to the playoffs in ways (arguably) that do not depend only on the previous games played.
(v) No set of game results trumps all others.	The results of the NFL playoffs serve as the effective "dictator" of a team's final ranking, supplanting any regular season results that may have been different.

Cardinal vs. Ordinal Comparisons

What does Arrow's impossibility theorem mean for the rankings determined by sports tournaments? Arrow's result will apply to any tournament that relies only on wins/losses and has more than two contestants. However, given the examples of violations above, the conditions may be less important in sport than they are in democratic choice. Furthermore, rankings in sport need not be based merely on wins/losses. For instance, margin of victory in a given game may be considered.

The parallel in social choice theory is to consider the differences in preference rather than simply the preference ordering. This requires cardinal preferences rather than ordinal preferences, and a social choice function must assume some meaningful way of comparing such preferences. This allows a way around Arrow's theorem [3,16]. Whether these exist and whether they can be meaningfully compared is a contentious issue in social choice theory. In sports contests, however, margins of victory certainly exist and can be easily compared. Indeed, point differences are often used in tiebreaking procedures for round-robin style tournaments. This, combined with the several ways in which tournaments violate the five conditions, suggests that Arrow's theorem is not as serious a constraint on sports tournaments as it may be on democratic choice mechanisms.

6. Conclusions: Implications for Sport Tournaments

The above considerations have numerous implications for how we should think about sports tournaments, weight alternative tournament structures, and understand tournament results. Here, I will briefly comment on different types of tournaments before concluding with an argument for championship pluralism.

6.1. Elimination Tournaments

Interestingly, certain tournament structures preclude the possibility of intransitive cycles in results. Because losers of single-elimination tournaments are removed from the competition, there is no opportunity for that team to generate a win-loop. This allows us to take the results of such tournaments as definitive. We can guarantee that there are no results from within the tournament that would contradict the champion's claim. This comes with costs, however. Seeding in elimination tournaments becomes paramount. If the two best teams in the tournament are paired in the first round, we will be unable to identify that contest as a kind of "true" championship game. Thus, we should not be confident that the loser of the championship game is actually the second-best team (or even third, fourth, etc.). Additionally, elimination tournaments will not and do not provide a complete ranking of teams (e.g., a ranking between all the teams that were eliminated in the first round). Finally, elimination tournaments are prone to upsets having a significant impact on overall rankings, something that some fans like about such tournaments. While this may be desirable for excitement purposes, it certainly is detrimental to identifying any "true" ranking of the teams in so far as there is one.

Some of these concerns can be addressed by making the tournament more complex, such as double-elimination tournaments, or elimination tournaments where teams play multiple games between one another. These can, at best, only partially address the costs and can also re-introduce the possibility of intransitive win-loops (e.g., win-loops are possible in double elimination tournaments). Finally, if genuine intransitive relationships do exist among the teams, it can be rationally optimal to make predictions for an elimination tournament that are logically inconsistent, such as predicting team A to lose in the first round but win in the second [17].

6.2. Round-Robin Tournaments

Round-robin style tournaments are susceptible to win-loops and other related concerns. They do, however, provide a method for generating a complete ranking of teams. Additionally, round-robin tournaments produce more game results than elimination tournaments, meaning that the results are more likely to be representative of the true relationships among the teams. However, as we have seen, this can mean they are more likely to generate intransitive win-loops and complicate finding a "true" ranking. For these tournaments to generate a full ranking, there must be an established way of weighting some results as more important than others (e.g., factoring in win-margins, or overall points scored). This is usually done in the form of tie-breaking procedures. It is also important to note that because these tournaments effectively score performance against the field, the winners of round-robin tournaments can be teams that will systematically lose to other teams in the tournament.

Mixed tournament styles, such as the FIFA World Cup finals, involve both round-robin elements (in the group stage) and elimination elements (in the knockout stage). Mixed tournaments can help address some of the seeding concerns in elimination tournaments, but only at the cost of facing the potential complexities generated by round-robin style results, such as win-loops.

There are also group-style tournaments that are distinct from round-robin style, such as a Swiss-style tournament, where competitors are paired with others that have a similar ranking or aggregate score. The idea is to match contestants that are "closely" ranked, and thereby facilitate coming to a complete ranking more quickly with fewer matches being played. There are several different kinds of Swiss-style tournament systems that vary in exactly how contestants are matched. The core idea of these systems is to get a complete ranking without a complete set of games by differentiating competitors of similar strength and extrapolating the entire rankings from those results. Note that such a method assumes a kind of transitivity among competitors, and yet still does not eliminate the possibility of win-loops in results.

6.3. Alternative Ranking Criteria

Social choice theory offers a plethora of different ways to rank options given voters preferences [18,19]. Different voting procedures have different strengths and weaknesses. There is arguably not a single correct or best method. Rather, there are a plurality of methods, some of which may be preferred to others on a variety of grounds depending on what the aim of the vote is. For example, do we want to identify the option that is most preferred by the most people, or find the one that minimizes dissatisfaction?

The parallel with social choice theory and sports tournaments allows us to conceive of novel ways to conduct tournaments and produce final rankings. For example, the Ranked Pairs method [20] considers each pairwise comparison between options in an election and ranks the pairings in order of largest margin of victory by votes among the pair. Then, it produces a ranking among the options by locking in the results with the largest margins first. If an intransitive cycle occurs, it discards the result with the lowest margin. Such a procedure would allow for a novel alternative way of ranking teams in a round-robin tournament.

The Ranked Pair procedure satisfies the Condorcet criterion, which holds that if one option (team) is preferred (wins) to all others in pairwise contests (games) that option ought to be preferred on aggregate. This condition, which seems highly intuitive in the context of sport, is not satisfied by many league structures. Take the Premier League in English association football for example. The Premier League follows a standard process in European soccer of having teams play a double-round robin, awarding three points for a win and one point for a tie. Teams are then ranked by the number of points they accumulate during the season. If there were a team that somehow won every game they played in their home stadium and tied every game they played away from that stadium they would amass 76 points across 38 games, never be defeated, and have beaten every other team on aggregate. However, 76 points would have been enough to win the league only once in its recent history. In many years, this total would have ranked third place or lower. The setup of the Premier League allows for a team to beat all other teams, never lose to any team, and yet not win the league. This violates the equivalent of the Condorcet criterion.

This is but one example. Social choice theory has produced a vast array of possible choice mechanisms and explored their effects and tradeoffs. Corresponding tournament rules or structures could be implemented that parallel virtually any voting or social choice mechanism. The parallel between social choice and sports tournaments allows us to draw on these ideas to re-consider how we conduct tournaments.

6.4. Championship Pluralism

Aaron Harper argues for what he calls "Championship Pluralism" [21], saying we should accept that one team may be the regular season champion, and another may be the playoff champion, and neither is strictly better. He argues for pluralism on the grounds that "no single format for measuring and comparing athletic excellence successfully captures all conceptions of excellence" [21] (p. 307). Considerations from social choice theory and the parallels with sports tournaments offer a distinct reason for embracing championship pluralism. Even if there were a tournament that could capture all aspects of athletic excellence, there is good reason to suspect there may be intransitive dominance among teams. In which case, the method of compiling results—the rules and structure of the tournament—may be the deciding factor. There is arguably no best tournament structure, just as there is no best social choice mechanism, but we (often) want to produce a winner nonetheless. Therefore, we should accept a plurality of tournaments and the plurality of champions that comes with it.

Funding: This research received no external funding.

Acknowledgments: I would like to thank the Rossetti Research Group at Northeastern for helpful discussion on social choice theory. Also thanks to Myraeka d'Leeuwen and two anonymous referees for helpful comments in revising this paper.

Conflicts of Interest: The author declares no conflict of interest.

References

1. Fry, J.P. Underdogs, upsets, and overachievers. *J. Philos. Sport* **2017**, *44*, 15–28. [CrossRef]
2. Dixon, N. On winning and athletic superiority. *J. Philos. Sport* **1999**, *26*, 10–26. [CrossRef]
3. List, C. Social choice theory. *Stanf. Encycl. Philos.* **2013**. Available online: https://plato.stanford.edu/entries/social-choice/ (accessed on 28 March 2019).
4. FIFA.com. Available online: https://www.fifa.com/worldcup/archive/usa1994/groups/index.html (accessed on 28 April 2019).
5. Condorcet, M. *Essai sur L'application de L'analyse à la Probabilité des Décisions Rendues à la Probabilité des Voix*; De L'imprimerie Royale: Paris, France, 1785.
6. Gehrlein, W.V. Condorcet's paradox and the likelihood of its occurrence: different perspectives on balanced preferences. *Theory Decis.* **2002**, *52*, 171–199. [CrossRef]
7. Bordner, S.S. 'All-things-considered,' 'better-than,' and sports rankings. *J. Philos. Sport* **2016**, *43*, 215–232. [CrossRef]
8. ESPN.com. Available online: http://www.espn.com/mlb/standings/grid/_/year/2017 (accessed on 28 April 2019).
9. Alonzo, S.H.; Sinervo, B. Mate choice games, context-dependent good genes, and genetic cycles in the side-blotched lizard, Uta stansburiana. *Behav. Ecol. Sociobiol.* **2001**, *49*, 176–186. [CrossRef]
10. Tenney, R.L.; Foster, C.C. Non-transitive dominance. *Math. Mag.* **1976**, *49*, 115–120. [CrossRef]
11. Arrow, K.J. A difficulty in the concept of social welfare. *J. Polit. Econ.* **1950**, *58*, 328–346. [CrossRef]
12. Arrow, K.J. *Social Choice and Individual Values*; Yale University Press: New Haven, CT, USA, 1963.
13. List, C.; Polak, B. Introduction to judgment aggregation. *J. Econ. Theory* **2010**, *145*, 441–466. [CrossRef]
14. List, C. The theory of judgment aggregation: An introductory review. *Synthese* **2012**, *187*, 179–207. [CrossRef]
15. Okasha, S. Theory choice and social choice: Kuhn versus Arrow. *Mind* **2011**, *120*, 83–115. [CrossRef]
16. Sen, A. The possibility of social choice. *Am. Econ. Rev.* **1999**, *89*, 349–378. [CrossRef]
17. Smead, R. On the rationality of inconsistent predictions: The March Madness paradox. *J. Philos. Sport* **2016**, *43*, 163–169. [CrossRef]
18. Brams, S.J.; Fishburn, P.C. Voting procedures. In *Handbook of Social Choice and Welfare*; Arrow, K.A., Sen, A., Suzumura, K., Eds.; Elsevier: Amsterdam, The Netherlands, 2002; Volume 1, pp. 173–236.
19. List, C. The logical space of democracy. *Philos. Public Aff.* **2011**, *39*, 262–297. [CrossRef]
20. Tideman, T.N. Independence of clones as a criterion for voting rules. *Soc. Choice Welfare* **1987**, *4*, 185–206. [CrossRef]
21. Harper, A. "You're the best around": An argument for playoffs and tournaments. *J. Philos. Sport* **2016**, *43*, 295–309. [CrossRef]

© 2019 by the author. Licensee MDPI, Basel, Switzerland. This article is an open access article distributed under the terms and conditions of the Creative Commons Attribution (CC BY) license (http://creativecommons.org/licenses/by/4.0/).

MDPI
St. Alban-Anlage 66
4052 Basel
Switzerland
Tel. +41 61 683 77 34
Fax +41 61 302 89 18
www.mdpi.com

Philosophies Editorial Office
E-mail: philosophies@mdpi.com
www.mdpi.com/journal/philosophies

www.ingramcontent.com/pod-product-compliance
Lightning Source LLC
LaVergne TN
LVHW071957080526
838202LV00064B/6770